OFFICE ✛ work *SPACES*

ROCKPORT

First published in the United States
of America by
Rockport Publishers, Inc.
33 Commercial Street
Gloucester, Massachusetts 01930-5089
Telephone: (978) 282-9590
Facsimile: (978) 283-2742

ISBN 1-56496-806-5

10 9 8 7 6 5 4 3 2

Design: Leeann Leftwich
Front cover photo by Jean-Marie
Monthiers, design by Atelier Christian
Hauvette.

Back cover photos as follows: top photo
by Farshid Assassi, Assassi Productions,
design by Herbert Lewis Kruse Blunck
Architecture; center photo by Walter
Smalling Jr., design by Ai; bottom photo
by Marco Lorenzetti ©Hedrich Blessing,
design by Elkus/Manfredi Architects Ltd.

Printed in China.

INTERNATIONAL PORTFOLIO OF *43* DESIGNERS

OFFICE ⊕ work SPACES

VERNON MAYS

GLOUCESTER MASSACHUSETTS

ROCKPORT PUBLISHERS

contents

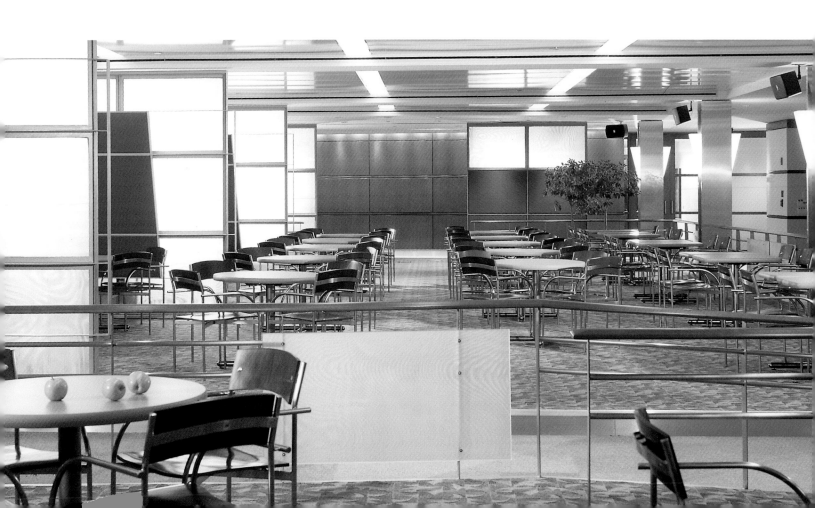

EVOLUTION AND CHANGE

Today's technology and manufacturing allows endless possibilities for the design of a workplace. From custom millwork to prefabricated workstations, the design community and its client base can improve the quality of life for corporations and institutions around the globe.

In their book, *The Demise of the Office*, Erik Veldhoen and Bart Piepers alert us to the need for change. "We are perched on the brink of a revolution in our society," they write. "The electronic highway, the digital city, the mobile telephone, the portable computer, listening televisions, talking computers, electronic mail, and teleworking are symptoms of a new era, a real one, and one that is very eminent."

At a recent group discussion, Duncan Sutherland, Jr., an office strategist for a major furniture manufacturer and adjunct professor in the School of Business and Public Management at George Washington University, suggested that "offices are not information factories, they are extensions of the mind."

Work process, new communication techniques, and office space are crucial for the functioning of any organization. An integrated approach is a necessity. Information technology, organizational development,

and facility are now inseparable from one another and are all integral to the success of the user.

This form of work is new to designers. The linkage of offices and work spaces with the social and political objectives of the sponsor's business plan requires a new and expanded definition of design—a definition not limited to form and function, but inclusive of aspiration for moral productivity, brand identification, management systems, and financial objectives.

The profession of interior design as we know it today was borne out of a merger of aesthetics, rational planning, and technology. The profession's relative youth is aptly chronicled by Cindy Coleman, executive editor of *Perspective* magazine, in her essay "Reflections of an Industry: The Role of the Designer Over History." Coleman notes how the modern architecture of the post-World War II era required a new and innovative approach to the design of interior corporate environments. A key element in initiating this new direction was the establishment of Knoll Associates in 1946 by Florence and Hans Knoll to design and manufacture furniture in the Bauhaus style. Florence Knoll, who trained in architecture under Eliel Saarinen and Mies van der Rohe, founded the Knoll planning unit, a design studio that provided furniture customers with interior architectural and planning services. Explains Coleman, "The unit became a laboratory for interior spaces, experimenting with the design, scale, and configuration of task-related furniture."

"Prior to this period, contract interiors—the planning and design of office environments—did not exist as a profession," she continues. "If a doctor, businessperson, or corporation wanted to arrange office space, they usually were referred to a furniture store, which would provide them with desks, chairs, and credenzas. As manufacturer representatives for the furnishing industry, furniture stores were responsible for sales, delivery, installation, and service to the customer base. As such, the selection of office furniture was primarily their domain. For most clients, hiring a professional designer was considered elitist."

In the early 1950s, the New York office of Skidmore, Owings & Merrill (SOM) became one of the first large architecture/engineering firms to offer interior design among its menu of professional services. SOM eventually established itself as the world leader in contract interiors, providing design services for major corporations including Pepsi Cola, Chase Manhattan, and Union Carbide.

"While the '50s saw the introduction of interior design services into existing architectural firms,"

Coleman notes, "the '60s bore witness to the maturation and transformation of these interiors studios into independent design firms offering a variety of services." The tradition of workplace design can be defined by five periods of modern history since the industrial revolution. Each period links social trends, dominant construction systems, and internal building systems with the design of offices and work spaces.

In the period before 1900, as American cities began to form and grow, the early technology of bearing wall construction and the inherent limits it placed on the creation of large continuous spaces gradually gave way to skeletal frame construction. This offered a new freedom that, along with the advent of elevators, allowed designers to move from individual office suites—inextricably tied to the structural limits of bearing walls—toward office spaces defined by an organization's size.

From 1900 to 1950, enormous economic growth brought forward the introduction of reinforced concrete. This structural development provided greater spans of leasable space. Expansive areas, along with the introduction of modular ceiling grid systems, created floor plates that could be utilized by larger organizational units. It was an era marked by building technology, which paved the way for the post-World War II building boom.

The period from 1950 to 1970 witnessed the growth of American corporate culture. The delineation of space by building modules gave birth to the organizational allocation of space by hierarchical standards. Organizations began differentiating job titles of staff and employees by the square footage of real estate assigned to them. This era was indelibly marked by the use of real estate as a noncompensation-based form of recognition. This period was also marked by the universal appeal of open planning—allowing large groups of individuals to be zoned together by function or organizational identity.

The years 1970 to 1990 were dominated by the explosion of information technology. Companies acquired the ability to pass information and shift capital investment rapidly from the building itself to desktop equipment, which in turn supported worker effectiveness. This era also was defined by the rising influence of the real estate developer in the form of the speculative office building. Before then, office building construction was dominated by corporations or institutions who were building for their own use. As speculative development increased, the built landscape became punctuated with stylistic, often arbitrary, and individualistic buildings.

The reliance on information technology provided the rationale for building interiors to be dominated by image and message rather than conservative planning. The ability of workers to communicate electronically freed them to inhabit alternative office settings. The workforce began to choose where and when the work was accomplished—either at home, in the car, on an airplane, or in a hotel room. Office design changed as a result, taking into account issues that went beyond the concern of mere efficiency toward examining issues of an organization's mission and identity. Sponsors looked to communicate the corporate culture of the occupants through the design of the workplace.

Buildings became intelligent through their management of voice and data. The capacity of electronically controlled security gave designers the freedom to explore new boundaries of functional relationships. The furniture industry, for example, responded by providing intelligent panel-based systems furniture that was modular, electrified, and movable. No longer were designers limited to defined groupings of people, but realized for the first time their ability to restructure such groupings on demand.

Moving from 1990 to the present, user control and employee empowerment have been supported by wireless technology. Adjustable seating and work surface ergonomics coupled with individual lighting and thermal environment control support the mobility of the worker to either collaborate or work independently in settings designed for specific tasks.

In her book *Citizen Office*, author Uta Brandes states, "New information and communication technologies throw fundamentally new light on our attitude towards the workplace." Brandes points out that, until recently, office organization had been based on old management concepts put forth by theorist Frederick Taylor. Taylor's "scientific management" model of the efficient factory—based on the notion that one worker equaled one unit of production—was later translated to the office. Hierarchy, order, and logistics of production and supervision became formalized within the office into a model of social organization based on virtues of order, which ultimately led to the dehumanization of the workplace.

Our current condition and the future of workplace effectiveness will allow us to abandon this rigid module. The new face of the interior design profession and the new design work depicted in Vernon Mays's *Office and Work Spaces* is the result of world-class design firms collaborating with some of the most prominent corporations, service firms, financial institutions, and telecommunication leaders. These projects benefit from the learning of cross-functional teams representing the disciplines of engineering, finance, human resources, the social sciences, and facility management. The result is a change in focus and priority.

The sponsor, or client, is no longer satisfied with identity. Today's goal is workplace effectiveness and performance along with an expression of corporate intent. The new criterion for design performance is the interactive relationship between the user and those who the user serves. Today, the hallmark of design achievement supports the union of social ambition with the technological aspiration of the user.

Neil Frankel, AIA, FIIDA

Prior to accepting the position of Fitzhugh Scott Distinguished Critic at the University of Wisconsin/ Milwaukee, School of Architecture and Urban Planning, Neil Frankel, AIA, FIIDA, was director of interior design for Skidmore, Owings & Merrill's Chicago architectural interiors practice. Internationally recognized through his numerous design awards, Neil Frankel's professional career has been characterized by a commitment to excellence in design and client services. Frankel was elected to the Interior Design Hall of Fame in 1994 and the International Interior Design Association's College of Fellows in 1997.

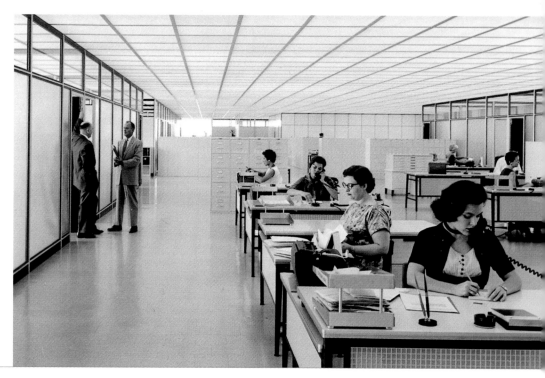

THEN AND NOW

Working on this book has forever changed the way I see—at least the way I see offices and work spaces. So it was with renewed vision that I recently took a personal tour of one of the modern era's prototypical suburban office buildings—the Reynolds Metals Headquarters in Richmond, Virginia. Designed in the mid-1950s by Gordon Bunshaft of Skidmore, Owings & Merrill, the aluminum company's elegant corporate offices have survived as a kind of time capsule—a tangible product of the corporate optimism that thrived in the post-World War II era. Its classically proportioned exterior, stately reflecting pool, and intelligent courtyard plan were all conceived to project an image of financial success, stability, and unparalleled accomplishment.

Aluminum, at the time, was a relative newcomer on the construction scene, having emerged as a versatile component of the war effort. Eager to demonstrate the material's potential applications, the company pressed Bunshaft to incorporate it wherever possible into the new building. He responded by using more than one million pounds (454,000 kilograms) of aluminum, mostly in the exterior cladding, but also in the custom furnishings, cellular ceiling panels, filing cabinets, and escalator enclosures. Even the carpets were woven with aluminum fibers. Having seen all

this first-hand, I was impressed by the logic and beauty of this icon of twentieth-century design and its masterfully executed interiors. But, at the same time, it struck me how the building constitutes the perfect foil against which the design of today's offices can be contrasted.

Stylistically the two are different, that's a given. But a more fundamental contrast, to my mind, is one of mentality. Although the Reynolds offices have long since been updated to accommodate new styles of working, documentary photographs of the original offices convey an attitude about business that today seems almost quaint. Bunshaft and his colleagues knew what an office was meant to be. They designed with that function in mind—and that function alone. That's how the 1950s were, of course: a male-dominated society in which the guys were executives and the gals were secretaries. It was orderly, controlled, predictable.

Would anyone dare say the same about business today? Technology advances at blinding speed. Yesterday's competitors are today's strategic partners. Wave after wave of corporate layoffs spell uncertainty, not security. How does one design for such realities? Culling through the sea of photographs submitted for use in this book, I discovered many firms that address the question by designing not for constancy, but for change. Somehow they find ways to accommodate today's organizational makeup without building roadblocks to tomorrow's. It's a symptom of the times. Rooms become freestanding boxes that don't disturb the building shell; walls pose as partitions that can be cheaply dismantled and discarded; ceilings are nonexistent, save for the view of overhead mechanical and lighting systems afforded by their absence; and workstations adhere to the concept of flexibility so literally that some are even equipped with wheels.

For me, the separation between today's offices and those of Bunshaft's time is embodied by the accompanying photograph of Vitale, Caturano and Company, a New England accounting firm that occupies offices renovated by ADD Inc of Boston. There, work is about a process, not simply a set of bureaucratic restrictions. Just look at the computer programmers, jeans and all, working comfortably in their Netsurfer divans—recumbent work chairs that elevate ergonomics to new levels. Compared to the buttoned-down version of American business portrayed in the Reynolds photograph of the 1950s, this environment exudes an informality that speaks volumes about the heightened value of employees and their role in the workplace today.

With increasing frequency, businesses have forsaken "big and bureaucratic" in favor of "lean and mean." That can be attributed partly to a lack of knowledge about what the future will hold six years from now, even six months from now. And while some would argue that this uncertainty offers today's designers opportunity for innovation, I suspect, in their efforts to meet a client's program, the burden of responsibility is heavier for them than for pioneers such as Gordon Bunshaft. Which, with my renewed sense of vision, gives me greater appreciation for what many of the world's leading architecture and interior design firms are contributing to the field. Their accomplishments are the core of this book.

Vernon Mays

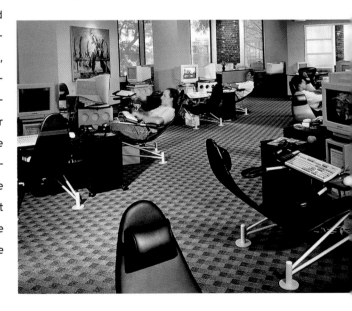

ADD INC

Winner of numerous design and building industry awards during its twenty-seven years in business, ADD Inc provides innovative architecture, interior design, and planning solutions for corporations, real estate and retail developers, institutions, and financial and legal services firms. It is a firm of talented professionals who are committed to providing design services and products that exceed client expectations and delivering the best design, value, and experience possible. ADD Inc also recognizes its environmental and social responsibilities through its commitments to reduce pollution, preserve natural resources, maximize the positive effects of its projects, as well as to give back to the community by supporting volunteerism and corporate gift programs.

OPPOSITE The design for this growing regional bank in Boston created shared conference rooms surrounding a dramatic two-story reception hub.
ALL PHOTOS BY LUCY CHEN

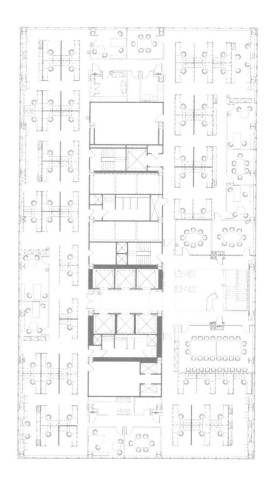

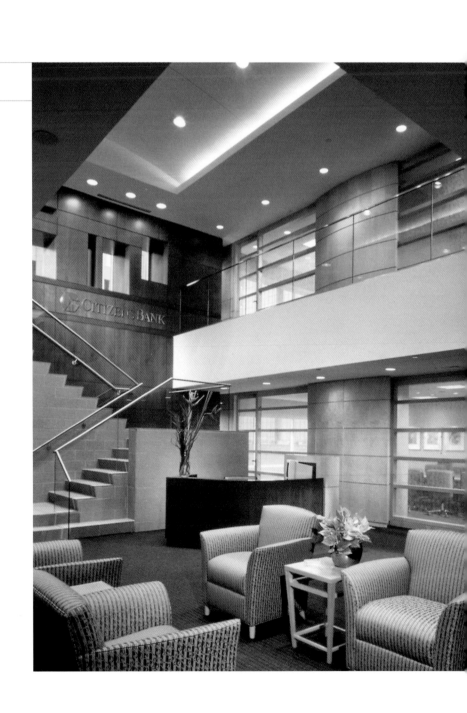

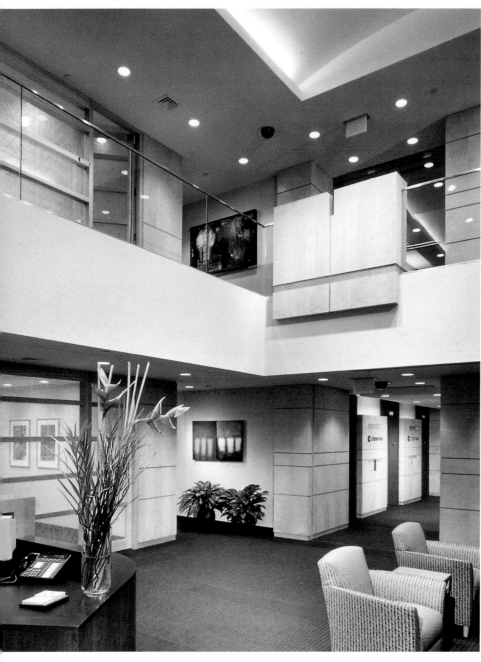

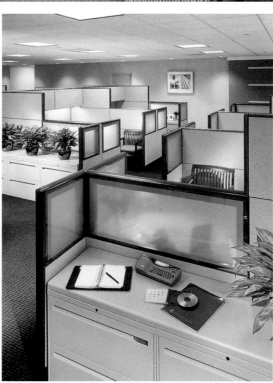

ABOVE Furniture and finishes express this bank's sensible approach by creating an aesthetic of fabric, wood, and frosted glass enhanced by the durability and cost savings of metal files and plastic laminate work surfaces.

RIGHT Workspaces emphasize openness and interaction, limit the number of closed offices, and convey a youthful, modern image.

FAR RIGHT Art niches with custom lighting were installed throughout the interior of this Boston firm to ensure that all staff members work with art in their surroundings.

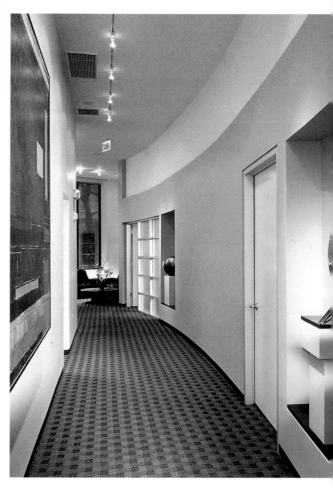

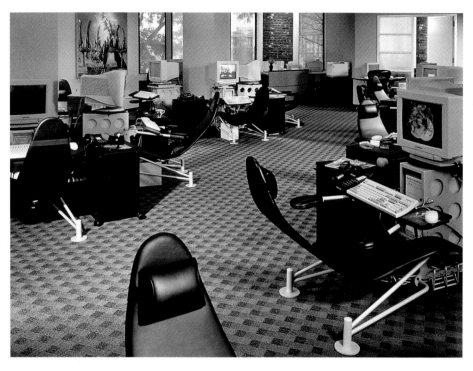

ABOVE The information services department conveys a high-tech image with an exposed server room and Netsurfer computer divans in which staff work at their computers in semi-reclining positions.

LEFT The design team worked with all of the firm's partners to customize the shape and granite selection for their desks. Twenty varieties of granite were specified, and each office received no fewer than three pieces of art.

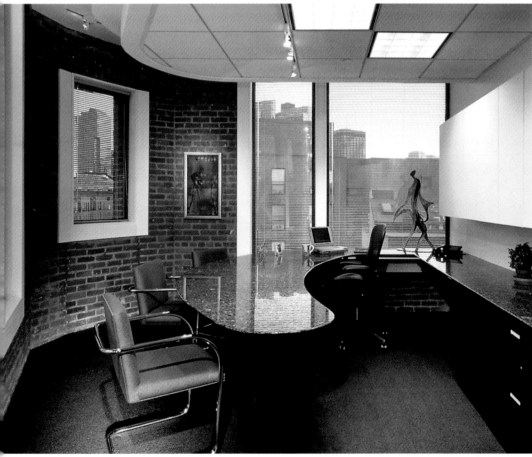

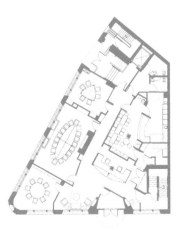

A i

Established in 1984, Ai has grown and diversified with a commitment to provide the services and resources necessary for its clients to maximize real estate assets. In an increasingly competitive marketplace, the principals believe that ideal translates into the design of facilities that reduce occupancy costs, provide maximum flexibility, and support worker productivity. In support of that goal, the firm helps its clients find new ways to do business through effective cultural changes and alternative approaches to planning and work styles. Ai offers integrated planning, design, and management services.

OPPOSITE Administrative staffers work in groups of three in spaces that open to the reception area. The design employs lively, sustainable finishes to achieve a loft-like environment.
PHOTO BY WALTER SMALLING JR.

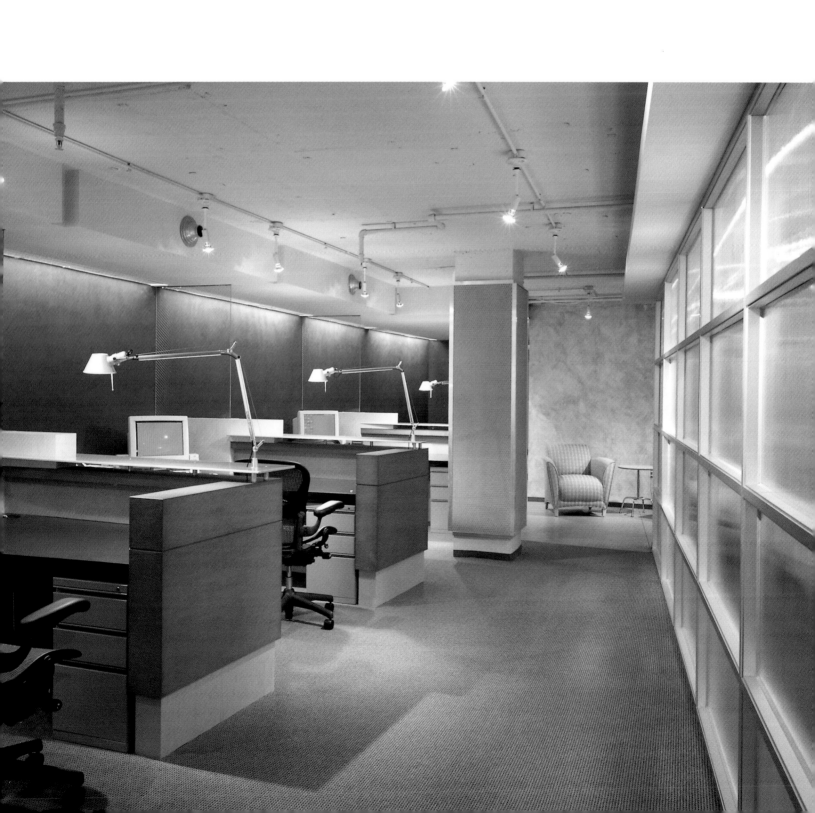

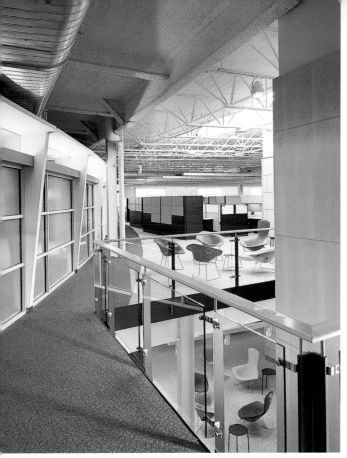

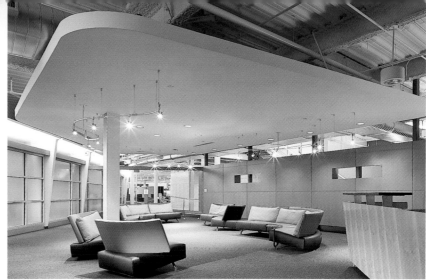

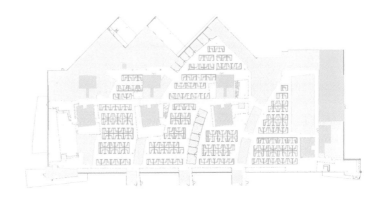

ABOVE LEFT Private offices with sensuous curved walls unite a composition that consists of numerous atria and conference pods. Expansive views of the interior space and landscape beyond enliven the offices and workstations.
PHOTO BY JEFF GOLDBERG/ESTO

ABOVE RIGHT In eight months, Ai converted a warehouse into a state-of-the-art office building, creating a flexible work environment, as well as an image appropriate for this global technology-based media company in Dulles, Virginia.
PHOTO BY JEFF GOLDBERG/ESTO

RIGHT The main conference room of this Washington, D.C., company is surrounded by partitions of anodized aluminum storefront systems infilled with plexiglass.
PHOTO BY WALTER SMALLING JR.

BELOW RIGHT The flexibility of this operations center in Reston, Virginia, is reflected in the dining area. Through the use of sliding opaque partitions, it can be divided into small seating areas or opened to create a single meeting space.
PHOTO BY WALTER SMALLING JR.

OPPOSITE From new rooftop monitors, light spills into informal seating areas used by employees for spontaneous team meetings and impromptu work sessions.
PHOTO BY JEFF GOLDBERG/ESTO

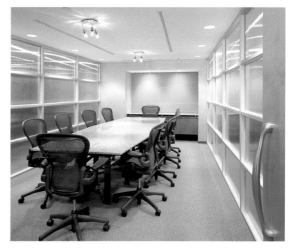

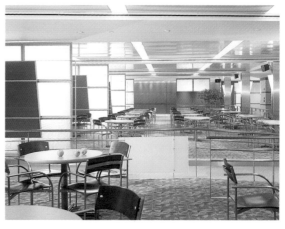

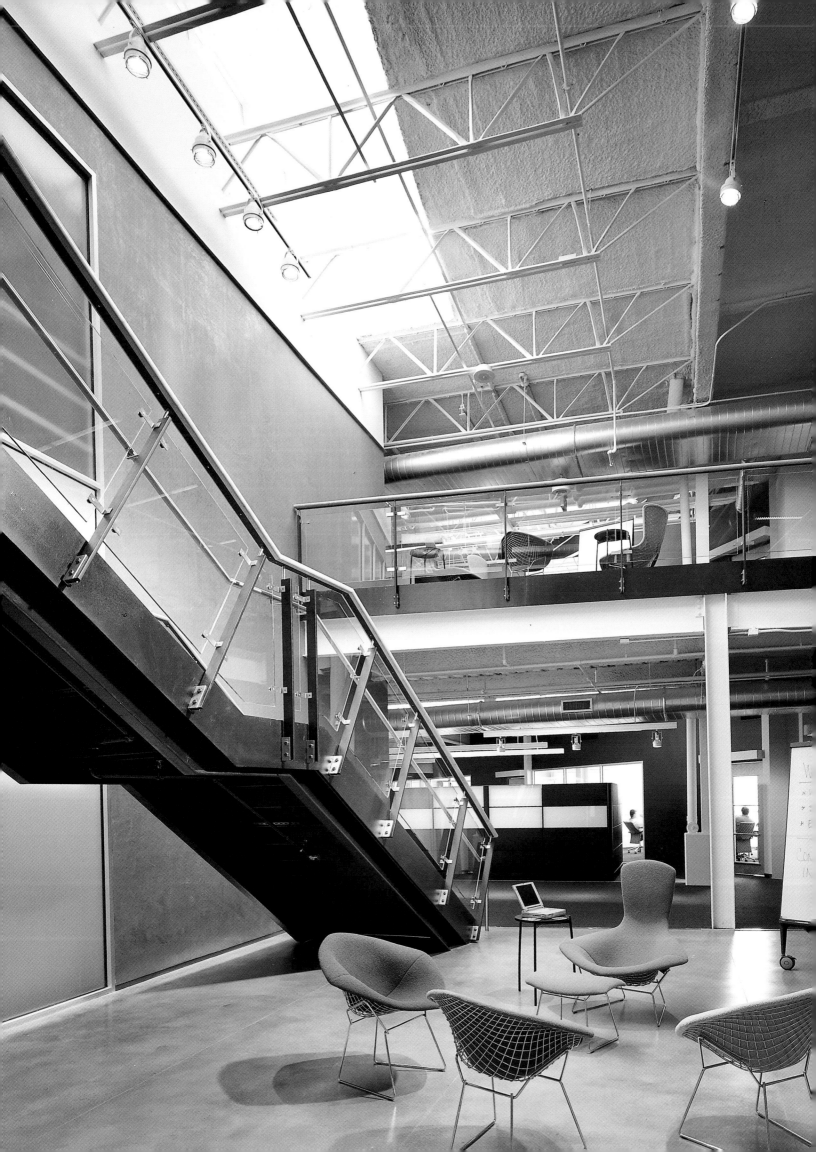

ARCHITECTURAL ALLIANCE

Architectural Alliance has built its success through a team-building approach, encouraging strong partnerships among employees, clients, contractors, and consultants. The firm services a wide range of clients including corporations, governments, institutions, property managers, retailers, airlines, and airports. Architectural Alliance joins with the most appropriate consultants for each project. The firm's architecture and interior design staff works closely with consultants to create quality projects in both renovations and new construction. The firm's longstanding relationships with clients have produced designs that are creative, functional, and responsive to physical and cultural influences. Founded in 1970, Architectural Alliance, Inc., is a multidisciplinary firm of seventy architects, planners, interior designers, and support staff providing architectural, planning, interior design, and construction observation services. The firm has received national and regional recognition and design awards, including the AIA Minnesota Firm Award in 1994.

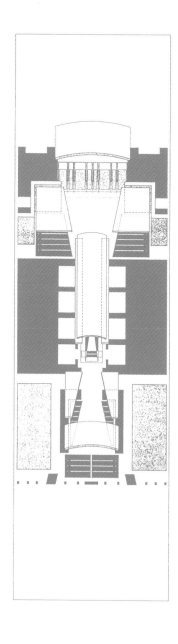

OPPOSITE CLOCKWISE FROM TOP LEFT The wood-paneled ceiling in the conference room bows slightly along the length of the space, its shallow arc complemented by a custom-designed translucent light fixture. The feature wall offers both privacy and openness; it combines clear and sandblasted glass framed by aluminum fins that incorporate uplights.

The design of these Minneapolis offices capitalizes on the opportunities of a single-tenant floor by integrating the elevator lobby with the firm's more public activities.

A neoclassical vocabulary in the base building gave rise to the diverse materials palette—terrazzo and carpeted flooring, brushed aluminum, clear and translucent glass, and a range of exotic wood types, including cherry, anigre, mahogany, and ebonized walnut.
ALL PHOTOS BY GEORGE HEINRICH

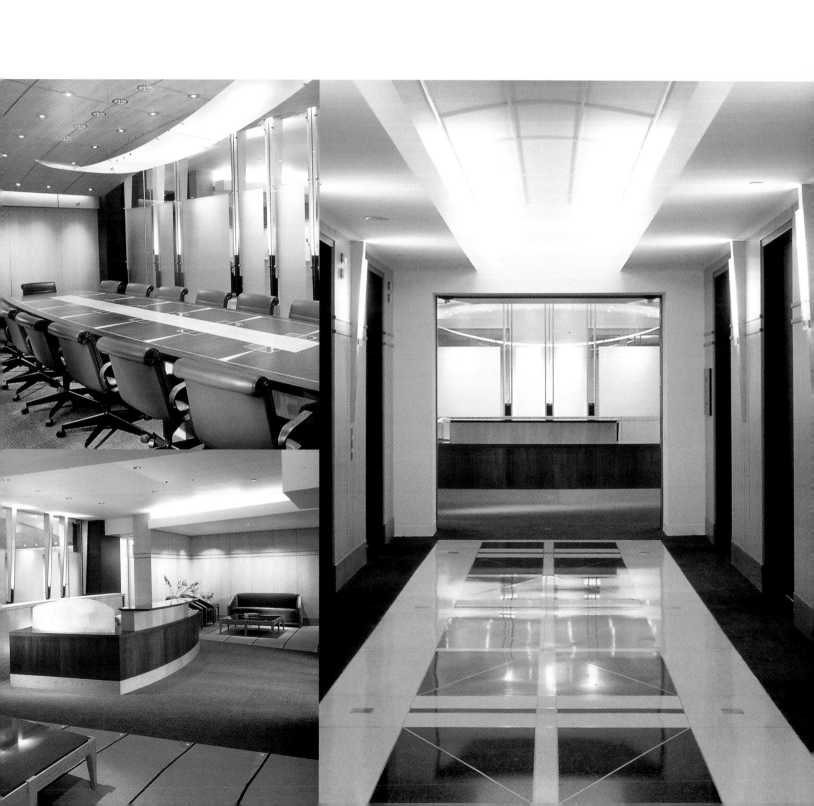

AREA

AREA bases its practice on entertainment, law, financial, and corporate firms, producing spaces with an architectural purity that is client-specific. Firm principals Walt Thomas and Henry Goldston, both registered architects, created the firm to serve clients who require a high level of personal attention and desire unique design solutions. Their past experience as managing principal of ISD Interiors and studio design director at Gensler, respectively, gives them the insight to realize that clients want spaces that express their individual image requirements, delivered on schedule and within budget. The firm's no-nonsense approach to the design process appeals to busy executives. AREA also strives to render and explain the character of its spaces to clients so that there are no surprises when the work is complete. While the firm's work is firmly based in the tenets of classic modern architecture, a palette of comfortable colors, lighting, furniture, and forms always take precedence over impersonal starkness or frivolous style.

OPPOSITE Taking advantage of the concrete structure in this vintage 1965 building, AREA left sections of the framework exposed and highlighted it with uplights in the public areas of these offices for a Beverly Hills talent management company.
ALL PHOTOS BY JON MILLER ©HEDRICH BLESSING

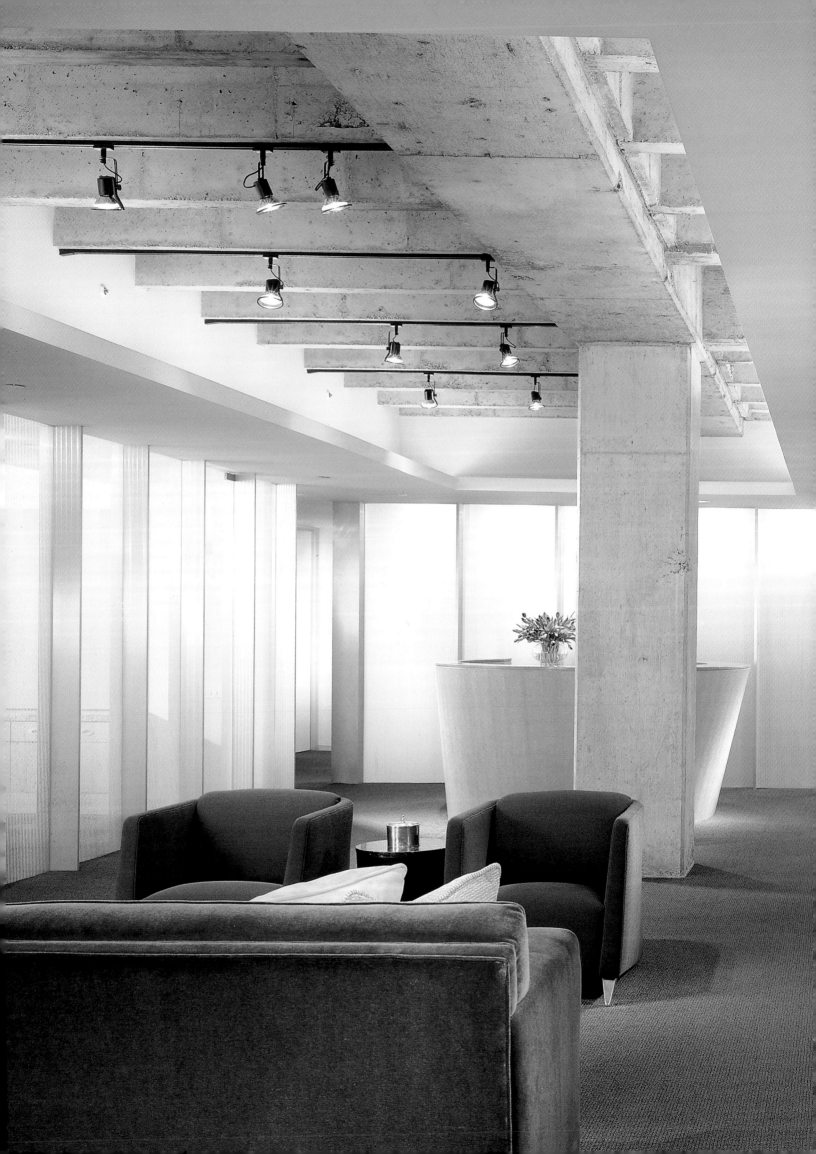

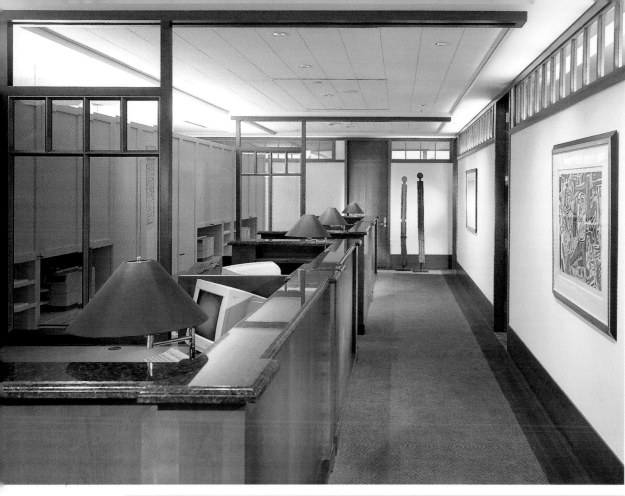

LEFT Stereotypes of glittery Hollywood are eschewed in these law offices, which feature clean architectural details. Rich olive green carpeting provides a backdrop for a range of wood species, such as English yew, East Indian laurel, wenge, and makore that were selected for inlays and supporting millwork.

BELOW To achieve the feeling of "California casual" requested by their client, the designers developed a color scheme that emphasized the mixing of multiple shades of green upholstery accented with shades of red. The design incorporates an existing collection of art and furnishings.

OPPOSITE In these offices for a prominent Los Angeles entertainment law firm, the client desired a sense of permanence and longevity. Common-grade, figured American cherry was selected as the main wood statement because of its unusual variations, sap marks, and swarthy character. Floors arc Brazilian cherry.

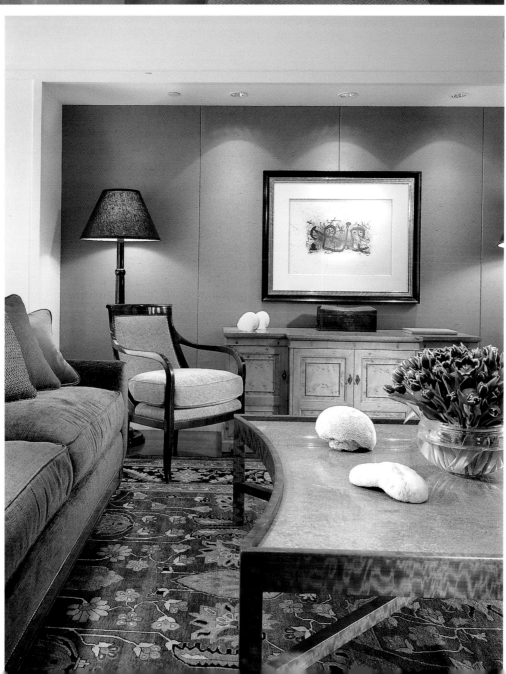

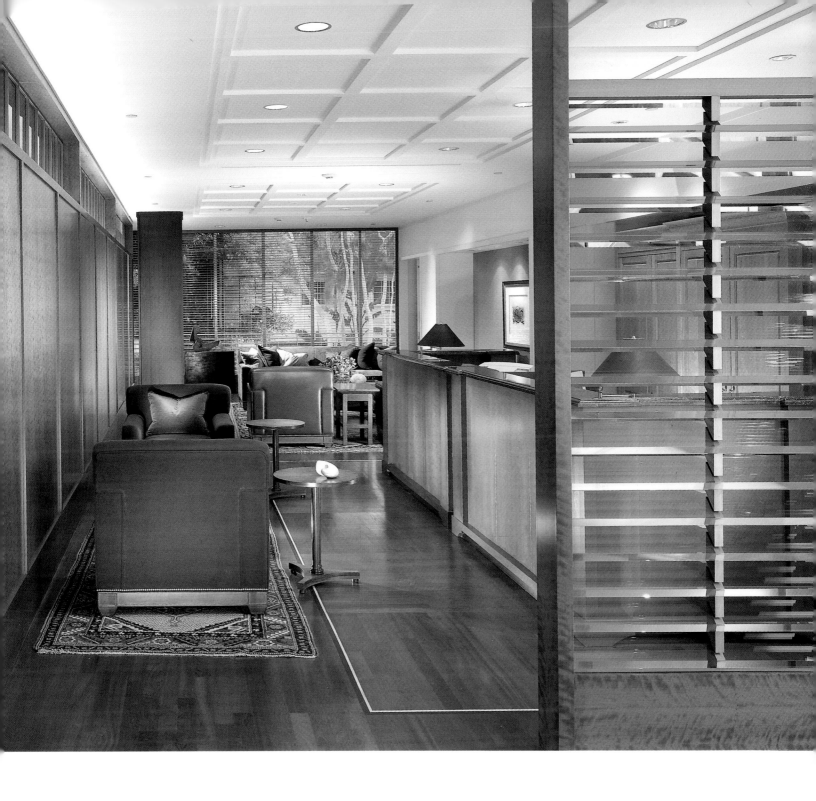

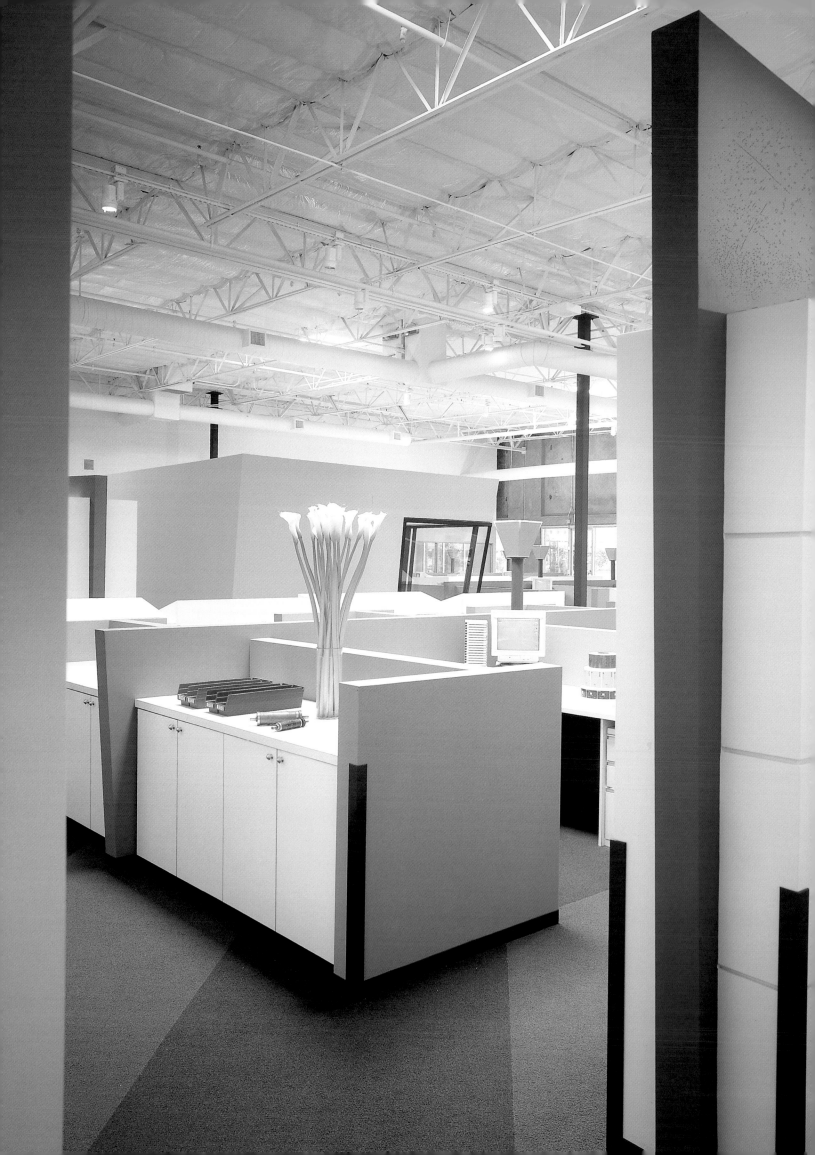

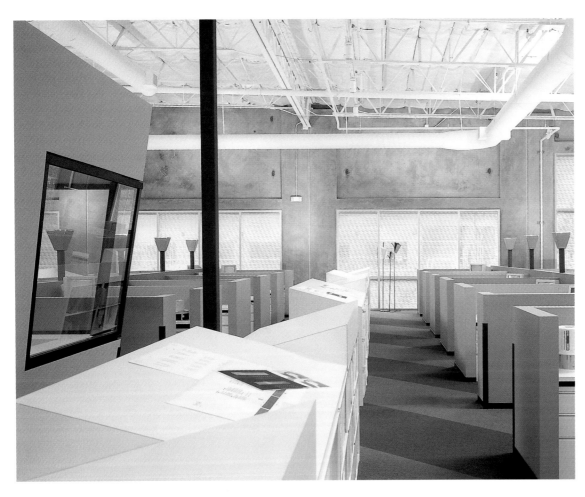

OPPOSITE Files are located in a storage wall that forms a partition embellished with a colored blade on top. At the center is the sales manager's cubicle, which is located strategically in the center of the building.

LEFT The sales manager's office occupies an enclosed space behind a canted yellow wall. It overlooks the open office area, where alternating sloped counters are arranged for viewing job tiles and customer artwork. Walls at the rear are unfinished tilt-up concrete panels.

BELOW LEFT The interior design solution in this low-cost tilt-up wall building blends a white "clean room" aesthetic with an infusion of geometric shapes and vibrant hues. Angled blades painted red, blue, and green sit atop banks of file cabinets, creating a colorful landscape.

BELOW RIGHT The 150-foot-long (45-meter-long) reception area for this TV animation studio in Burbank, California, includes a green room/employee lounge partially hidden behind a curved, orange "Googie" wall and a dripping, green slime staircase that leads to the mezzanine.

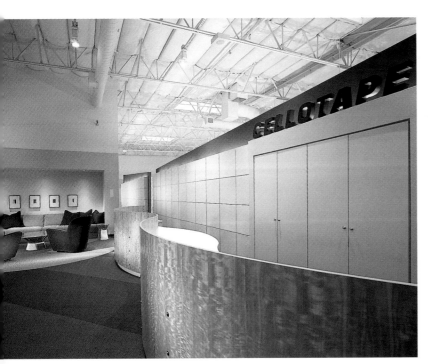

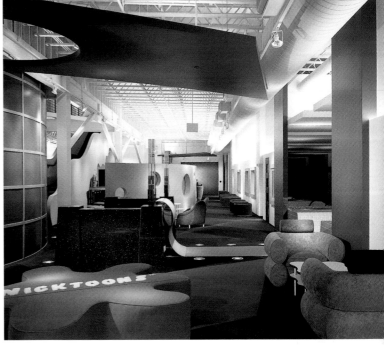

BERGMEYER ASSOCIATES, INC.

Founded in 1973, Bergmeyer Associates, Inc., is a seventy-five-person full-service architecture and interior design firm specializing in retail and food service design, housing, commercial buildings, and corporate interiors. Additional areas of expertise include image and identity analysis, prototype store design, and media technology. Bergmeyer works nationally as well as in Japan, Canada, and the United Kingdom.

OPPOSITE An inviting kitchen and informal arrangements of tables and lounge chairs encourage impromptu meetings and brainstorming sessions. Bright fabrics and colors reinforce the company's departure from a stale corporate image.

BELOW Using existing structural elements and raw building materials, Bergmeyer created a casual office developed around the way people work in the space.
ALL PHOTOS BY LUCY CHEN

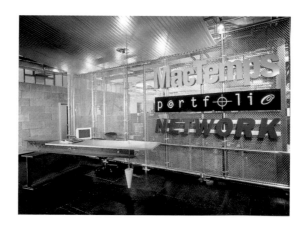

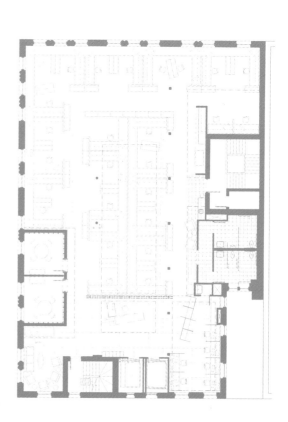

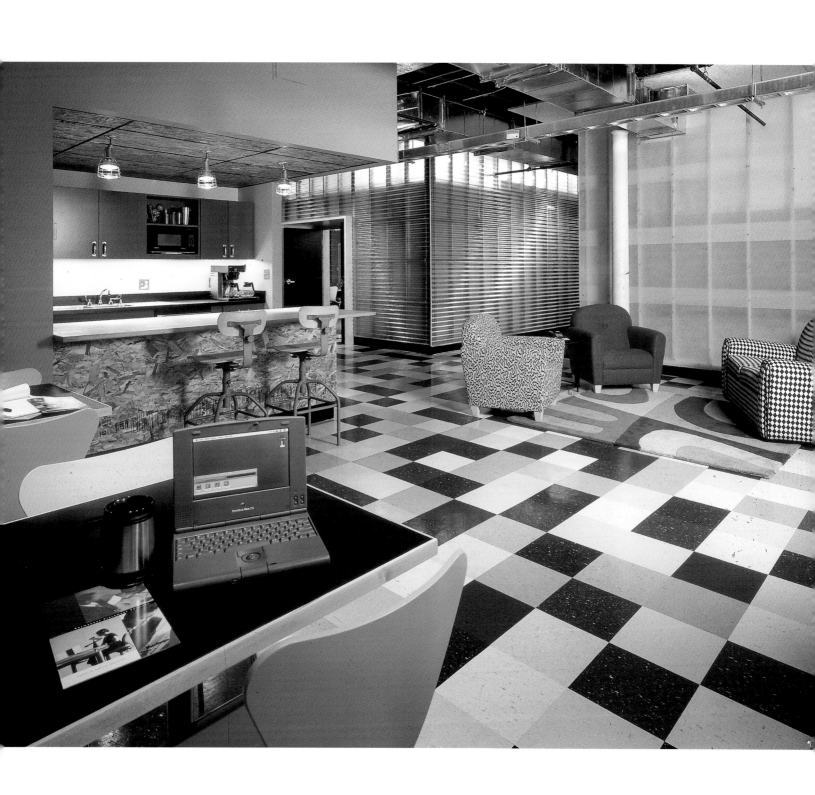

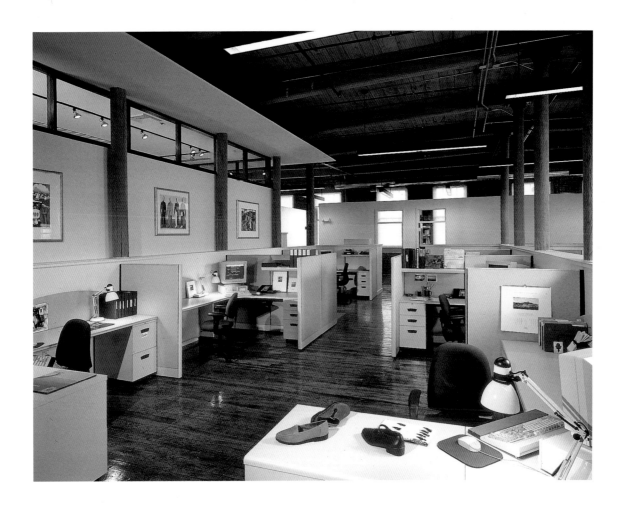

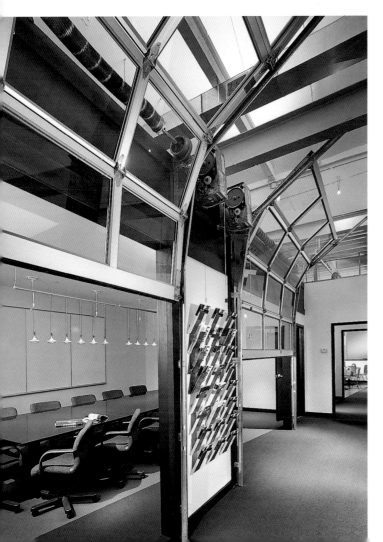

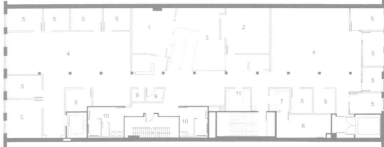

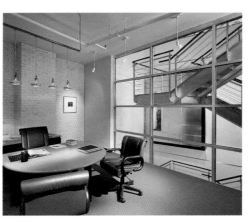

ABOVE Original features of a reno vated mill building—hardwood floors, beams, and high ceilings—are combined with wood, leather, graphics, and storefront elements in these corporate offices for a specialty shoe manufacturer.

FAR LEFT When opened, the garage doors that enclose this firm's conference room become an awning extending into the reception area.

LEFT One of the firm's partners has an office that overlooks an atrium—and across the atrium into a galvanized steel bay that contains the office of his counterpart.

OPPOSITE The cantilevered atrium stair is made of exposed structural steel, pigmented concrete treads, stainless steel cable guards, and ebonized poplar rails.

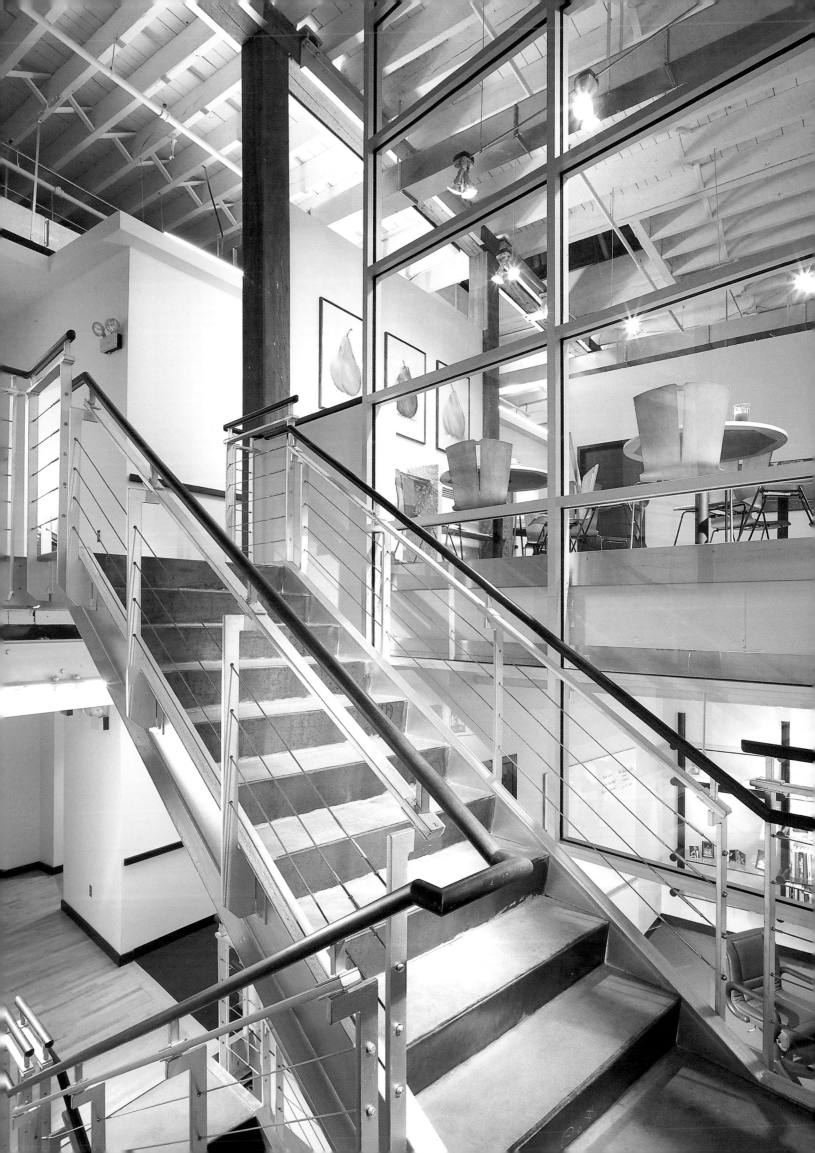

THE BOMMARITO GROUP/
GRAEBER, SIMMONS & COWAN

The Bommarito Group/Graeber, Simmons & Cowan has earned a reputation for design that is both innovative and sensitive to client requirements. Recognizing that design is a business as well as an art, the firm works with clients as an interactive team, searching for unique design solutions that also make good business sense. The design team possesses a diverse project portfolio, with experience in commercial, institutional, health care, hospitality, and advanced technology design. The firm offers comprehensive commercial interior architecture, interior design, and space planning services, incorporating the skills of interior designers and architects to provide clients with personalized service.

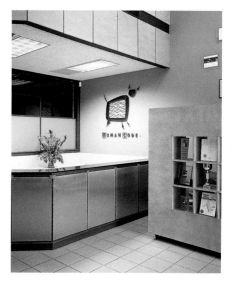

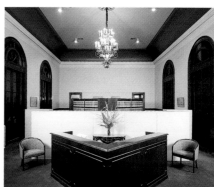

ABOVE RIGHT The juxtaposition of natural fiberboard and raw metal in the entry desk and mobile display unit reflect this multimedia firm's identity: both rough and modern, primitive and slick.

RIGHT The reception area of this law office houses the original judge's bench, platform, and witness stand that occupied the building when it was a federal courthouse in the early 1900s.

OPPOSITE Canted corridors and walls, stonelike portals, and ever-changing color are among the elements designed to reflect the creative nature of this Austin software games company and inspire its employees.
ALL PHOTOS BY PAUL BARDAGJY

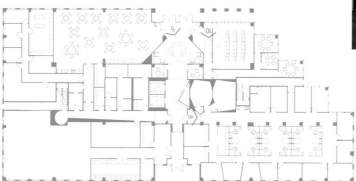

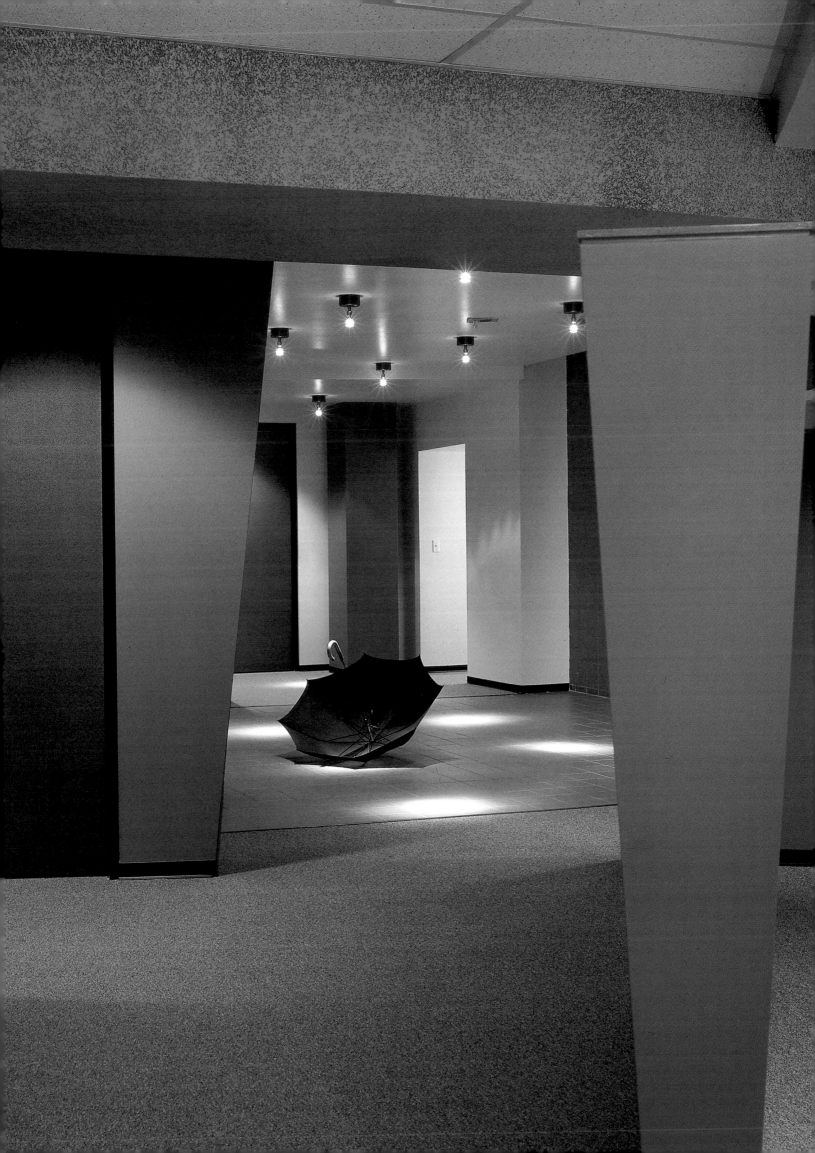

BRAYTON & HUGHES DESIGN STUDIO

Founded in 1989 by Richard Brayton, who was later joined by Stanford Hughes and Jay Boothe, Brayton & Hughes has cultivated a design approach that offers unique solutions to each design by emphasizing the particulars of program and regional design influences. The firm serves both American and international markets, providing comprehensive architectural and interior design services for projects throughout the Pacific Rim, Europe, the Middle East, and the United States.

RIGHT An 11,000-square-foot office and lighting showroom in San Francisco combines a wide variety of functions within an existing concrete shell. Materials and details embody new construction techniques and finishes, with gestures such as the historic acorn pendant fixture introduced as a direct reference to a transcended past.

OPPOSITE Lateral bracing required in the existing facade provided a rich opportunity for its redesign. Openings that once held industrial sash windows were filled with concrete and punched with small squares filled with cast blue glass that transmits light into the mezzanine-level cafe.
PHOTOS BY JOHN SUTTON

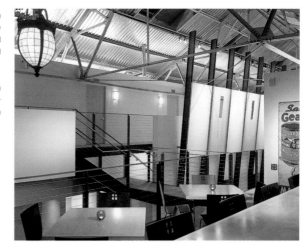

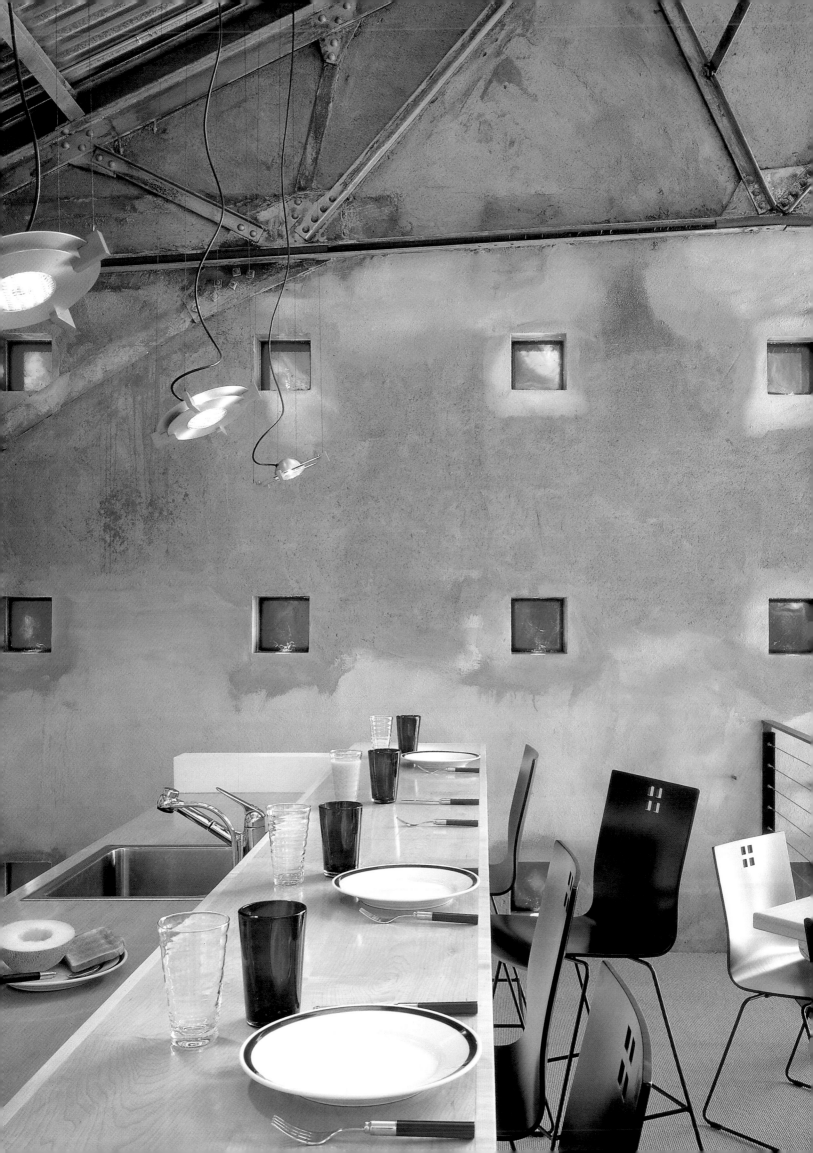

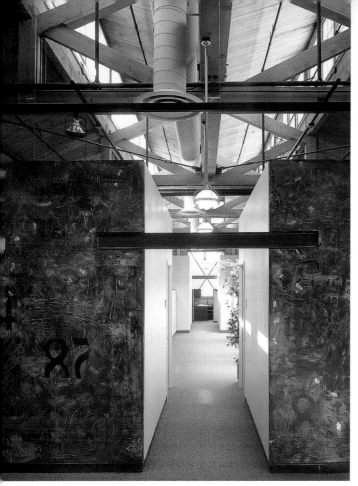

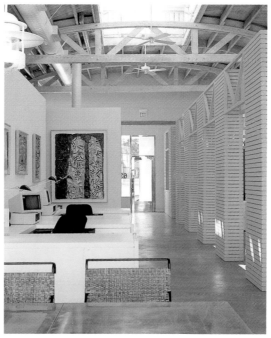

FAR LEFT Raised drywall panels painted by a local artist suggest a mixed message of billboards, urban calligraphy, and industrial decay in these temporary quarters for an Emeryville, California, company. These openings, framed by lintels of cold rolled steel, lead to "court-yards" that accommodate work groups.
PHOTO BY CHAS MCGRATH

LEFT Solid elements play against a garden-like trellis of lattice screens and structural portals at an invest-ment banking firm that moved into a former glass factory in Palo Alto, California. Custom furniture includes plastic laminate desks and a zinc-topped conference table; existing concrete floors were stained a deep earth color.
PHOTO BY JOHN VAUGHN

BELOW Asian design themes lend a feeling of serenity to these San Francisco offices. The executive reception area features a banquette with silk pillows and restrained col-ors; indirect light washes across the grid-patterned beech wall.
PHOTO BY JOHN SUTTON

OPPOSITE Clean modernist space provides a showcase setting for the Cubist cabinet and screens that divide the conference areas at an Alameda, California, investment banking firm. The cabinet conceals audio-visual equipment while pro-viding an ideal showcase for an eclectic collection of artifacts.
PHOTO BY JOHN SUTTON

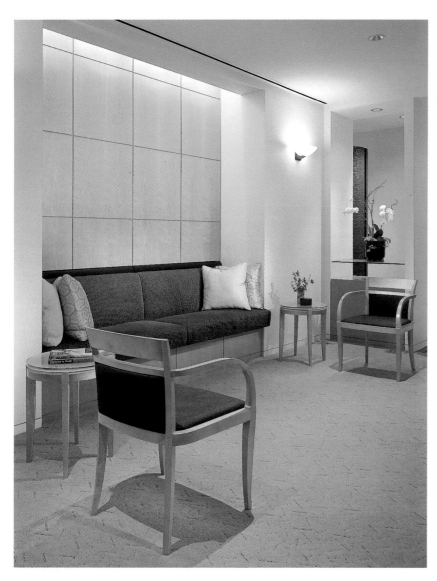

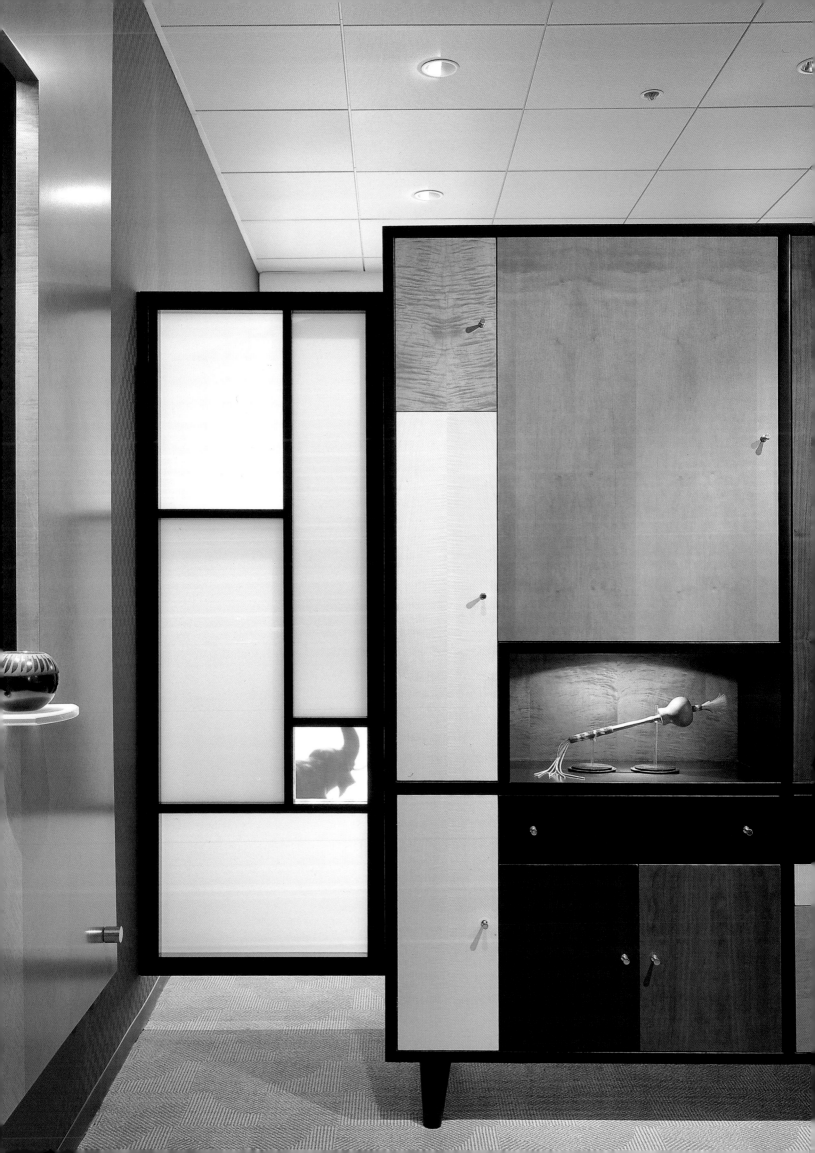

BRENNAN BEER GORMAN MONK / INTERIORS

Brennan Beer Gorman Monk/Interiors focuses on creating solutions for each client's unique requirements, achieving more than budget and schedule compliance. The firm provides efficient, effective, and dynamic interior environments that support each client's goals. Responsible for more than 10 million square feet (900,000 square meters) of interior construction, the firm has experience spanning a variety of industries, including insurance, construction, pharmaceuticals, law, real estate, entertainment, hospitality, and retail. The firm was established in 1987 by the founding partners of Brennan Beer Gorman/ Architects with Julia Monk as president. In 1989, an additional office in Washington, D.C., was established to serve the ongoing needs of clients in the Southeast. The firm's interiors staff is comprised of space planners, designers, and renderers; 3D computer modeling/CADD technicians, project architects, and many other specialists. Collectively they produce work that is internationally recognized as unique and innovative, which leads to the best reward of all— satisfied and prosperous clients.

OPPOSITE Wood tones are carried throughout the office in the desks, tables, cabinetry, and doors to create a warm and inviting environment. To complement the richness of wood, the designers selected khaki-colored carpet and upholstered seating.
PHOTO BY DAN CUNNINGHAM

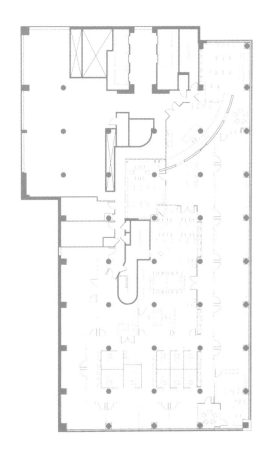

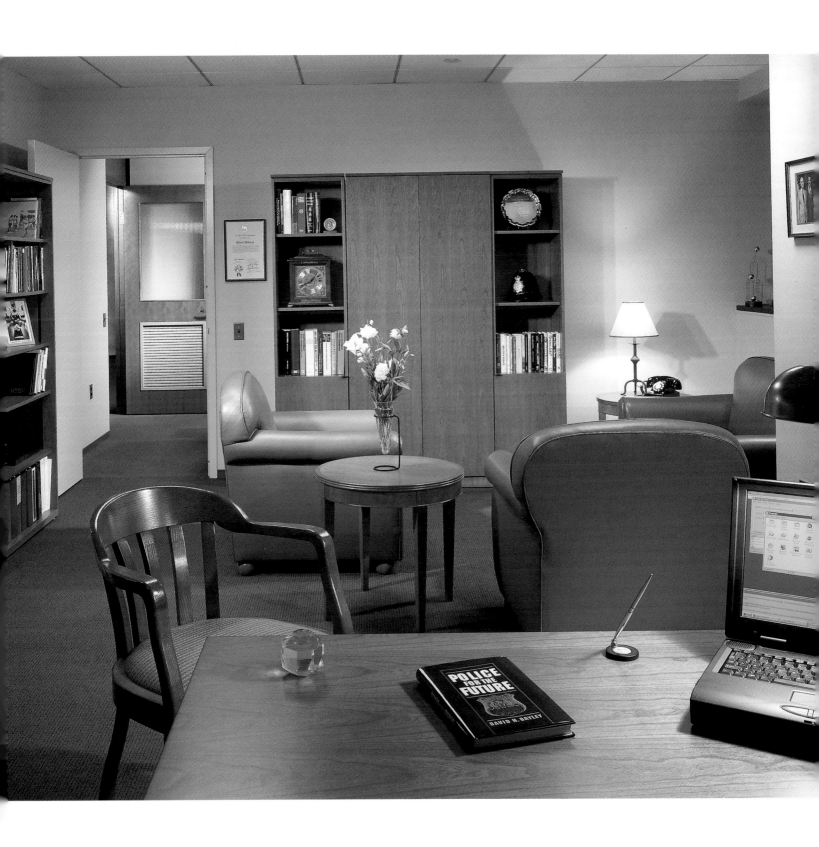

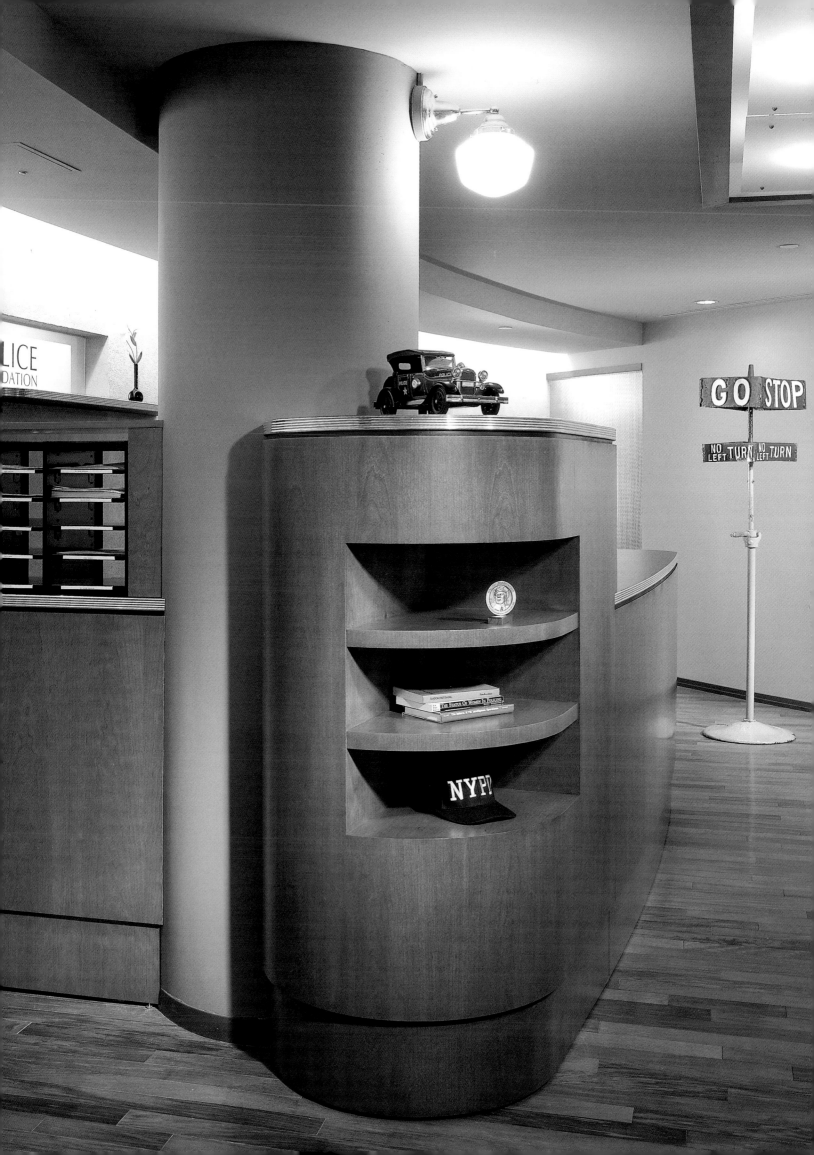

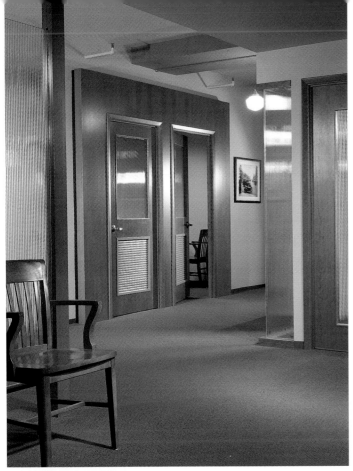

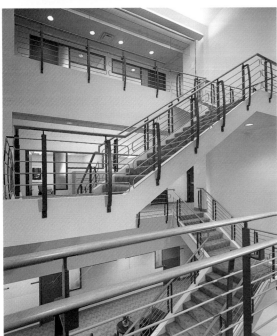

OPPOSITE Unusually large columns posed a challenge to the designers, who integrated this one in the lobby with the custom cherry reception desk. The curved wall behind is a textured backdrop with cove lighting and a cut-out for sandblasted signage.
PHOTO BY DAN CUNNINGHAM

ABOVE Retro décor—paneled door surrounds, ribbed glass, and stout wooden chairs—recall a movie set image of a 1940s police precinct at these offices for a police support organization in Washington, D.C.
PHOTO BY DAN CUNNINGHAM

LEFT A new internal stair was constructed by removing two floor slabs to link several departments in this New York City office.
PHOTO BY PAUL WARCHOL

BELOW LEFT Dropped ceilings were removed from this existing office to reveal beautiful vaulted slab construction. Alternative furniture mockups were erected for employee review before final selections were made.
PHOTO BY PAUL WARCHOL

BELOW RIGHT Poor availability of natural light was compensated for by designing custom ceiling fixtures that bounce light off the newly exposed vaults.
PHOTO BY PAUL WARCHOL

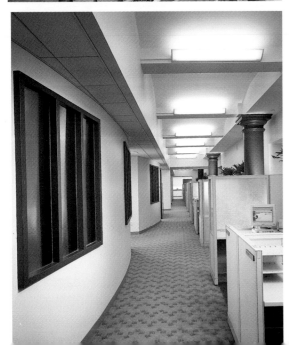

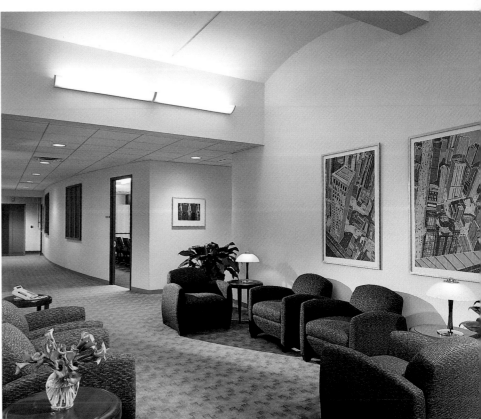

CALLISON ARCHITECTURE

Callison maximizes the design potential of each project through a balance of art, business, and technology. Founded in 1975, the firm develops innovative solutions in partnership with its clients, creating value by enhancing the clients' success. Callison provides full-service planning and design services to retail, hospitality, residential, health care, and corporate clients throughout the world. Services include architecture, master planning, interior design, graphic design, corporate facility consulting, and purchasing. The firm's specialties include corporate offices and campus planning, health care facilities, retail-based urban mixed-use developments, and a wide range of retail, entertainment, and hospitality projects. Based in Seattle, Callison is one of the largest architectural design firms in the United States, with a staff of more than 400 professionals. The firm also maintains offices in Hong Kong.

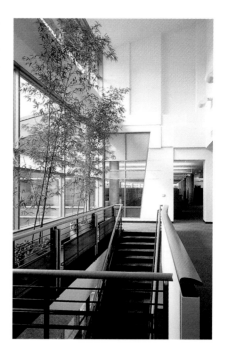

RIGHT Abundant natural light and awareness of the outdoors are emphasized in the design of this corporate headquarters in Redmond, Washington. Clerestory windows spill light into the informal gathering areas on the second-level gallery.

OPPOSITE The stone walls and recycled wood floors of the waiting lobby outside the executive wing reflect the design team's efforts to connect indoors and out. Mission-style furniture is from the client's own product line. ALL PHOTOS BY CALLISON ARCHITECTURE, INC.

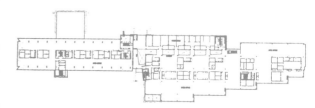

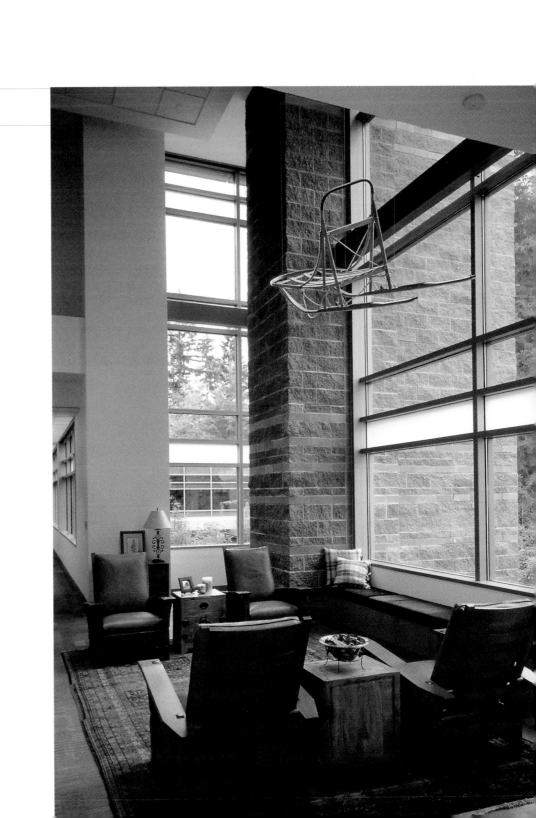

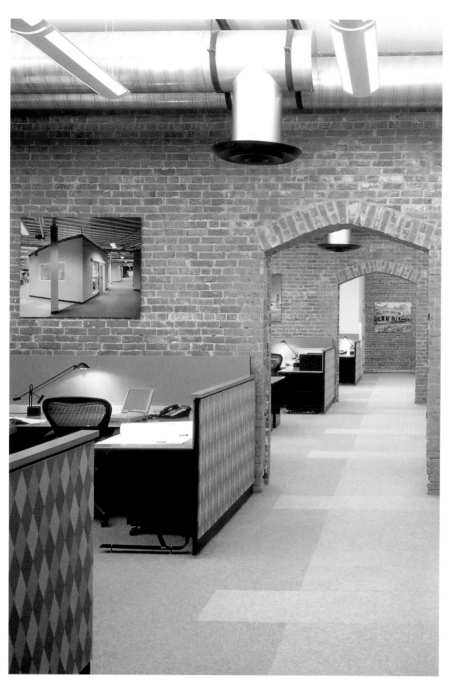

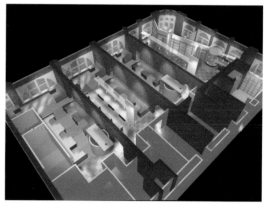

LEFT A contemporary palette of form, materials, color, and detail complements the historic building that houses this construction company's Seattle offices. The blue, green, and ochre color scheme evokes associations with the natural setting of the Pacific Northwest.

BELOW Wheeled workstations arranged on a raised floor allow the creative groups of this 3D animation software company to reconfigure swiftly into new combinations as assignments change.

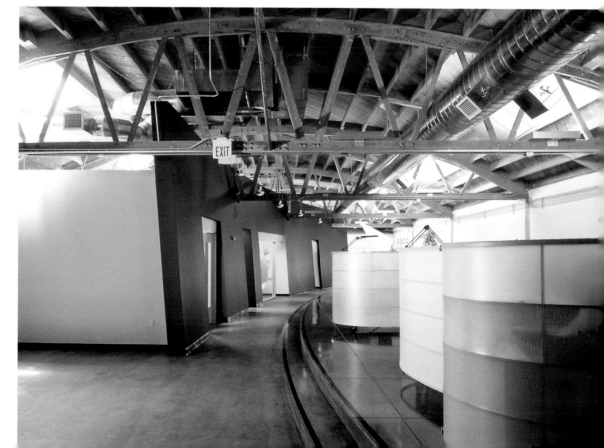

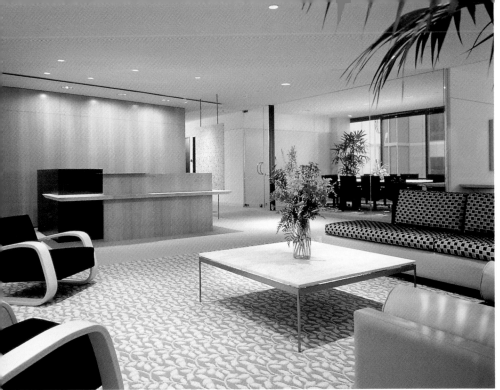

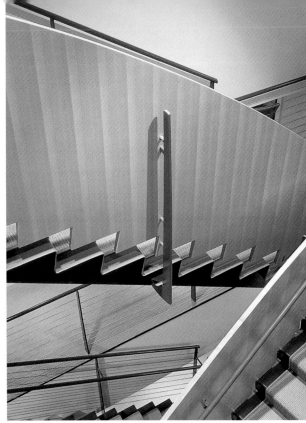

ABOVE LEFT To achieve the greatest impact on a tight budget, the office upgrade of this San Diego law firm refreshed and reused materials wherever possible. Soft muted colors and natural wood finishes reflect the context of the Southern California desert and evoke a sense of tranquility.

ABOVE RIGHT The redesign of this office minimized space previously dedicated to circulation while adding a three-level staircase to create more flexible, efficient circulation and establish a visual tie between floors.

CAMAS ASSOCIATES ARCHITECTS PA

Established in 1983 by Wayne H. Camas, AIA, Camas Associates Architects PA is a multi-service firm offering architecture, space planning, and interior design services. The firm is uniquely qualified to assist clients based on its in-house capabilities to handle every phase of a project—from the initial design and space planning to working drawings and finish selection—and to respond to clients' time requirements and budget constraints. While the firm has provided services to clients throughout the Southeast, most of its completed projects are located in or near its home city of Charlotte, North Carolina. These projects include single-family homes, commercial and retail facilities, and institutional projects.

RIGHT The lobby wall and stair screen recall the curved exterior wall of this three-story suburban office building in Greensboro, North Carolina.

OPPOSITE The rotunda room is a pivotal component of the suite containing reception, executive dining, and the board room in this 174,000-square-foot (16,165-square-meter) regional headquarters for an insurance company. Movable mahogany-framed panels allow easy flow into the reception area and conference room opposite it.

ALL PHOTOS BY RICK ALEXANDER & ASSOCIATES, INC.

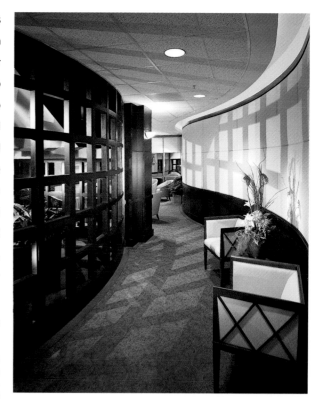

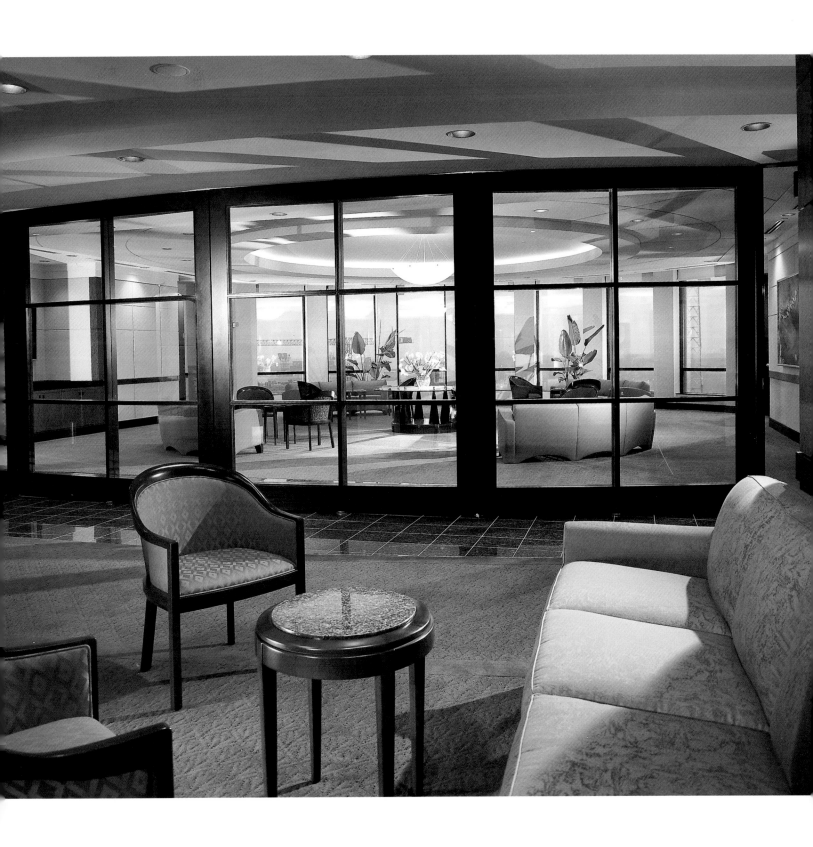

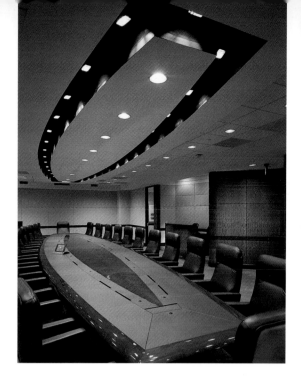

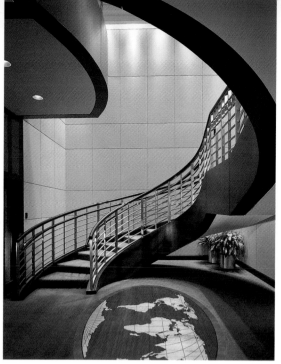

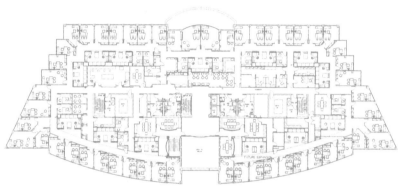

ABOVE LEFT The tenth-floor board room is a high-tech television studio in disguise. Features include three-way teleconferencing, power and data at each seat, and the ability to operate a/v functions from the podium, recorder station, or conference table, which was custom-designed by Camas Associates in mahogany and black leather.

ABOVE RIGHT Used for circulation between the executive floor and the floor below, which holds training facilities and other operating companies, the monumental stair is a graceful element of sculpted mahogany and stainless steel.

RIGHT The second floor stair landing connects the building's multistory atrium to the client's office space. Carpeting was selected to pick up on the muted green of the window mullions.

OPPOSITE The unusually tall floor-to-floor height in this older downtown Charlotte building allowed for added architectural interest. The cherry-and-marble reception desk was designed by the architect.

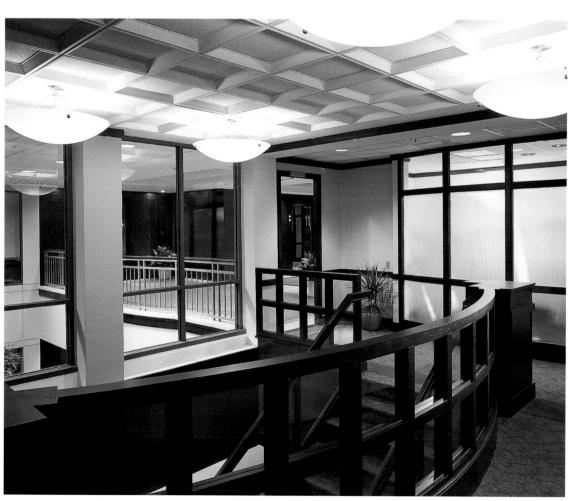

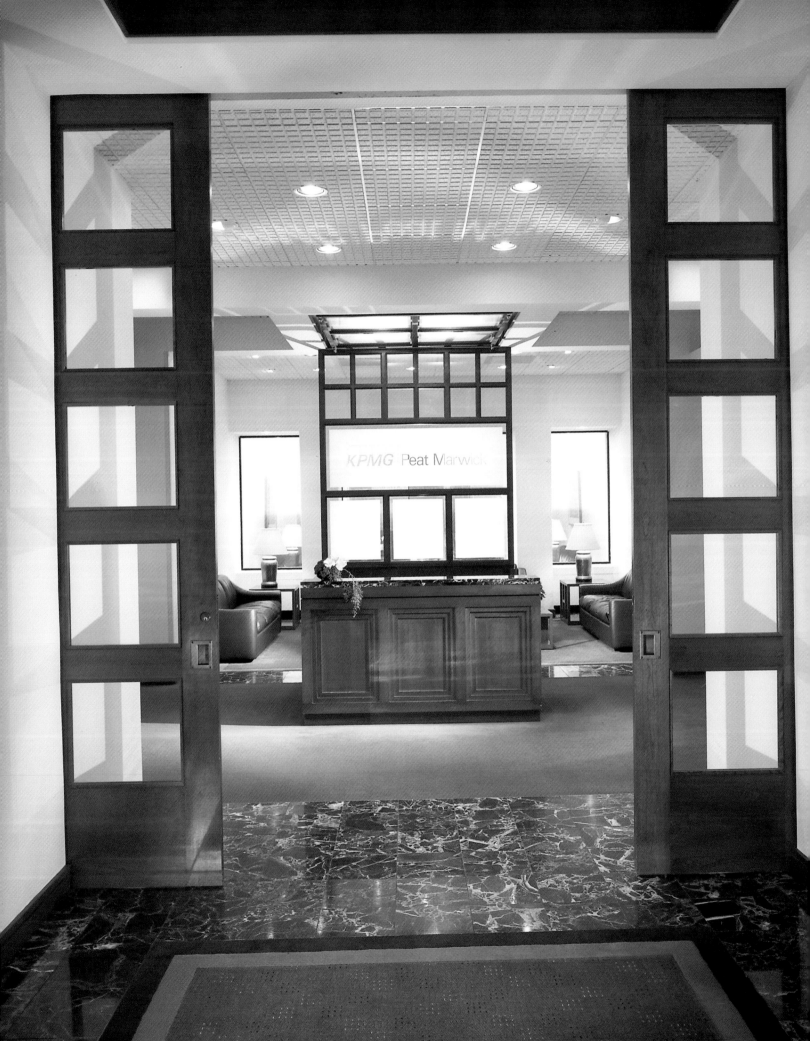

CANNON

The firm's unique form of organization—a "single-firm/multi-office" practice—enables Cannon to focus staff resources to meet client needs from the most convenient location. By providing all disciplines under one roof—planners, interior designers, architects, and engineers—the firm offers clients a single point of responsibility and accountability, a team working with commitment to ensure each project's success. Cannon strives to create environments that are a thoughtful response to the program mission, physical setting, and functional purpose—spaces that reflect the spirit and personality of each owner. The firm of 300 delivers services through seven regional centers located in the U.S.

OPPOSITE Mahogany framing around balcony windows and three shades of granite on the floors add warmth and contrast to the soaring six-story atrium of a Buffalo bank.
PHOTO BY PATRICIA LAYMAN BAZELON

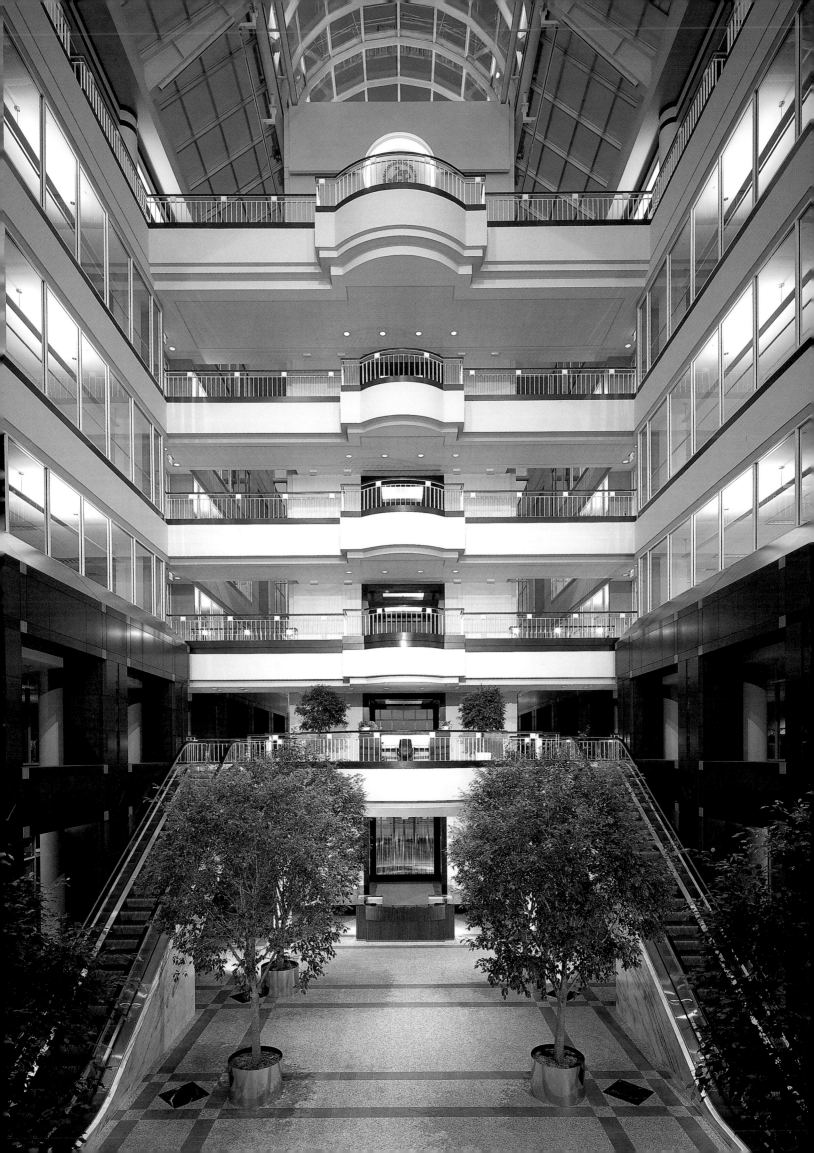

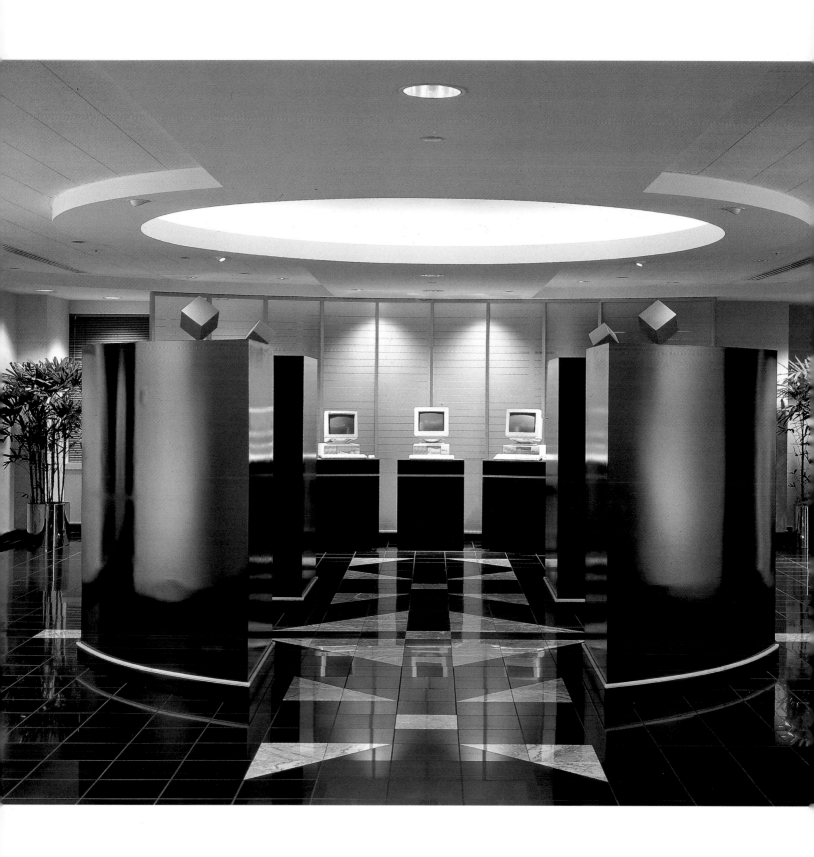

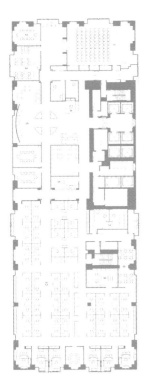

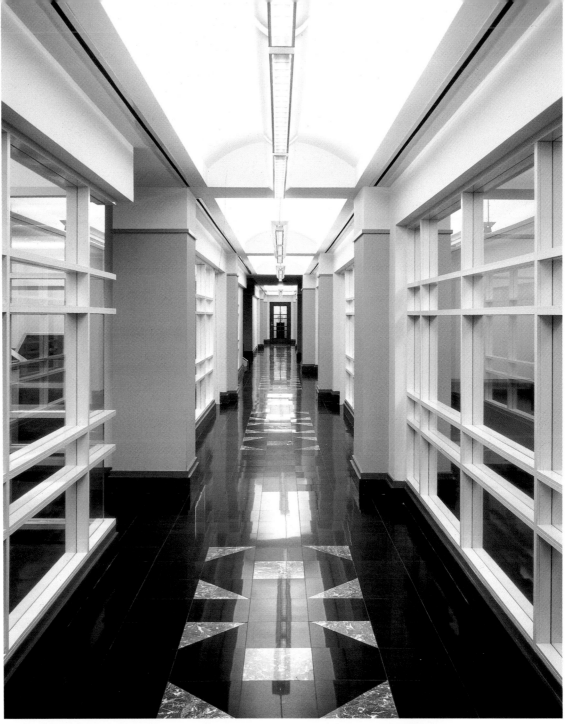

OPPOSITE The demonstration area of this business machines company in San Francisco is designed in the manner of a computer showroom. Glass corridor walls give visitors an instant view of the company's wide range of products.
PHOTO BY JEFF GOLDBERG/ESTO

ABOVE RIGHT The interior streetscape of these New York City offices is typified by black and gray marble floors, an articulated ceiling, maple-and-sandblasted-glass screen walls, and "rice paper" wall coverings.
PHOTO BY ELLIOTT KAUFMAN PHOTOGRAPHY

RIGHT The reception area of this international software company has a serpentine perforated metal wall, wire-grid ceiling with track lighting above, interactive computer terminals, and blue-box demonstration room to showcase the firm's education and training programs.
PHOTO BY PETER PAIGE ASSOCIATES PETER PAIGE

FAR RIGHT This New York City elevator lobby makes a sweeping statement articulated by an alternating tile floor pattern and raised ceiling. Perforated metal awnings conceal electric blue accent lights.
PHOTO BY PETER PAIGE ASSOCIATES PETER PAIGE

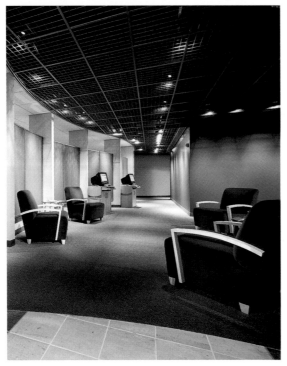

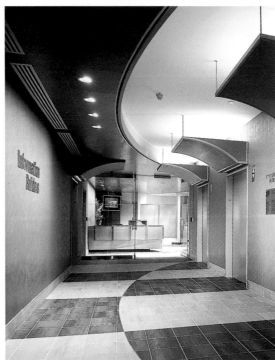

CDFM² ARCHITECTURE INC

A diversified architectural services firm, CDFM² provides its clients with complete solutions through a full-service approach integrating architecture, interiors, and facility management. CDFM² believes that the most rewarding results are the product of a dynamic collaboration between owner and architect. The firm builds on the principle that a successful design concept is formed from equal parts of clear-eyed analysis and creative problem solving. CDFM², therefore, focuses on designing buildings from the "inside out," which means determining clients' needs in relation to an individual project's goals—then designing facilities around those needs. The intent is to achieve a creative, flexible, and practical scheme that will perform well into the next century.

OPPOSITE A small conference room, situated between two private offices, includes a custom conference table and leather chairs highlighted by a canopy light fixture, fabric panels, and anigre trim.
PHOTO BY TIMOTHY HURSLEY

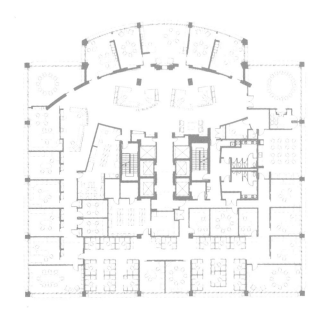

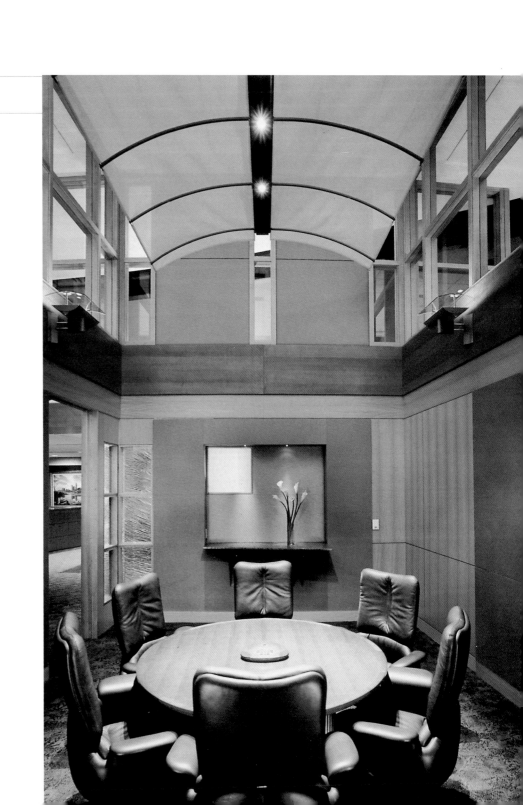

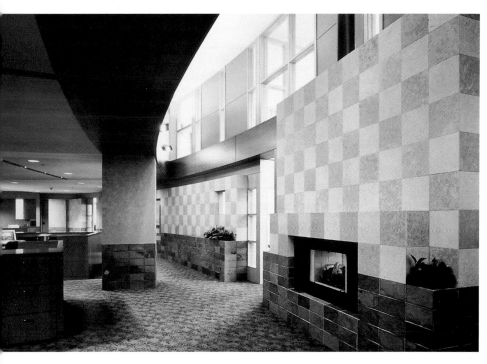

ABOVE Sandblasted and honed limestone create a checkerboard effect along the curvilinear back wall of this Kansas City company's reception area.

RIGHT The elegance of this large conference room is accentuated by a suspended glass light fixture. Patterned glass and the limestone wall continue into the reception area beyond.

PHOTOS BY TIMOTHY HURSLEY

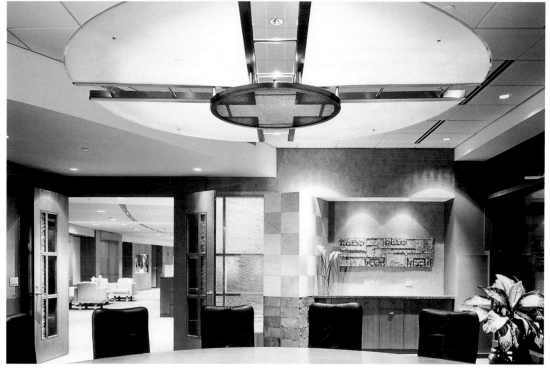

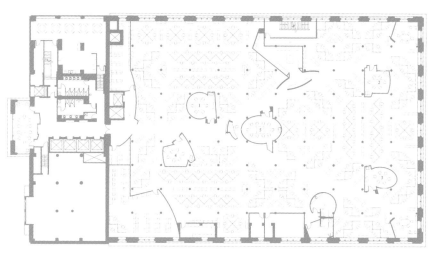

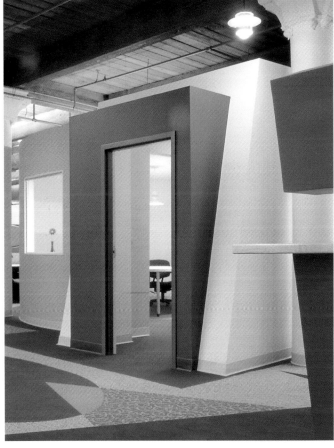

RIGHT Located along the internal street of this Kansas City company are seven "community centers" signaled by unique and colorful entry-ways. The centers are cross-functional spaces that accommodate conferencing, team meetings, and project work groups.

BELOW LEFT Changes in color, form, and lighting distinguish the resource zone from the idea and collaboration zone that exists within each community center.

BELOW RIGHT A free-flowing furniture layout with lower panel heights, body-pocket work surfaces, paper management toolbars, and mobile pedestals supports the user's change in work philosophy.

PHOTOS BY MIKE SINCLAIR

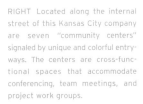

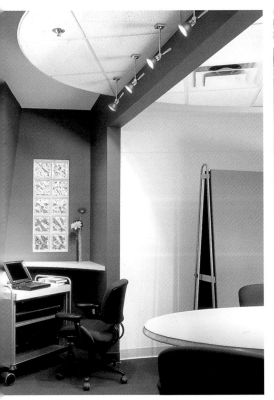

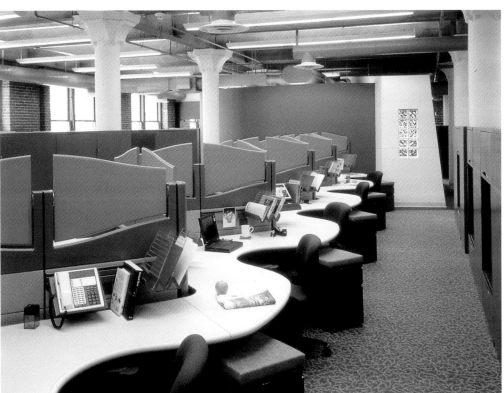

CORE

CORE cultivates a professional culture focused on producing high-quality work and delivering client satisfaction. Its primary business is design, with capabilities including architecture, interior design, master planning, historic preservation, and graphic design. Specializing in creative problem solving, CORE has a reputation for total image development. The firm pursues innovation in every aspect of its work, devising methods that respond to each client's unique and changing needs.

RIGHT The sculptural supervisor's tower creates a focal point between two open workstation areas and allows easy monitoring of operations on the floor. Existing structural glazed tile walls in some areas of the base building complement the new material palette.

OPPOSITE The company's focus on electronic warranty service is underscored by the display of antique electronic artifacts throughout the space. The building perimeter is reserved for private offices and a conference room, seen here behind one of the large sloped drywall partitions that create a series of colorful backdrops in the windowless environment.
ALL PHOTOS BY MICHAEL MORAN PHOTOGRAPHY

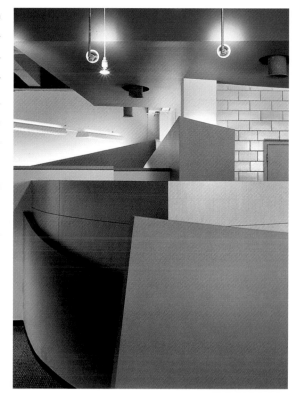

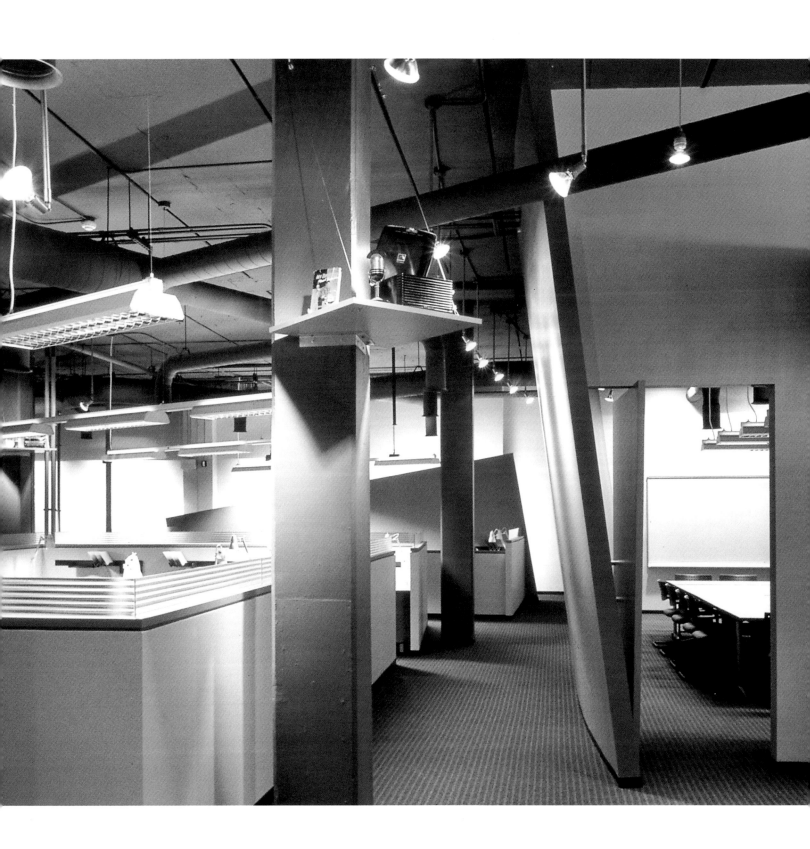

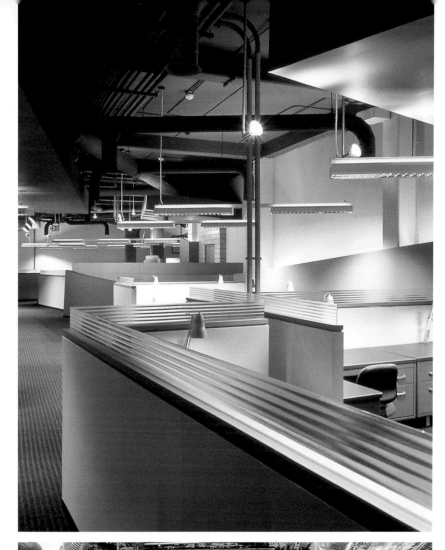

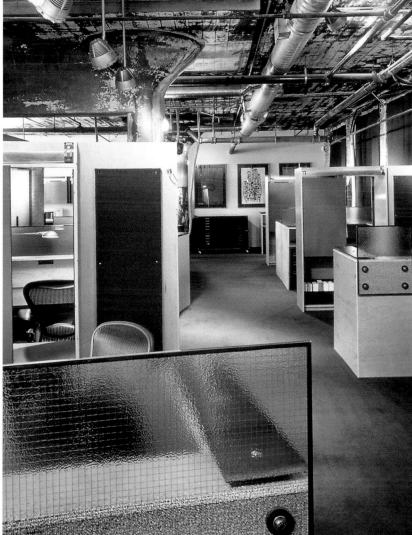

ABOVE Free-floating workstations in this Washington, D.C., graphic design firm are constructed of birch veneer plywood, medium density fiberboard, and cold rolled steel. Framed wire safety glass adds a level of privacy to each station, along with a movable panel that slides to allow communication between stations.

LEFT The layout of this call center in Great Falls, Montana, is composed of a series of open workstations organized in team clusters. Surrounding the clusters are low partitions that feed power and data cabling to the workstations. Panels of fluted glass on top of the partitions reinforce the retro look of metal desks.

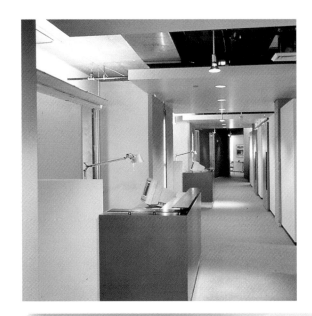

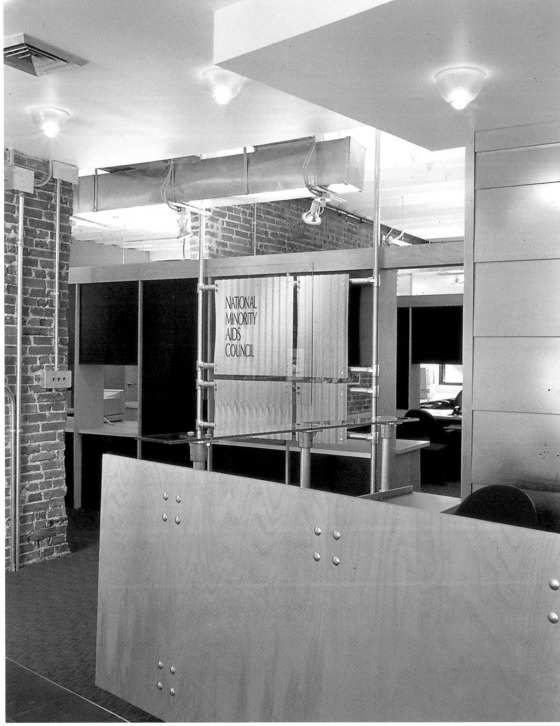

ABOVE RIGHT General work spaces at this Washington, DC, firm incorporate birch sliding doors, exposed concrete ceilings, and industrial carpet and light fixtures.

RIGHT By converting two derelict townhouses into a single building, the architects created new offices for their client. Counters, desks, shelves, filing cabinets, and chairs were designed to maximize space-efficiency and achieve dramatic results on a $700,000 budget.

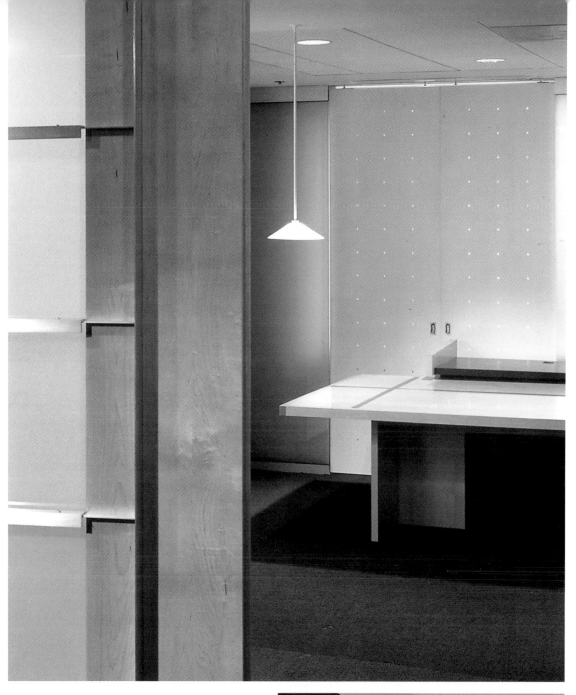

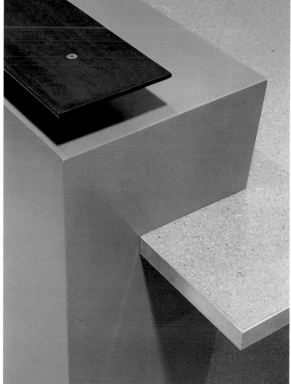

ABOVE LEFT By employing a series of sliding and pivot doors, this conference room doubles as a meeting space or well-equipped reception area. Movable conference tables convert to buffets and, when its doors are open, the pantry doubles as a serving bar.

LEFT The minimalist aesthetic of the custom millwork and furniture reinforces a straightforward design approach borne of budget constraints, while allowing for an expressive use of color.

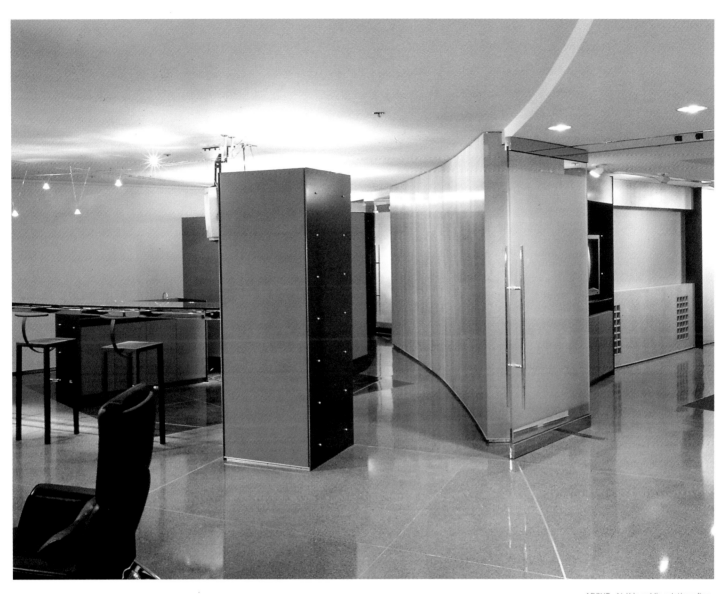

ABOVE At this public relations firm, the designers created a dynamic environment by layering lines, planes, and volumes. These elements interact to frame vistas and define informal spaces where employees work alone or on teams.

ELKUS / MANFREDI ARCHITECTS LTD

Founded by Howard F. Elkus, FAIA, RIBA, and David P. Manfredi, AIA, Elkus/Manfredi Architects Ltd, is a full-service design firm providing architecture, master planning, urban design, interior architecture, space planning, and programming. In its ten-year history, Elkus/Manfredi has been selected by CEOs and decision-makers around the country to make their goals tangible. The firm has helped clients evaluate their business processes and analyze future trends, at times leading to the development of a new prototypical design or implementation of a new way of doing business. Elkus/Manfredi's portfolio includes a rich diversity of projects that energizes the firm's work by a cross-pollination of ideas.

OPPOSITE Groupings of European-styled furniture and custom sculptures create focal points of interest in this two-story atrium, which is flanked by large conference rooms. Floors are polished concrete.
PHOTO BY MARCO LORENZETTI ©HEDRICH BLESSING

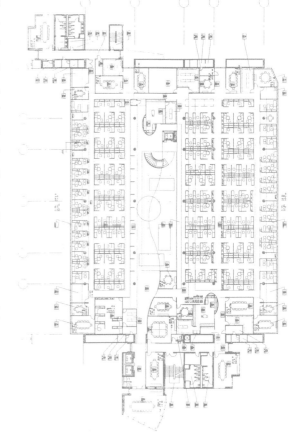

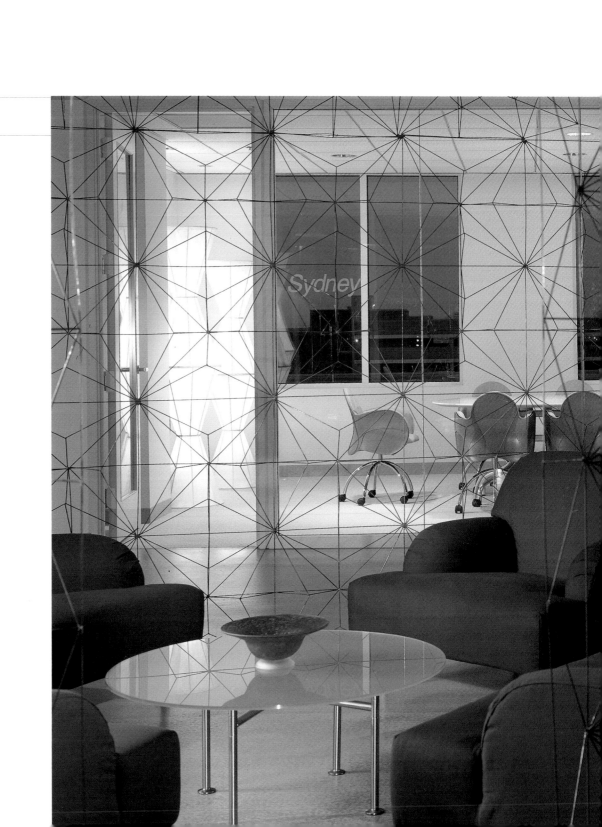

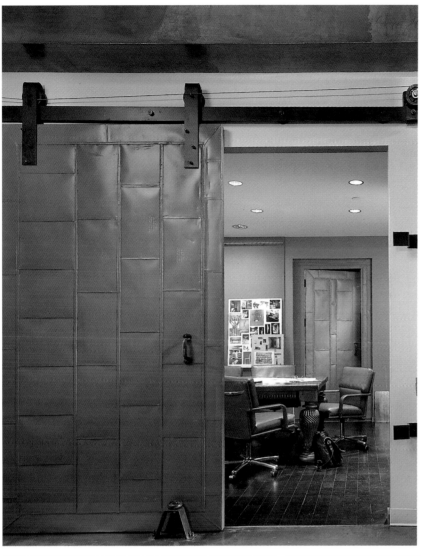

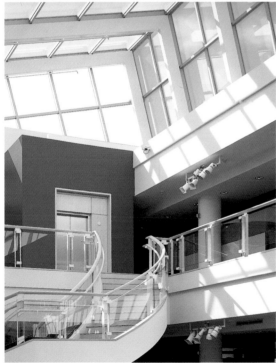

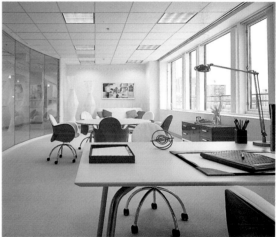

ABOVE Leather-tile flooring and Moroccan furnishings combine with iron-clad pulley doors to create a unique old-world feel in this conference room for a Boston ad agency.

FAR LEFT A new three-story atrium runs through the center of the entire building, spilling sunlight into the open office environment that surrounds the spaces. Both an elevator and curved staircase offer easy access between floors.

LEFT Large offices accommodate work, meeting, and seating areas. Typical offices in this six-floor interior are glass-walled to bring daylight into the rooms and provide visual connections between interior spaces.

PHOTOS BY MARCO LORENZETTI
©HEDRICH BLESSING

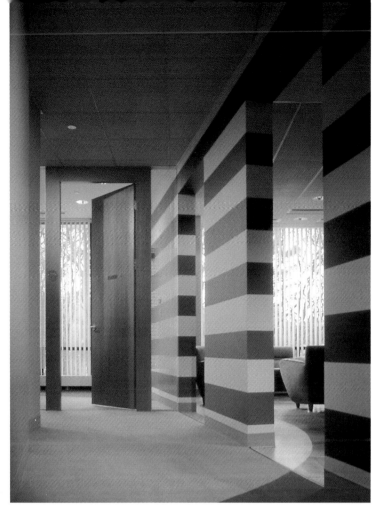

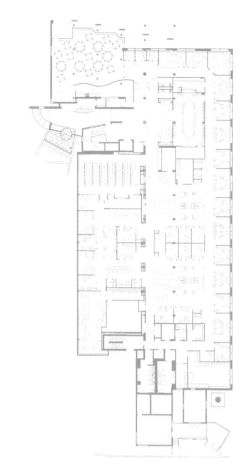

ABOVE Open seating areas (right) are intermingled among the private offices of this international consulting firm, whose spaces were designed with a flexibility to accommodate unpredictable growth.

RIGHT Large-scale photographic murals lining the interior "Main Street," such as the baseball players opposite the coffee bar, add vibrancy to the space and evoke themes of teamwork for this company, a longtime sponsor of the Olympic games.

PHOTOS BY GARY QUESADA
©HEDRICH BLESSING

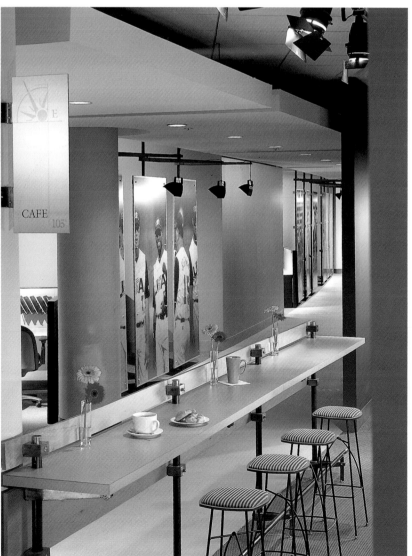

THE ENVIRONMENTS GROUP

Founded in 1991, The Environments Group is a service organization providing master planning and facility programming, interior design, and facility management. Although the firm's projects range in size from 2,000 square feet to nearly 2 million square feet (180 square meters to nearly 180,000 square meters), its mission on each assignment remains the same: to provide the highest standard of professional service and personnel to guarantee the fulfillment of clients' ongoing facility needs. The integration of planning, design, and management services throughout The Environments Group's project work has been vital to the growth of the firm and fosters a sharing of expertise among the different disciplines. The firm's service delivery approach addresses current and long-term business plans—providing clients with efficient means of utilizing their facilities.

OPPOSITE The reception area and entry to private work-spaces in these Sears Tower offices are framed by shell-stone and eucalyptus with brushed metal accents.
PHOTO BY STEVE HALL ©HEDRICH BLESSING

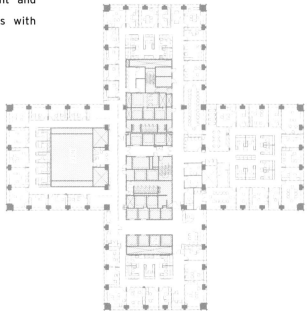

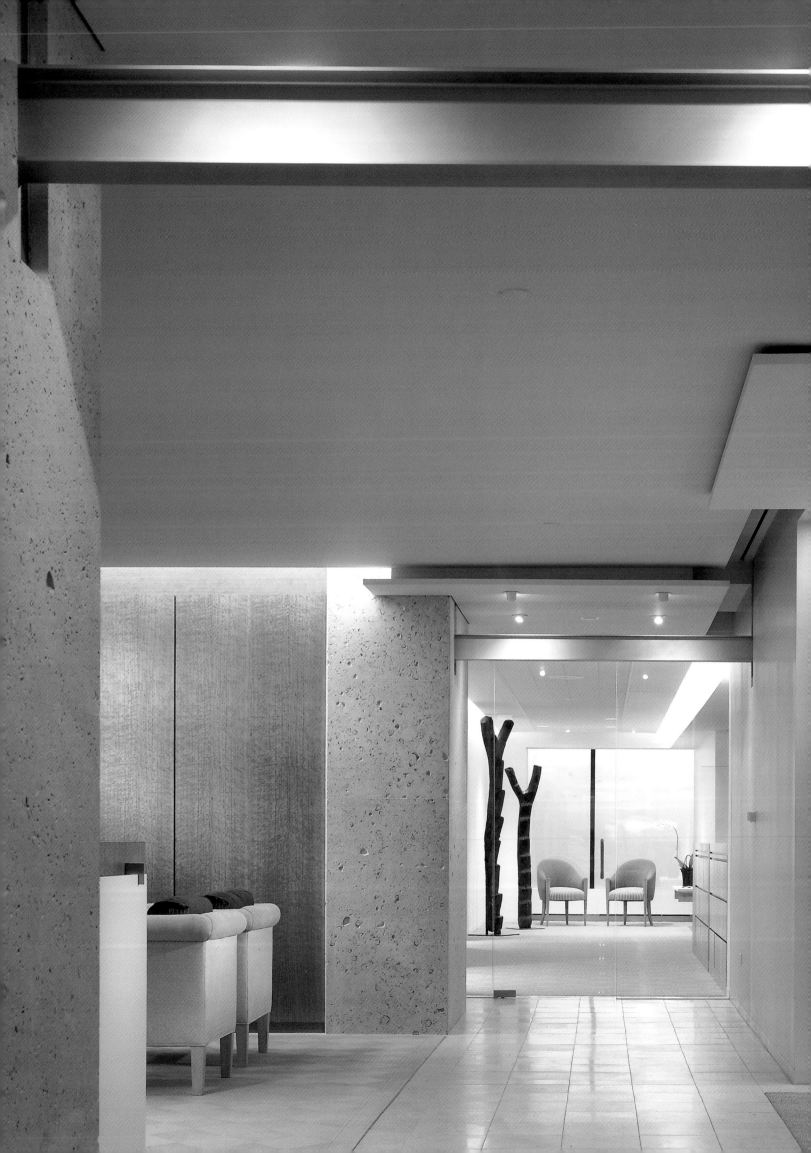

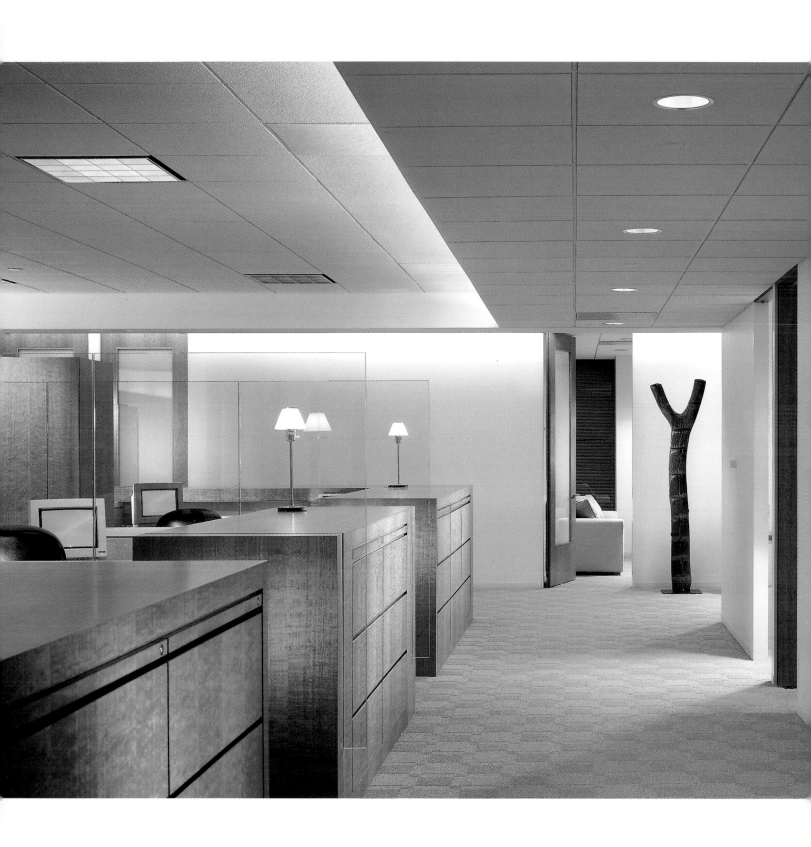

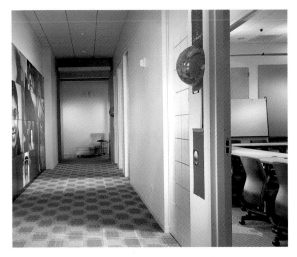

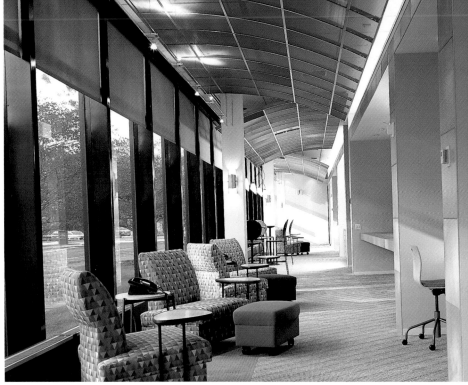

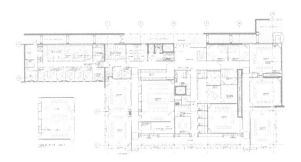

OPPOSITE The work area for executive assistants integrates filing and storage. Eucalyptus and glass enhance the work spaces and the entries to private offices.
PHOTO BY STEVE HALL
©HEDRICH BLESSING

ABOVE LEFT Muted colors and diverse images from around the world create a pleasing environment in the block of training rooms for this international company.
PHOTO BY CHRIS BARRETT
©HEDRICH BLESSING

ABOVE RIGHT Meeting rooms in this corporate training center open to a shared lounge where employees can contact their home office, download files, and send e-mail during breaks. Arched open ceilings, a rich mixture of colors, and flexible furniture create a relaxed feel.
PHOTO BY CHRIS BARRETT
©HEDRICH BLESSING

RIGHT The meeting and presentation space in The Environments Group's offices incorporates a glass wall with custom walnut millwork and layered blinds, allowing free circulation along the office perimeter without affecting light and views. The meeting table can be configured for a variety of uses.
PHOTO BY STEVE HALL
©HEDRICH BLESSING

BELOW RIGHT The firm's resource library is located along the perimeter circulation path, which is kept open to allow natural light to penetrate the space. Project storage is placed at the base of the curtain wall.
PHOTO BY STEVE HALL
©HEDRICH BLESSING

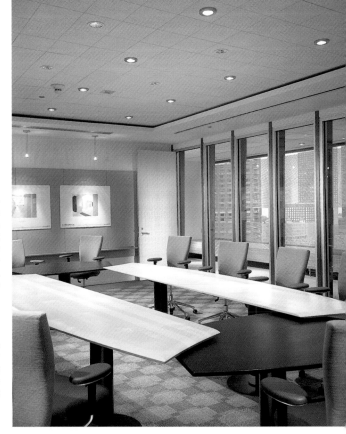

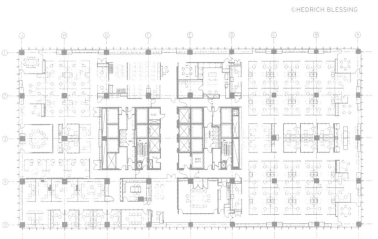

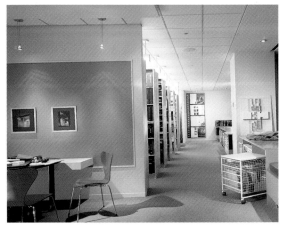

FOX & FOWLE ARCHITECTS, P.C.

Fox & Fowle Architects, P.C., is an architectural, interior design, and planning firm of fifty people. The firm provides a complete range of services including feasibility studies, program analysis, site selection, and post-occupancy evaluation for projects of every size and scope. Robert F. Fox, Jr. and Bruce S. Fowle formed the practice in 1978, establishing a diverse practice with much repeat work in the planning and design of investment-grade office buildings, corporate and institutional interiors, cultural and institutional facilities, residential buildings, and mixed-use, adaptive reuse, and renovation projects. Fox & Fowle's long commitment to interior design continues strong today. Heading the firm's interior architecture projects are design director Peter Jensen and studio director Rodney VenJohn. The interiors work covers a wide range of project sizes and types, from public spaces to boardrooms, from showrooms to educational facilities, and from high-end residential to back office spaces. A hallmark of the studio is its innovative use of "green" materials and the implementation of sustainable design guidelines throughout its work.

OPPOSITE The maple-floored "gallery" space connects the staff offices and showroom. Tack surfaces and chalkboards provide low-tech interactive elements that foster easily customized presentations.
ALL PHOTOS BY MARCO LORENZETTI ©HEDRICH BLESSING

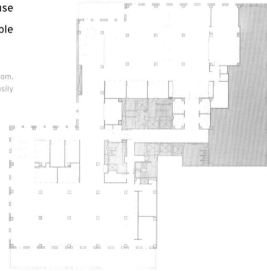

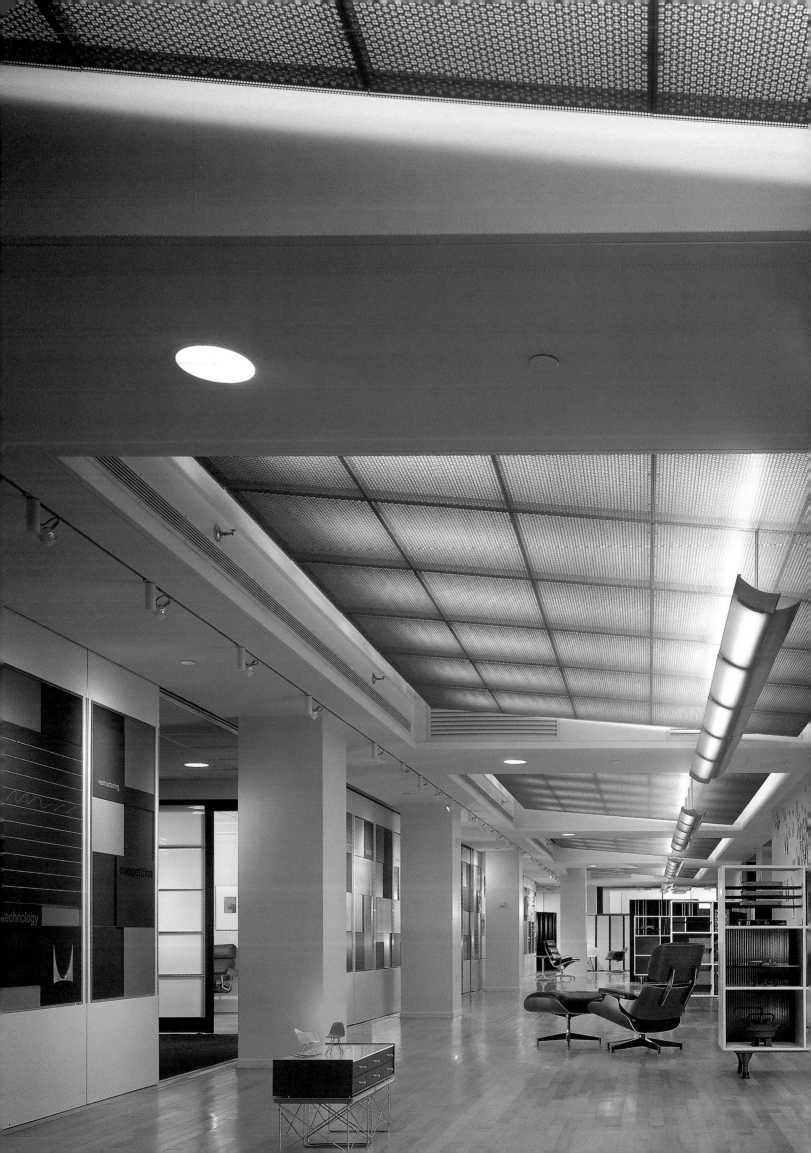

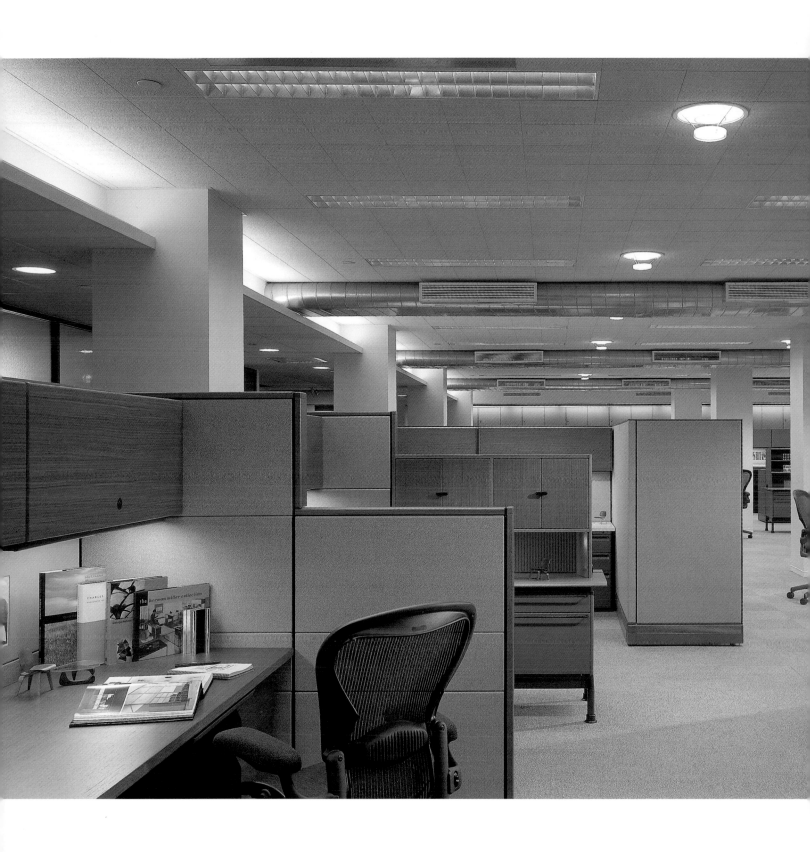

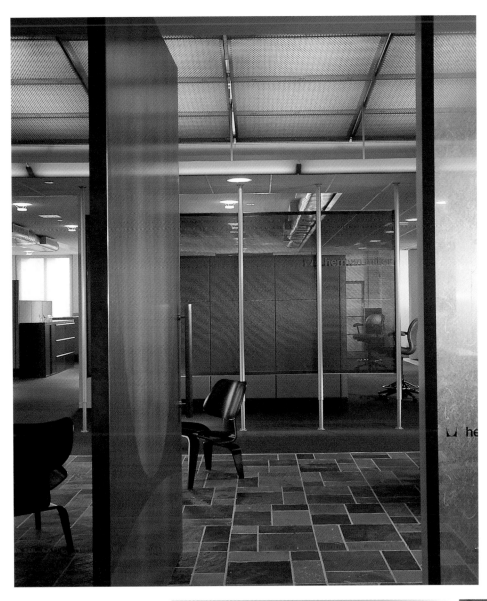

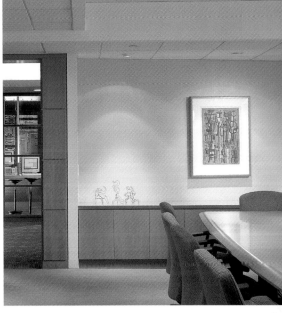

OPPOSITE Staff offices exhibit a cross-section of available system furnishings in a conventional office configuration. Oval ductwork is exposed beneath the ceiling to reinforce the column/bay rhythm and allow the finished ceiling to be as high as possible.

ABOVE LEFT The office/showroom entry off the elevator lobby features an oversized panel door inlaid with the client's corporate logo, a fabric screen wall supported by aluminum poles, a multicolored slate floor, and layered mesh ceiling.

ABOVE RIGHT Views from the main conference room look into the technology demonstration rooms across a central waiting area. A warm palette of luxurious materials contrasts with the firm's high-tech products.

RIGHT This office entry features a sloping gridded wall with a custom, etched-glass logo set in a pearwood surround. Behind the metallic reception desk a mesh curtain wall obscures coat closets.

FAR RIGHT The conference waiting area is punctuated by pearwood portals "rotated" out of the surrounding wall and leading into conference rooms of various sizes.

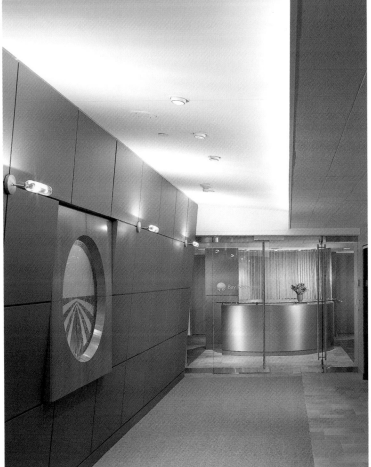

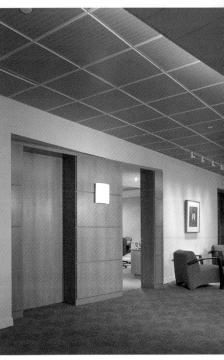

G.A. DESIGN INTERNATIONAL

G.A. Design is an international interior design firm whose projects range from full renovation to new construction of commercial offices, hotels, resorts, restaurants, and clubs. The firm's practice integrates the skills of architects and interior designers to offer clients the full scope of services needed to take a project from initial space planning and design through construction documents, furniture purchase, and installation. G.A. Design operates as a team, selecting the most qualified designer for each project from among the twenty designers in the studio. This expertise, combined with the many years of diverse design experience of the four principals—Werner Aeberhard, Harry Gregory, Terry McGinnity, and Maria Vafiadis—enables the firm to provide clients with unique and creative design solutions. Working within a wide range of budgets, the firm's designers welcome the challenges of creating both attractive and successful working environments.

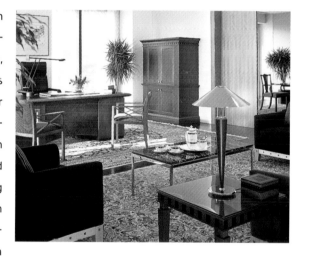

RIGHT Contemporary furniture is mixed with the more traditional lines of the armoire unit adjacent to the chairman's desk. Door at right leads into the adjoining private dining room.

OPPOSITE This executive's office in Canary Wharf offers spectacular views of downtown London. Black leather upholstery complements the beige color scheme, with cherry and maple woods used for the desk, sofa, and side tables

PHOTOS BY NIALL CLUTTON

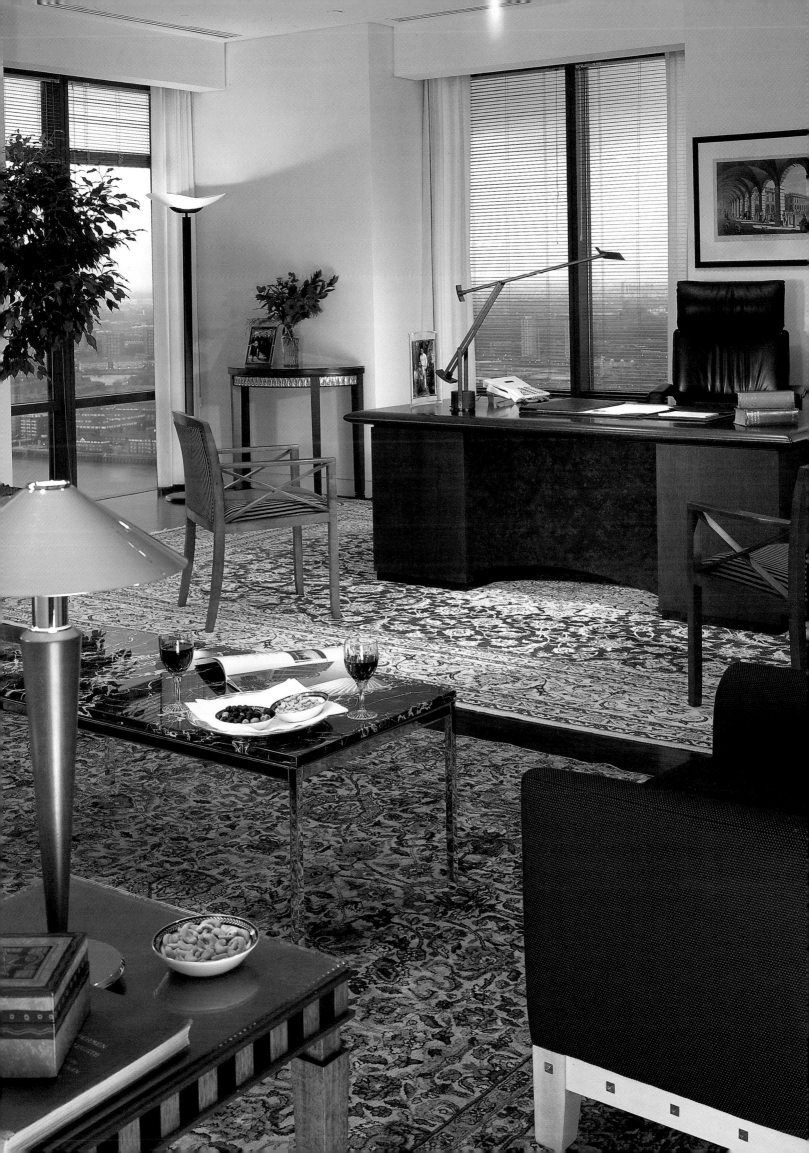

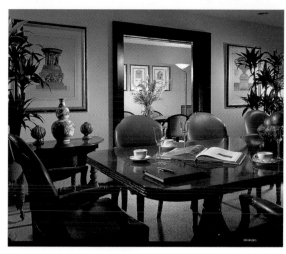

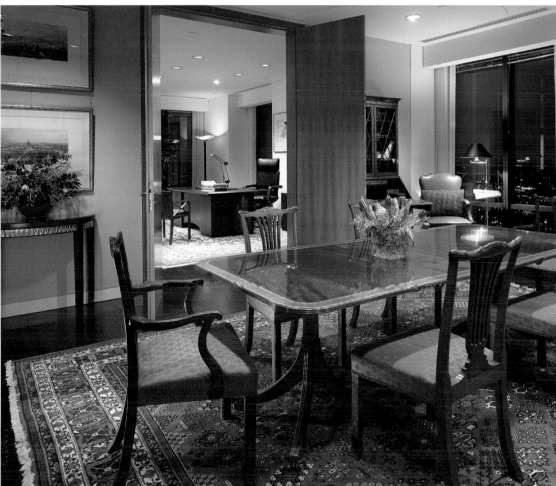

ABOVE A custom-made focal table and padded leather chairs enrich the luxurious boardroom. Sliding mahogany doors allow access to the partners' offices located on either side of the boardroom.
PHOTO BY ROBERT MILLER

LEFT The private dining room makes use of an existing collection of traditional furniture, but existing artwork was relocated and contemporary pieces such as consoles were added to update the space.
PHOTO BY NIALL CLUTTON

BELOW LEFT A richly detailed Oriental rug adds a warming and classical touch to the contemporary interior. The custom-designed armoire, seen at right, houses a television and mini-bar.
PHOTO BY NIALL CLUTTON

OPPOSITE A sunken, black granite entrance well leads into the London design firm's main reception area, which is anchored by a sleek mahogany desk. The space is finished with a polished oak floor; walls are lined with a warm Tuscany faux stone finish.
PHOTO BY ROBERT MILLER

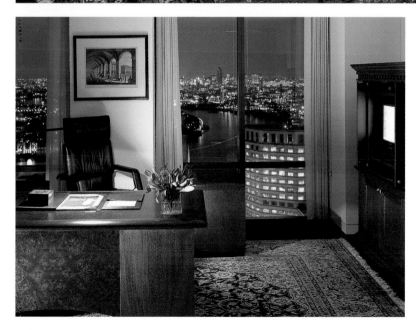

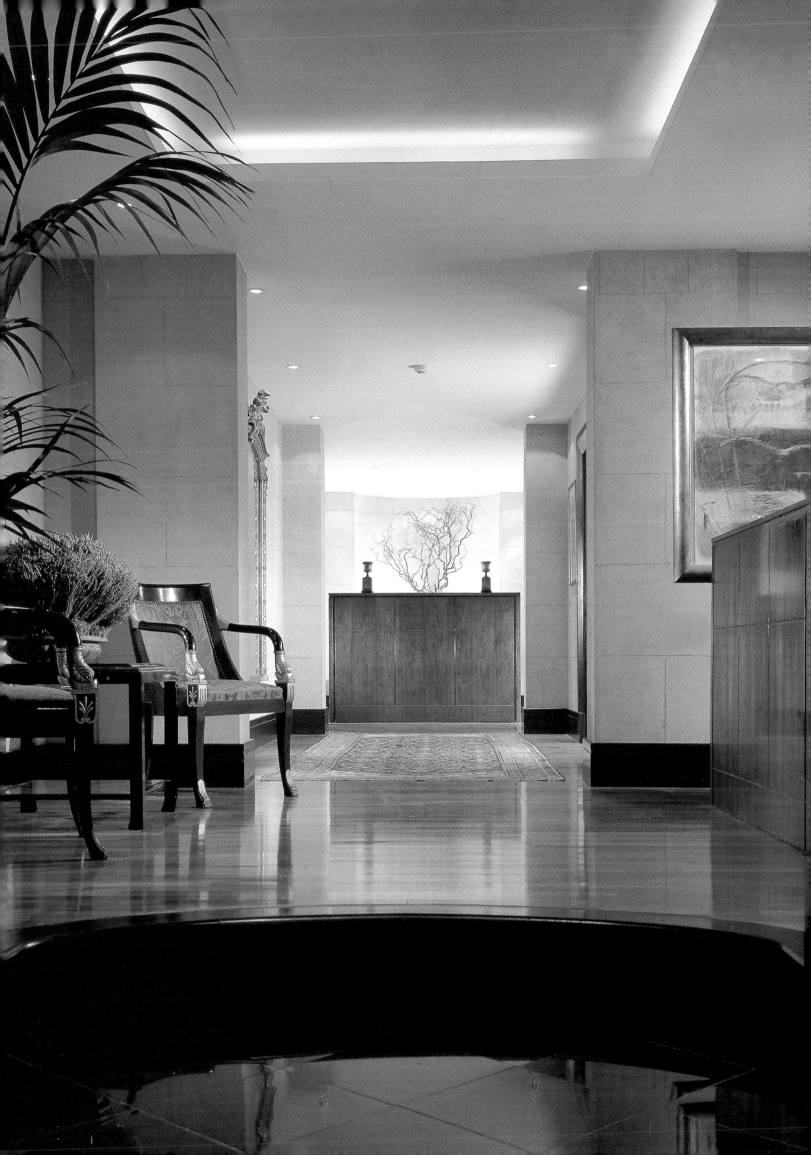

GENSLER

Described by *Fast Company* magazine as one of America's largest and most influential design firms, Gensler provides a full spectrum of comprehensive services in architecture, interior design, branding and communications, retail design, master planning, and design management. The small San Francisco-based group assembled in 1965 by M. Arthur Gensler Jr., FAIA, has grown into a team of more than 1,300 people in 16 offices. In fact, for nearly two decades, Gensler has been recognized as the largest U.S. interior design firm by *Interiors* magazine. In 1998, Gensler received the prestigious Arthur Andersen International Enterprise Award for Best Business Practices in Motivating and Retaining Employees. Progressive management, combined with team members who share a common philosophy, is at the heart of the organization. Beyond that, intangibles such as personality and character have given the firm its leading position in the design community.

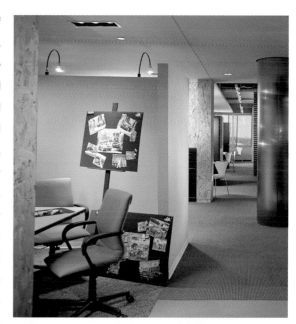

ABOVE RIGHT The main corridor is enlivened by walls with colorful finishes that range from bright green sheetrock to brick and particleboard. This informal gathering area, one of several in the work environment, reflects the client's vision of a "brand team" approach to office organization.

RIGHT Simple, sleek materials respond to an ad agency's desire for a lively industrial aesthetic in its offices. The atrium's curved particleboard, tall aluminum-clad pillars, and vaulted skylight create an airy environment for employees to eat lunch or hold casual meetings.

OPPOSITE The chairman's office at this Hawaiian bank has a large lounge seating area where meetings are conducted in an informal setting. The executive's desk and personal work area can be concealed with a sliding wood-and-glass shoji screen. Twelve-foot-high windows frame panoramic views of Honolulu's skyline. Appointments include maple floors, a large antique oriental rug, silk-covered walls, and classic modern furniture.

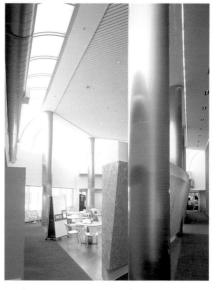

PHOTOS BY MARCO LORENZETTI ©HEDRICH-BLESSING

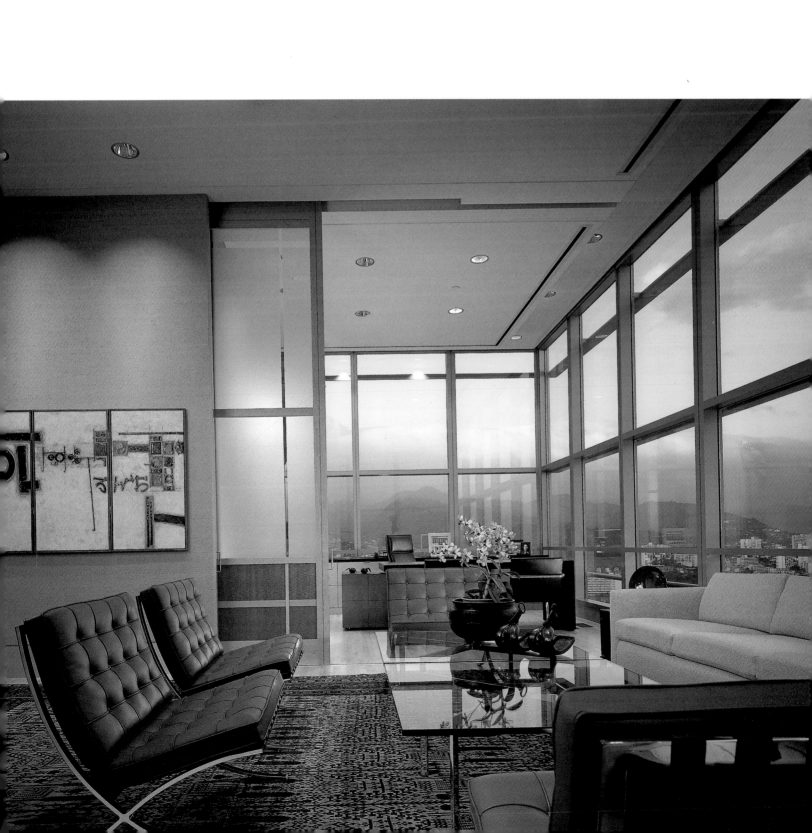

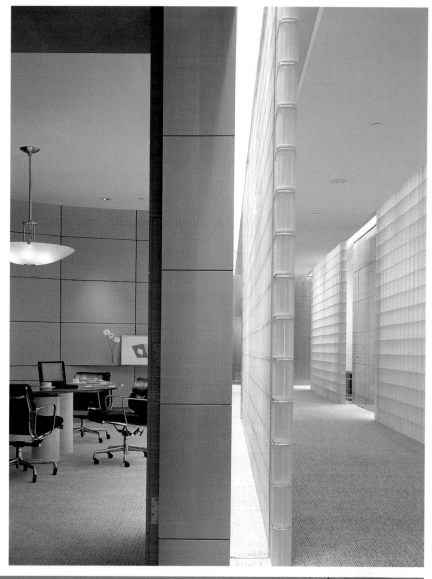

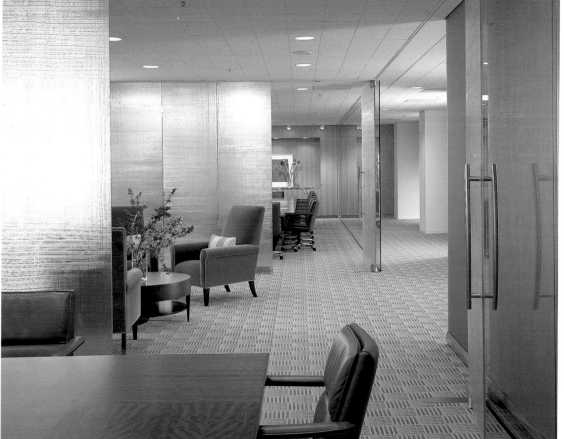

ABOVE LEFT The main corridor at this Swiss company's conference center features a layering of wood and sandblasted glass that screens off executive conference/dining facilities. The strong architecture and cool elegance typify the Swiss propensity for contemporary style.
PHOTO BY NICK MERRICK
©HEDRICH-BLESSING

LEFT Two large client conference rooms flank the reception area. All three spaces can be joined together for staff events by sliding the obscure glass walls into adjoining pockets. The green glass wall is a movable privacy screen chosen in lieu of drapery for the busiest conference room. Glass walls are textured cast glass, carpeting is woven in an oversized pattern, and movable walnut tables are custom designed.
PHOTO BY CHARLES MCGRATH

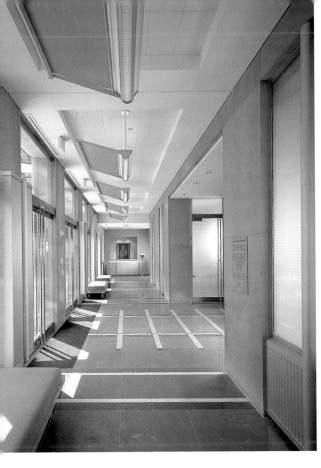

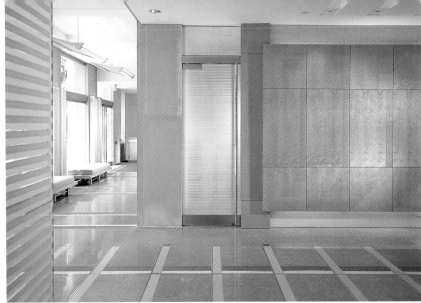

ABOVE LEFT This firm's original exterior arcade was enclosed in glass to provide a ceremonial connection between the main lobby and conference center reception area. The new arcade serves as a transition zone, juxtaposing patinated limestone, textured slate, and exterior steel with the interior's figured maple paneling, patterned glass, and polished stainless steel.
PHOTO BY JON MILLER
©HEDRICH-BLESSING

ABOVE RIGHT This lobby's figured wood paneling, floor pattern, and ceiling treatment coordinate to create a rhythm through space. Wood paneling was suspended in front of the wall and treated as artwork, facilitating a tight schedule by allowing millworkers to begin fabrication prior to demolition of the existing interior. The opaque glass door leads directly to the bookstore, a key contact point for public distribution of the firm's publications.
PHOTO BY JON MILLER
©HEDRICH-BLESSING

BELOW LEFT This client's CEO envisioned a contemporary yet classic design for new executive offices on the penthouse of a prominent downtown high-rise. Among his foremost desires: the suite had to make a powerful statement about the firm's solidity and leave a memorable impression on potential investors. Lighting enhances the color of the English sycamore wood, and provides ambient illumination in the CEO's private suite.
PHOTO BY JON MILLER
©HEDRICH-BLESSING

BELOW RIGHT The designer's goal for this Hawaiian bank's private dining and conference center was to create a contemporary space with strong Asian influences. Finishes in the elevator lobby include Botticino marble floors with inset custom wool carpets, walls paneled in honey-toned Anigre, and a custom wing-shaped ceiling of brushed and polished stainless steel. The lobby is prelude to a series of dining and conference spaces that seat as few as twelve and as many as 120 people.
PHOTO BY MARCO LORENZETTI
©HEDRICH-BLESSING

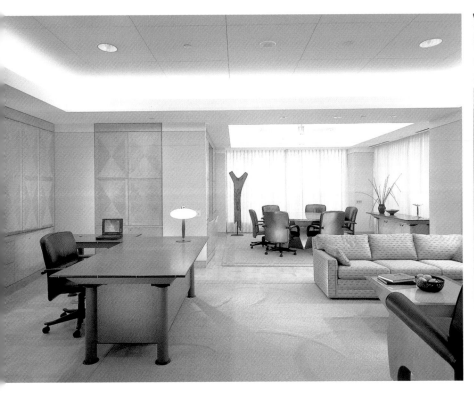

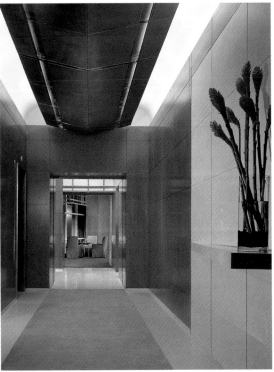

GREENWELL GOETZ ARCHITECTS, P.C.

In addition to its primary focus on interior architecture and design, Greenwell Goetz also provides an array of consulting and advisory services, including construction administration, on-call tenant interiors work for building owners and property managers, strategic facilities planning, space planning, building evaluation, and project coordination.

BELOW The public boardroom is a full-function, state-of-the-art meeting facility with ultimate flexibility to change configurations. Sound panels and carpeting in the space minimize noise and further soundproof the room.

OPPOSITE The reception area and bridge connect the entry portal to the building core. Because a large part of the client's business deals with excavating for water, themes relating to the earth and descent into the earth's crust are introduced by angled stairwells and stone and terrazzo flooring.
PHOTOS BY MAXWELL MACKENZIE

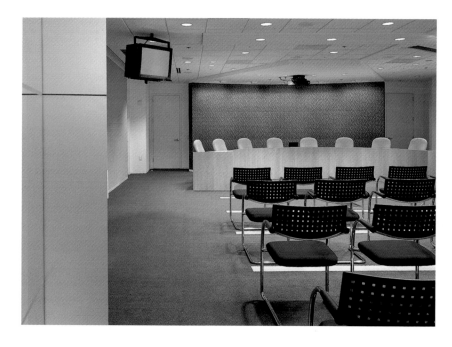

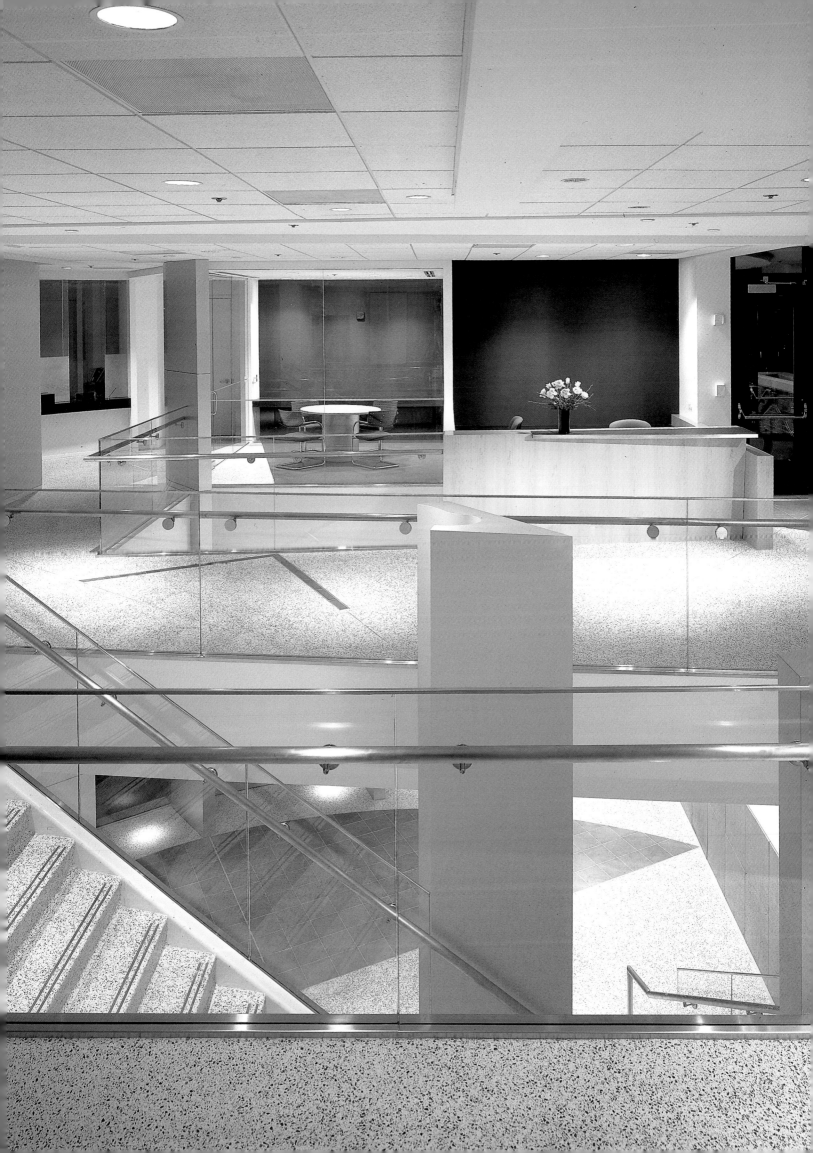

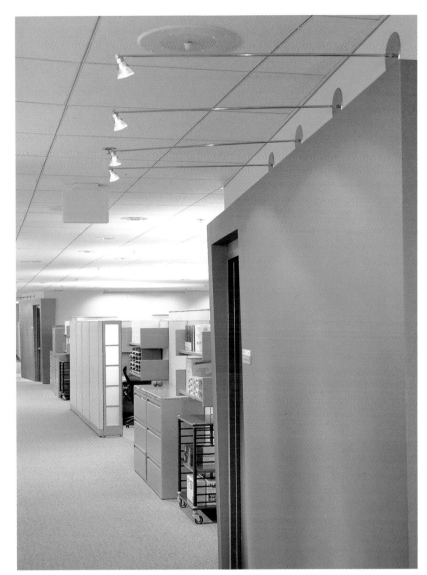

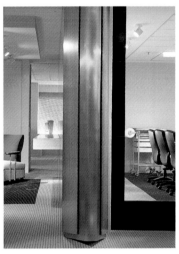

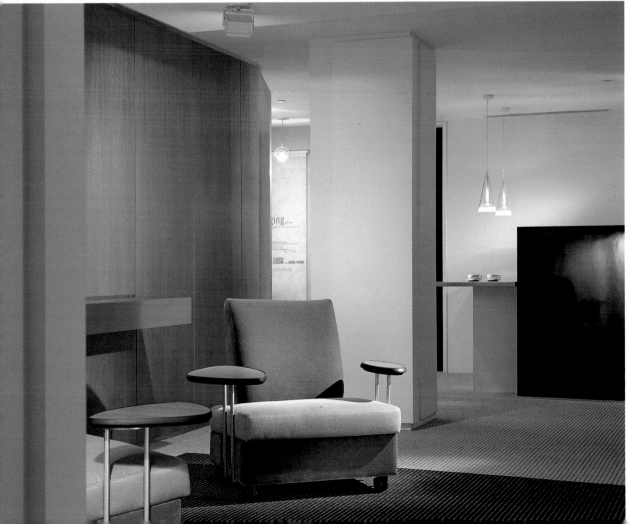

ABOVE LEFT The warm color palette in the workspaces complements the humane aspects of the firm—in sharp contrast to the cold look that often prevails in software companies. Because of heavy computer use by the staff, the designers specified indirect lighting above workstations.

ABOVE RIGHT Separating the reception seating area from the conference room, the thickened wall of eucalyptus panels tapers at each end to reveal a layer of brushed stainless steel beneath.

LEFT Foreground seating in the reception area allows for laptop hook-ups for visitors and office staff. The cafe beyond—which creates an informal environment where sales staff can meet with clients—incorporates a coffee bar and service area.

OPPOSITE In the reception area, a boldly patterned checkerboard terrazzo floor defines public and private zones. High-tech lighting was left exposed as an object in space. Unconventional finishes—such as metallic copper, orbitally sanded aluminum, and frosted glass—were used throughout.

PHOTOS BY JON MILLER
©HEDRICH-BLESSING

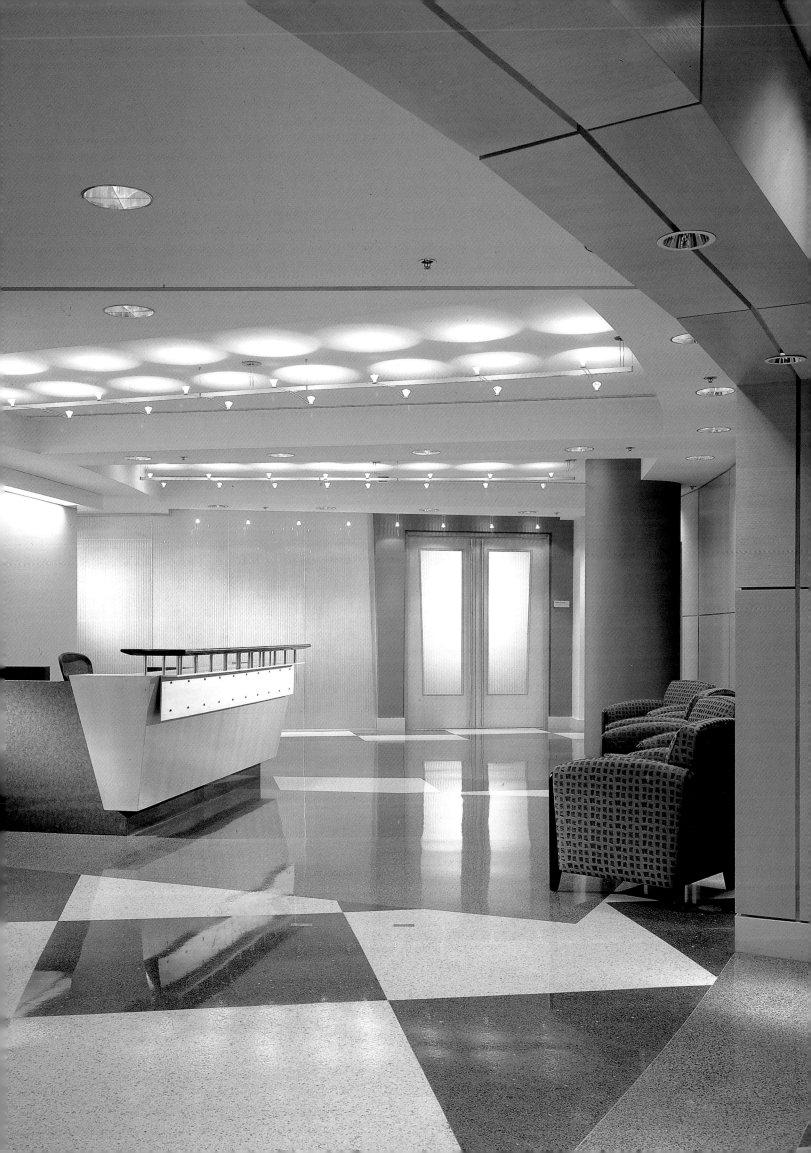

GRISWOLD, HECKEL & KELLY ASSOCIATES, INC.

Griswold, Heckel & Kelly Associates (GHK) designs workplaces that support the business processes of its clients and invigorate their office environments. Incorporated in 1955, GHK maintains a national network of offices located in Chicago, New York, Boston, Baltimore, San Jose, and Washington, D.C., with real-time communication and information exchange capabilities. The firm's design and facility planning and management professionals assist corporations in industries such as insurance, finance, consulting, high technology, biotechnology, and health care to create facilities that help reduce costs, improve workflow, and enhance productivity. GHK's ability to exceed expectations accounts for the firm's success with multiple Fortune 500 clients, some of whom have remained clients for more than twenty-five years.

OPPOSITE The customer center of this health care company is outfitted with ample seating, beverage and snack service, and even coat closets. The company's operating principles are outlined on the wall near the presentation room door.
PHOTO BY JON MILLER ©HEDRICH BLESSING

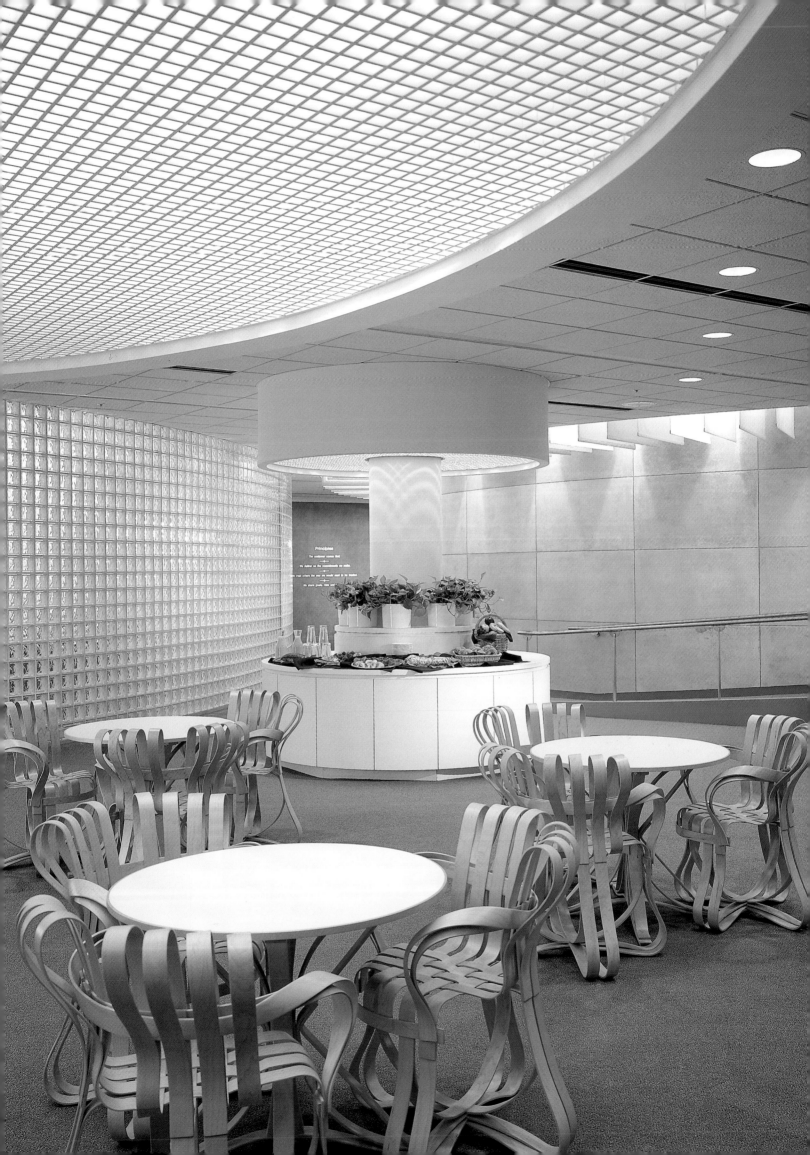

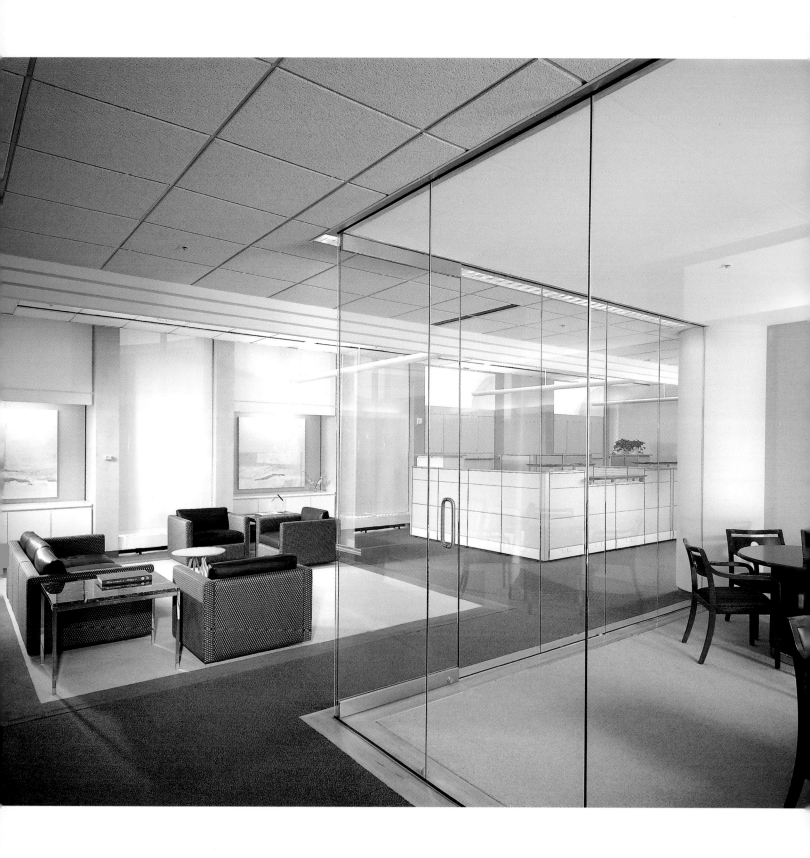

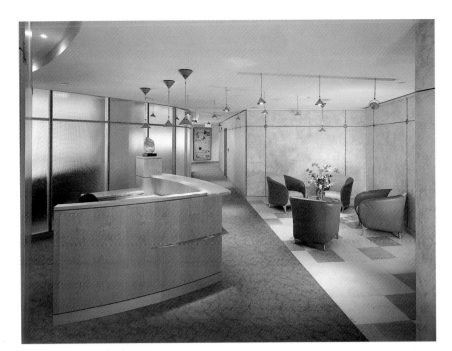

ABOVE RIGHT Two curved walls—one made of wood and the other textured glass and metal—define the firm's reception area. The sculptural desk, accentuated with metal fins, was placed where the two walls merge for dramatic effect.
PHOTO BY CERVIN ROBINSON

RIGHT GHK's design challenge was to create offices that emphasize teaming and flexibility. A modular facility that can be reconfigured overnight was created by using movable walls, lighting, and furniture.
PHOTO BY CERVIN ROBINSON

OPPOSITE Executive offices located near small, informal seating areas are walled in glass to make the company brass more accessible to the staff.
PHOTO BY JON MILLER
©HEDRICH BLESSING

BELOW LEFT To reflect the high-tech nature of this insurance company claim center, designers developed a futuristic theme that is reflected in the reception area and throughout the space.
PHOTO BY STEVE HALL
©HEDRICH BLESSING

BELOW RIGHT On the executive floor of this razor manufacturing company, the interior design relies on a muted palette, high-quality finishes, and attention to detail to create elegant and functional space.
PHOTO BY MARCO LORENZETTI
©KORAB/HEDRICH-BLESSING

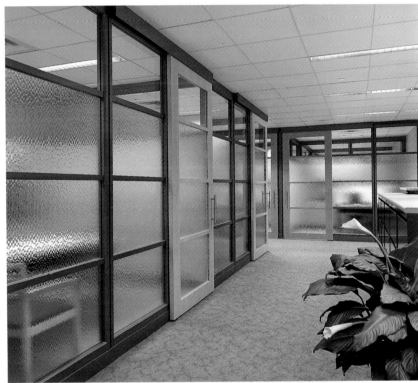

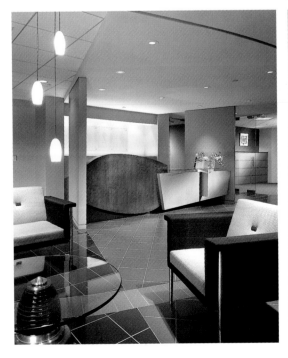

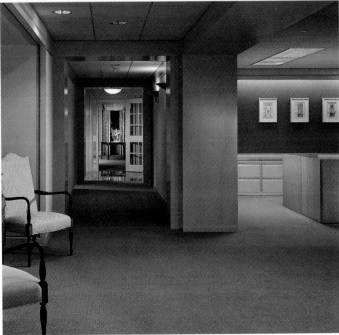

HAMMEL, GREEN AND ABRAHAMSON, INC.

At Hammel, Green and Abrahamson, Inc., company headquarters are no longer seen as static interpretations of the past. Instead, designers at the firm view corporate offices as dynamic, multi-use, interactive centers for work, research, and production. The firm believes evolving building technologies require highly specialized interior design expertise. Topping the list of considerations for each project are appearance, usefulness, safety, accessibility, cost, maintenance, and return on investment. HGA strives to achieve design excellence and an image that is appropriate to the client—all within the constraints of budget, user, needs, history, and time. The firm believes that design does not begin and end with appearance; it is a process that culminates quite naturally in a measurement of utility.

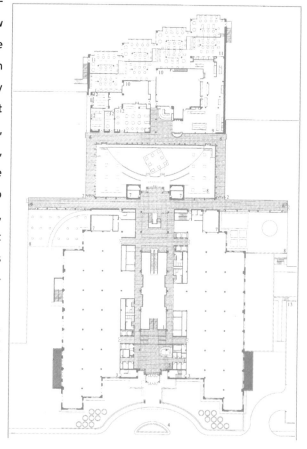

OPPOSITE-CLOCKWISE FROM FAR RIGHT In the massive complex for a St. Paul manufacturer, HGA met the client's goals of improving opportunities for spontaneous interaction and communication among employees by providing delightful common areas.
PHOTO BY GEORGE HEINRICH PHOTOGRAPHY

Within a limited budget and tight time frame, HGA designers combined unique uses of color and space to create this fresh, dynamic office in Uptown Minneapolis.
PHOTO BY DROEGE PHOTOGRAPHY

Movement is the theme for the corporate offices of this car rental company, whose lobby is animated by curved forms on the ceiling, floor, and walls. Cherry paneling, slate floors, color-saturated fabrics and carpeting, champagne-colored metals, custom glass, and commissioned artwork fill the space with a rich variety of colors and textures.
PHOTO BY DROEGE PHOTOGRAPHY

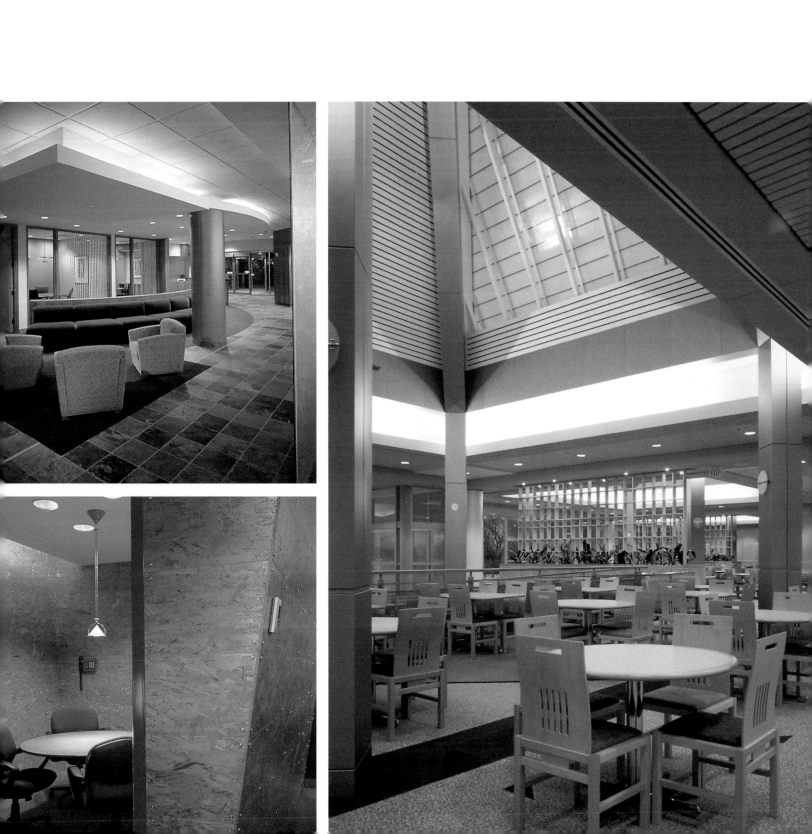

ATELIER CHRISTIAN HAUVETTE

"Christian Hauvette is the principal structuralist architect in France today," wrote Wojciech Lesnikowski in *The New French Architecture.* "Preoccupied with the study of mechanical aesthetics, he believes that the structuralist movement in architecture was shelved too quickly. In the final account, architecture for Hauvette consists of the making of images that generate visual messages in two different ways—in the spirit of structuralism... and in the spirit of descriptive, literary motifs that serve to formulate 'discovery journeys' for the users throughout the building." Hauvette describes himself as "a product of an engineering culture," attempting to explain, perhaps, his rejection of Romanticism and his ambiguous relationship with space. His architecture is both highly pragmatic and unabashedly preoccupied with expressive concerns, such as the power of light and shadow. Hauvette believes buildings must respond to the functional brief and, at the same time, imaginatively organize space, light, form, and structure. "The search for this conceptual clarity is associated with the search for tranquility and calm, which Hauvette believes architecture should always convey," writes Lesnikowski.

OPPOSITE Natural light from above floods the first-floor council room lounge of this large Paris bank. The space is furnished with Arne Jacobsen chairs; walls are finished with perforated cement-wood panels fit into an aluminum frame.
PHOTO BY JEAN-MARIE MONTHIERS

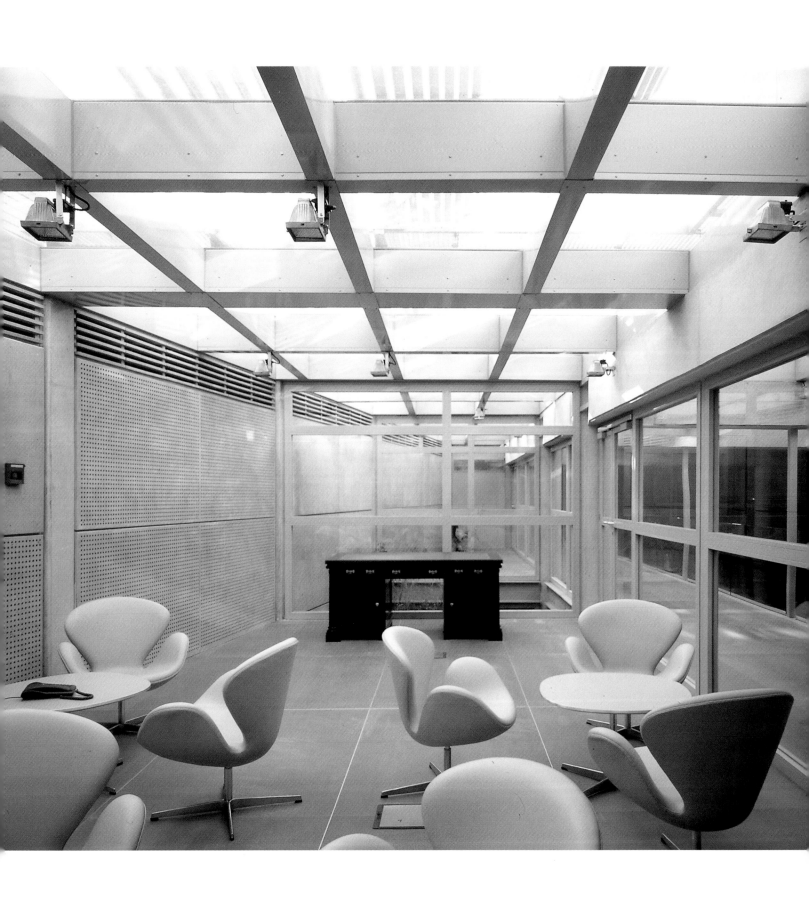

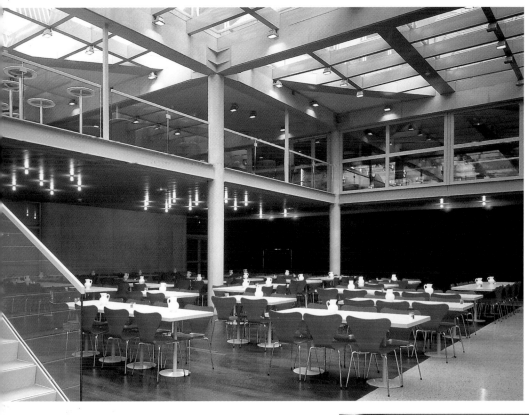

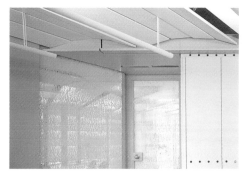

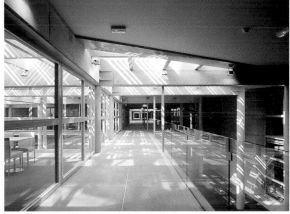

ABOVE LEFT Up to 280 employees are accommodated in the company restaurant, with cafeteria-style dining on the balcony level. Metal stairs leading down to the seating area have rubber-coated treads and a glass railing. Deep-stained wood floors have a broad terrazzo border.
PHOTO BY GEORGES FESSY

ABOVE RIGHT Offices are fitted with radial ceiling panels that produce a soft ambient light. Glass leading to the corridor is embellished with an herb pattern; metal dividing walls can be dismantled to accommodate changing space needs.
PHOTO BY GEORGES FESSY

MIDDLE A covered walkway runs the length of the building beneath the triangular office cores. The upper level, shown here, passes alongside a glassed-in dining area for company management.
PHOTO BY JEAN-MARIE MONTHIERS

LEFT Rows of private offices line a wood-paneled corridor in one of the triangular office blocks. A thin aluminum strip separates the flax-and-goat hair carpet from the wood border.
PHOTO BY GEORGES FESSY

OPPOSITE Leftover space outside the elliptical council chamber serves as a changing room. Flooring is aluminum-colored rubber; the coat rack on left is stained wood and stainless steel.
PHOTO BY JEAN-MARIE MONTHIERS

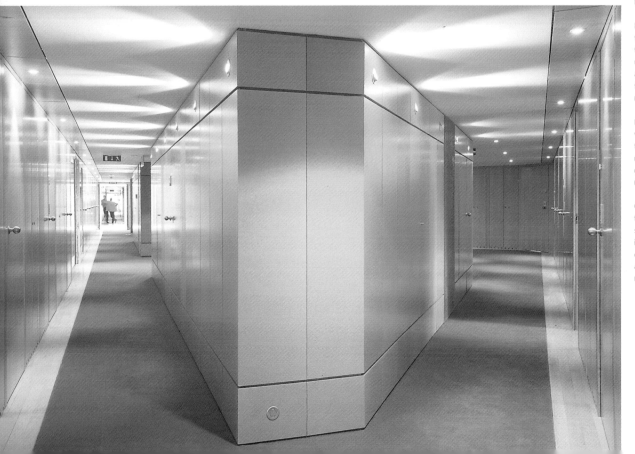

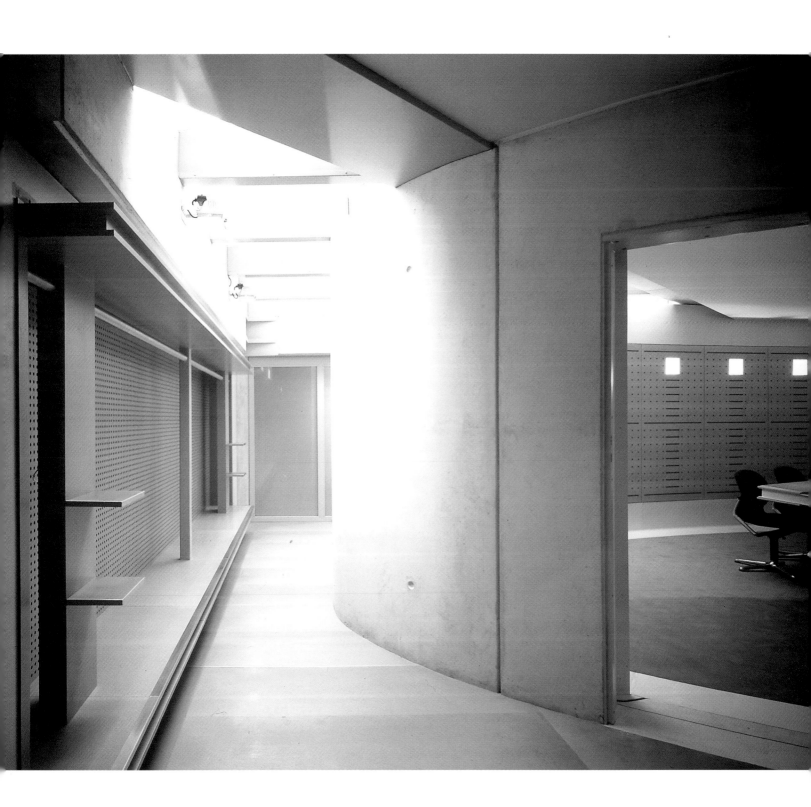

HERBERT LEWIS KRUSE BLUNCK ARCHITECTURE

Herbert Lewis Kruse Blunck Architecture is a growing continuation of the original architecture firm established in 1961. This collaboration of talents continues a tradition of high quality architecture–a tradition that has generated some of the region's most significant and enduring buildings. The firm displays a commitment to serve its clients by working hard to adhere to their needs. The diversity of projects accomplished over the past thirty-seven years is a testimony to the firm's architectural philosophy that deals with each client and project as a unique opportunity to teach and learn.

OPPOSITE In this project for a nationally recognized computer animation company, contrasting values of wood provide a range of tones that accent and enrich a composition of metal and glass planes.
ALL PHOTOS BY FARSHID ASSASSI, ASSASSI PRODUCTIONS

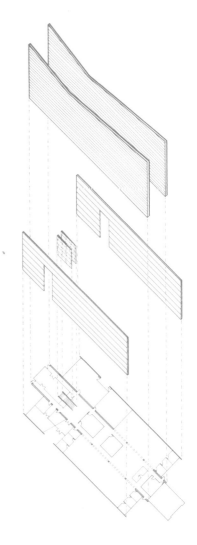

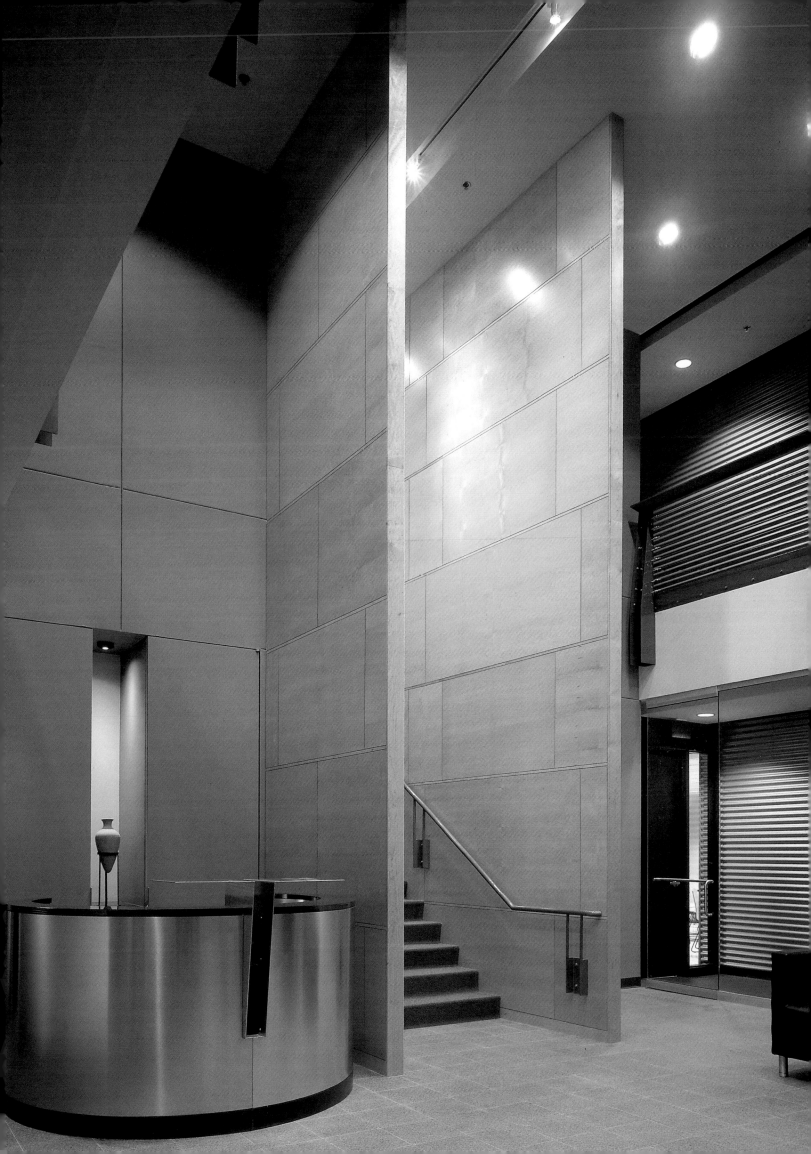

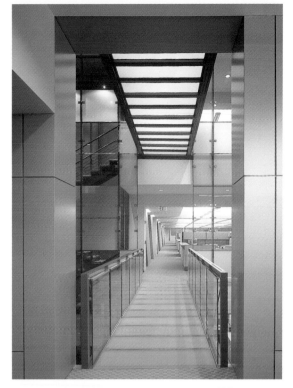

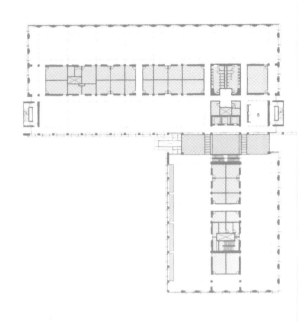

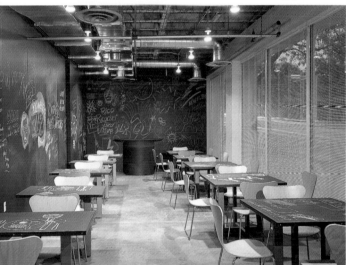

ABOVE Private offices and conference rooms in the headquarters of this Des Moines magazine publisher are placed at the building core rather than lining the perimeter, allowing daylight to illuminate most of the open offices.

LEFT Typical of the design for this advertising agency in Des Moines, simple everyday materials—cedar studs, plastic sheet, gypsum board, birch veneer plywood, chalkboard, and steel plate—are assembled with straightforward and exposed connections.

BELOW LEFT A skylight spine in the roof of this university's athletic department allows natural light to flood the interior court between rows of offices.

BELOW RIGHT Exploiting the existing building's warehouse aesthetic, the design for this food distributor's offices integrates glass block, masonry, and exposed structural steel into tactile, spatial experiences.

OPPOSITE In the central boardroom for this ad agency that caters to agribusiness clients, the scale and atmosphere of a lowly Iowa corncrib is convincingly recreated. Light drifts through the humble slat-wall enclosure; even the conference table's corrugated metal base picks up the theme.

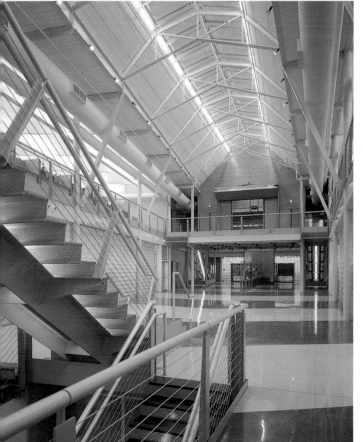

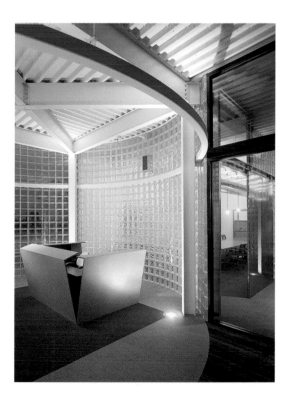

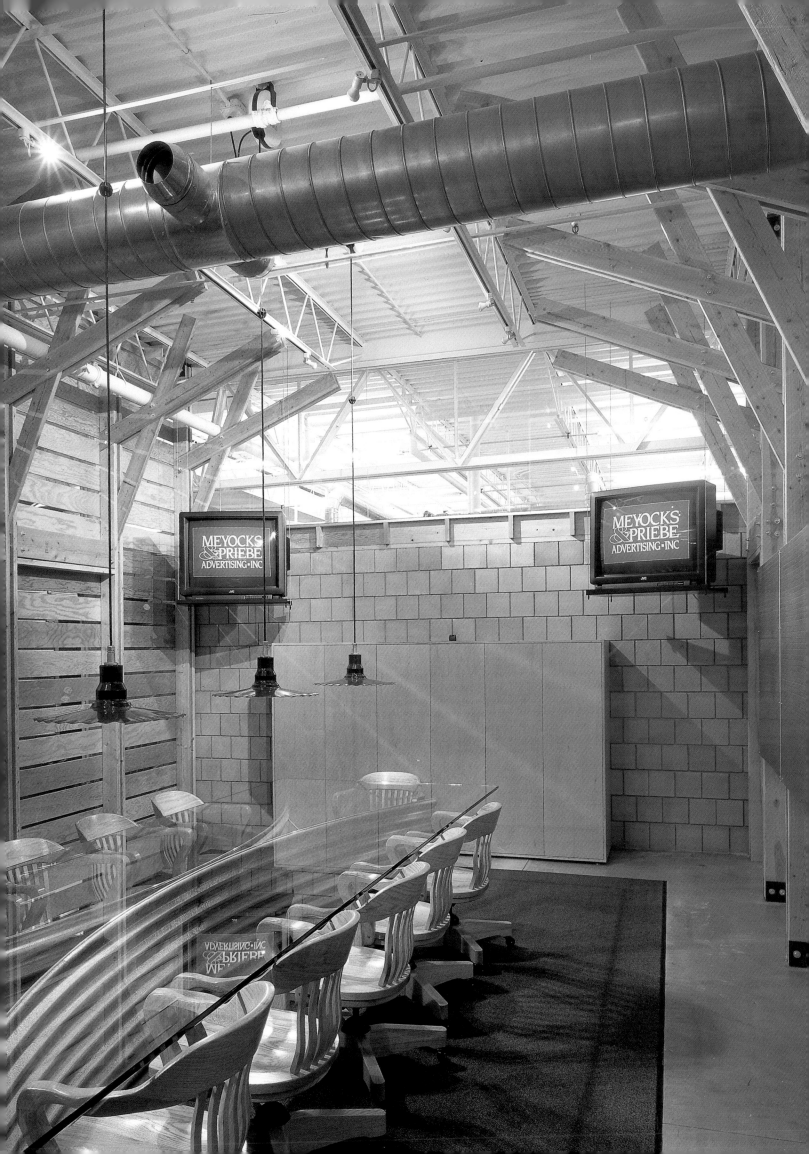

HKS INC.

Throughout its fifty-year history, HKS has been involved in programming, space planning, and interior design. In 1973, HKS Interiors, the interior architecture division of the firm, was founded to better control overall quality and complement the firm's range of services. Since its formation, this division has become one of the largest interior architecture firms in the nation. HKS Interiors has provided creative, efficient workplace solutions for corporate clients—solutions that include flexible planning, real estate options, and work environments that promote communication and interaction. In addition, HKS Interiors can incorporate current and future technologies into workplace design that will simplify facility and space management over the life of a building.

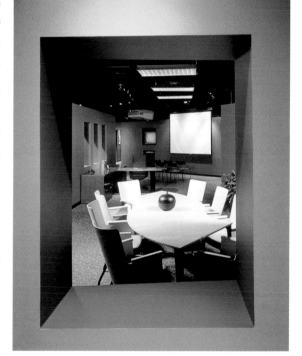

RIGHT Bold colors in this unique workshop setting enable organizations to look into the future of health care. The area is designed with yellow rubber flooring, an open-grid ceiling system, and punched windows that open toward a simulated park.

OPPOSITE The entry area of this health-care consulting group incorporates varying ceiling heights, downlighting, and hardwood floors to create a futuristic, home-like setting.

PHOTOS BY RON ST. ANGELO

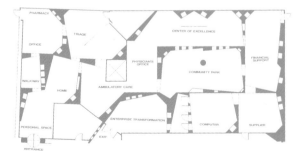

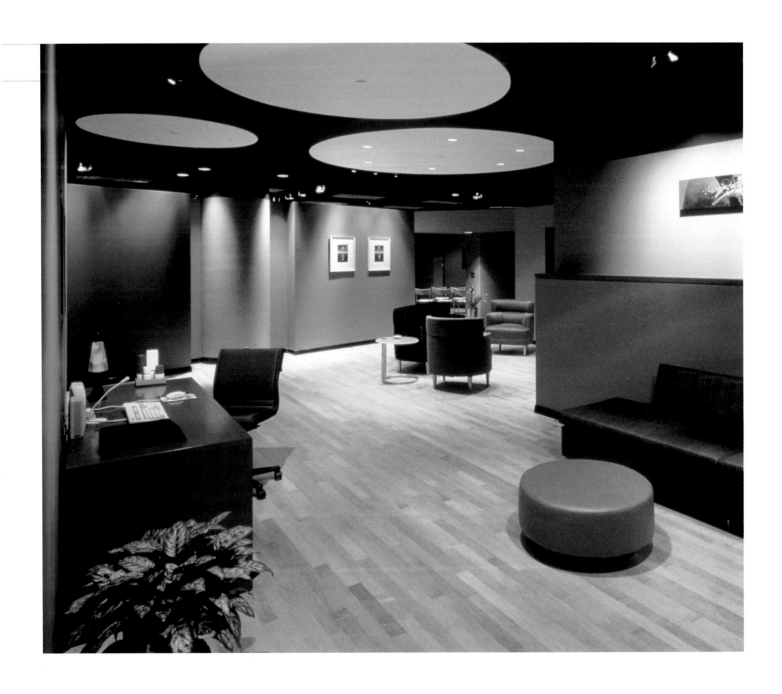

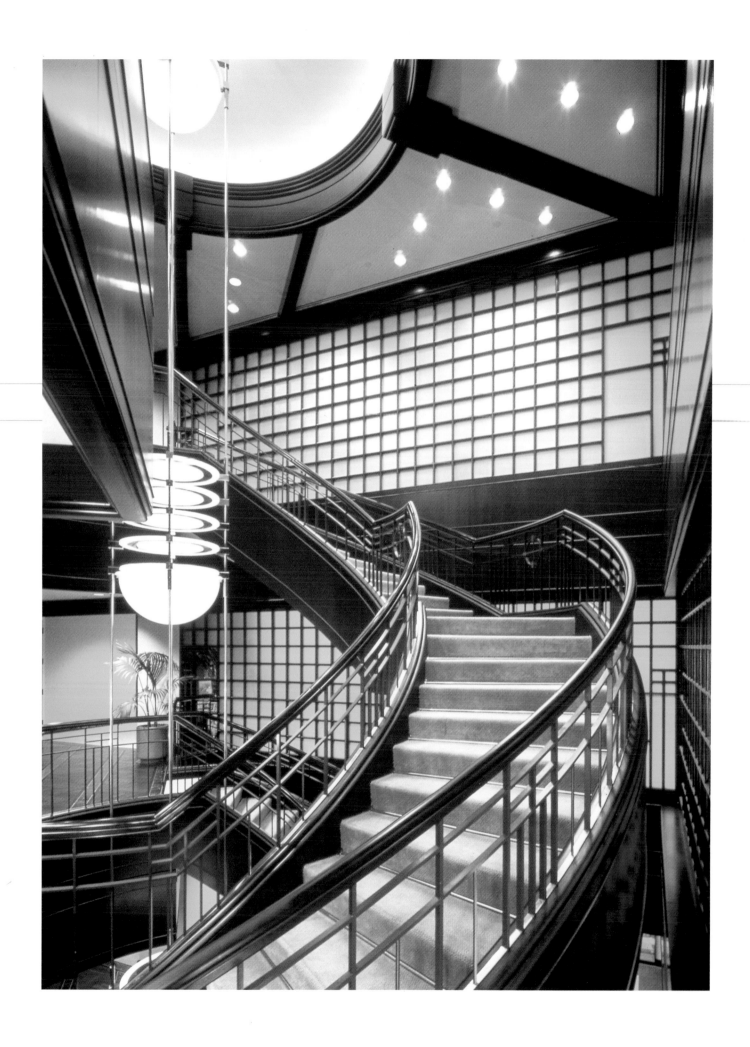

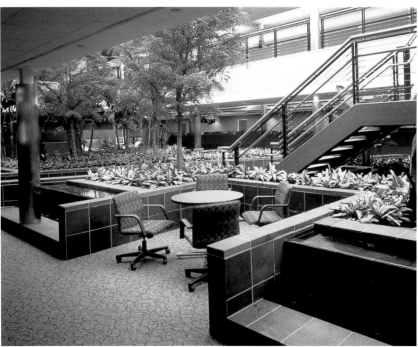

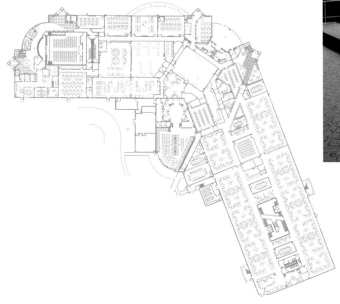

OPPOSITE At the new headquarters for this soft drink company in Dallas, an interconnecting stairwell adjacent to the main lobby provides access to corporate meeting rooms, training areas, and executive office.
PHOTO BY WES THOMPSON

ABOVE A second-level mezzanine was inserted into the high-bay warehouse space of this Denver telecommunications company. New skylights allow natural light to flood the windowless space.
PHOTO BY WES THOMPSON

RIGHT The corporate headquarters of this oil and chemical company in Plano, Texas, was designed with an open plan concept throughout the facility, including the president's office shown here.
PHOTO BY CHAS MCGRATH

FAR RIGHT The building's ground floor houses a full-service cafeteria with an adjacent multipurpose room providing dining areas and space for large meetings and other company events.
PHOTO BY CHAS MCGRATH

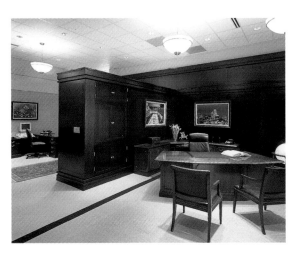

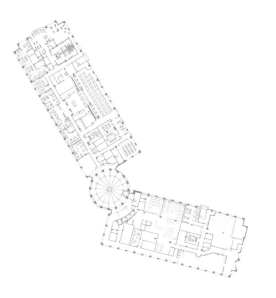

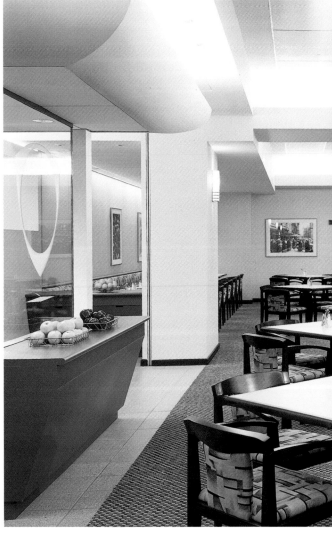

INTERIOR ARCHITECTS, INC.

Interior Architects, Inc. (IA) was founded to meet the workplace needs of corporations, professional service firms, and developers. The firm balances creativity and innovation with pragmatic concerns, such as budget and schedule, to achieve unique design solutions. IA believes that successful projects result from the combination of the hands-on involvement of IA senior management and the goals, insights, and vision of clients. An understanding of business objectives, workplace processes, values, and culture provides a basis for anticipating future project needs. From that understanding, the project team can develop solutions in response to specific workplace issues. Established in 1984, IA has grown to eleven offices providing services internationally. The firm's reputation for innovative and full-service solutions has propelled it into a leadership role within the interior design industry. A 1998 survey by *Interior Design* magazine ranked IA as the number one U.S. firm that exclusively provides interior architecture services. In the same survey, IA was rated the number one firm providing services to financial services firms.

OPPOSITE Visitors to the San Francisco offices of this independent energy provider are greeted with the presence of a two-story water feature illuminated from behind by fiber optic lights that refract through laminated glass. Polished limestone surfaces in the reception desk and flooring lend the interior a fitting sense of formality.
ALL PHOTOS BY BEATRIZ COLL

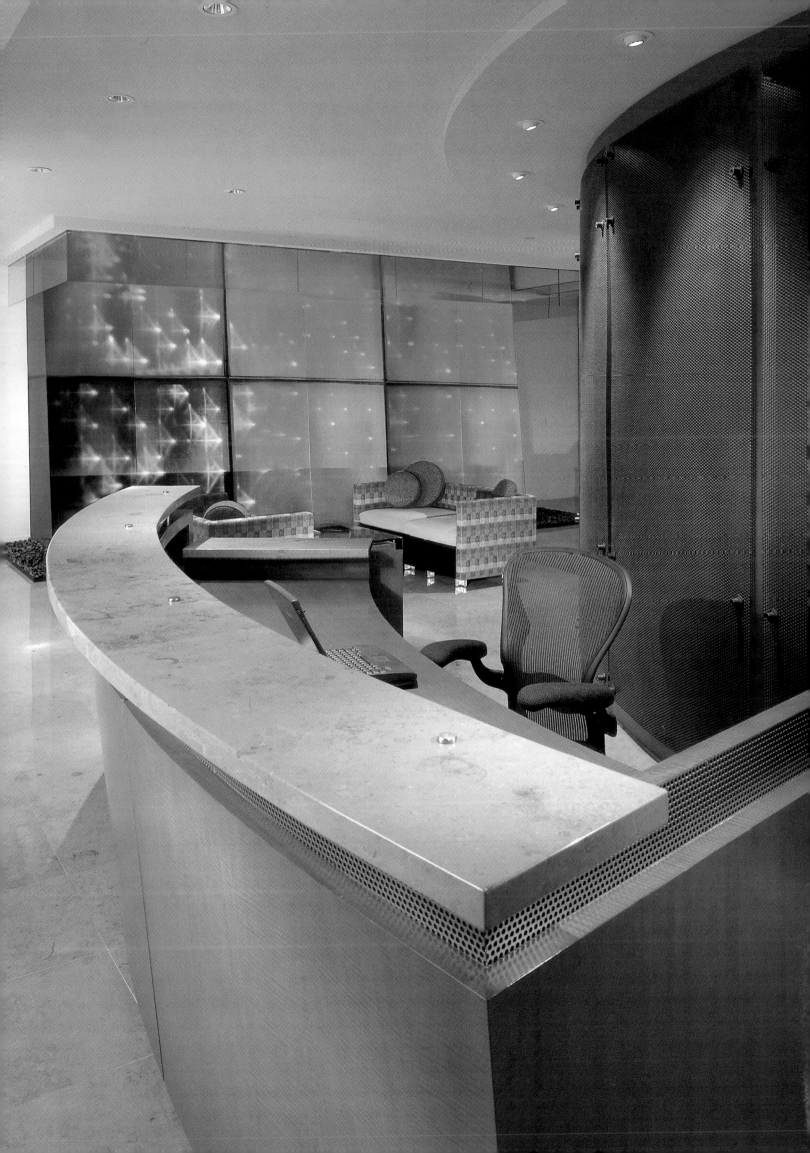

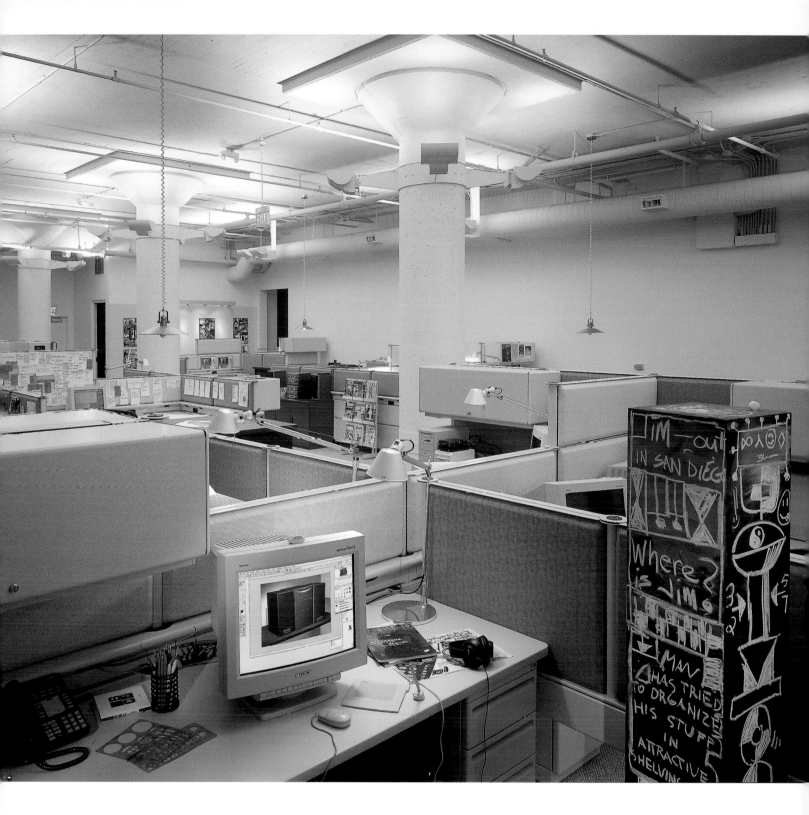

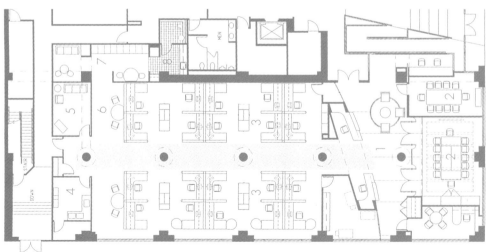

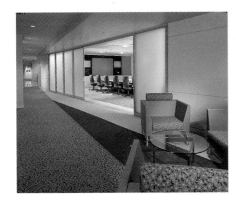

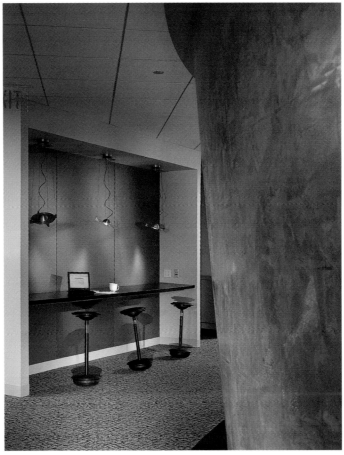

OPPOSITE In the design studio for a large consumer electronics manufacturer, a high priority was placed on conveying a light-filled, loft-like spatial quality while eschewing costly materials. Indirect lighting with specially lamped H.I.D. exterior fixtures mounted to concrete columns provide color-corrected, shadow-free illumination. Workstations are a combination of Haworth Race System and Crossings mobile tables and storage pedestals.

FAR LEFT Controlled aberrations in the carpet pattern articulate a seating area outside the main conference room. Sliding doors made of translucent patterned glass give privacy to occupants of the room while admitting light into the corridor. The limestone conference table is wired with microphones at each seat to aid videoconferencing.

LEFT German-made stools resting on beanbag-like bottoms are merely a perch—not a resting place—at the firm's "conference bar," which is tailored for brief business discussions. The curved Tuscan-red wall, finished with a troweled-on encaustic plastic pigment, separates the circulation space from the company's in-house coffee bar.

BELOW LEFT The high-bay spaces in this video production company made for a number of lighting challenges. In the firm's conference room, aircraft cables were strung overhead across the room and hung with MR-16 low-voltage lights, with two expressive Italian pendants suspended from the ceiling. The video monitor used for client presentations is housed in a custom-made, orange-stained particle board cabinet.

BELOW RIGHT In IA's own offices, the resource library is combined with the staff kitchen, in part to illustrate to clients that kitchens—if well maintained—don't have to be hidden in out-of-the-way places. The plastic laminate island is detailed with routed slots adjacent to the shelf where coffee cups are placed after washing.

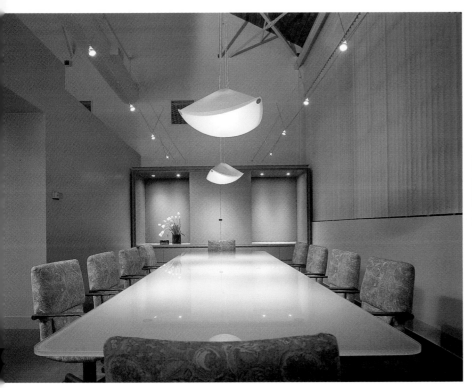

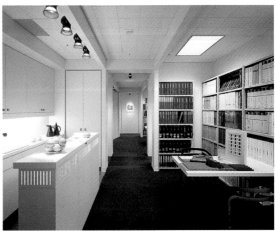

JUNG / BRANNEN ASSOCIATES, INC.

Jung/Brannen's deep experience, commitment to understanding its clients' needs, and innovative use of materials result in beautifully designed, cost-effective solutions for interior design projects. Since its founding in 1968, Jung/Brannen Associates, Inc. has built its reputation as a leading international architecture, interior design, and planning firm by consistently delivering superior solutions to even the most complex projects. The firm offers every client the diversified services of a large organization along with the individual attention associated with smaller practices.

OPPOSITE Teams determined by function within the company are located in a pattern radiating from the free-form central stair that links the separate product groups of this manufacturer of high-design electronic products.
ALL PHOTOS BY RICHARD MANDELKORN

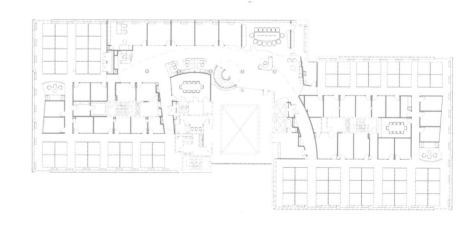

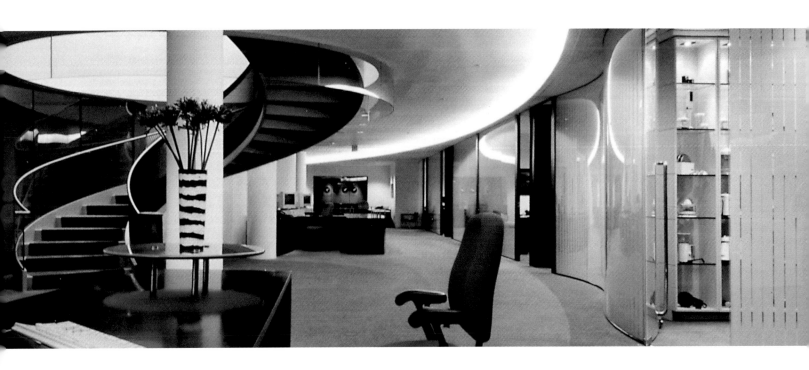

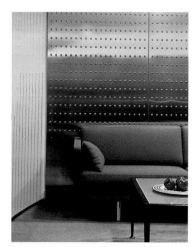

ABOVE The owner's product lines and materials are reflected throughout the interior—in this instance, by the textured metal wall and cobalt blue sofa.

RIGHT Designed as a point of congregation and informal gathering, one of the cafe-style "oasis areas" features a coffee bar, 150-gallon salt-water aquarium, and Internet access station. The perforated stainless steel screen references the styling of the company's products.

BELOW Guests arriving in the richly paneled reception area of this Boston firm are enticed by an obscured view through the translucent glass of the adjacent conference room.

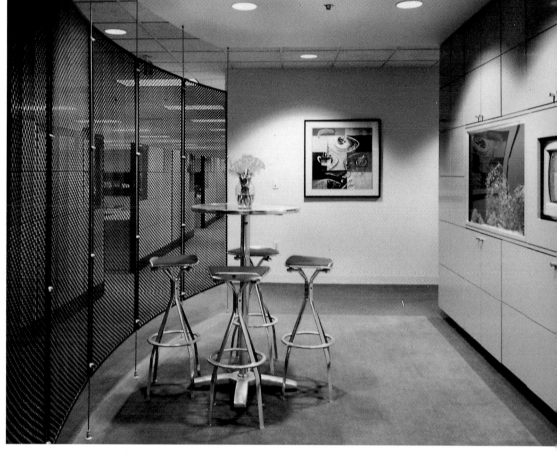

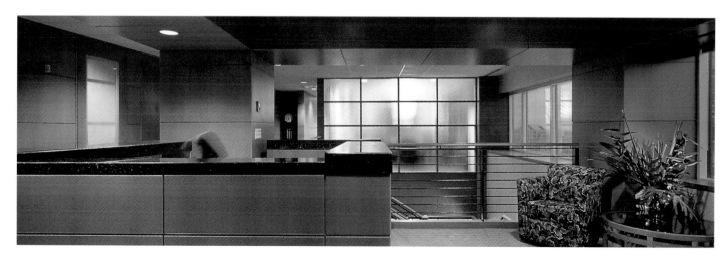

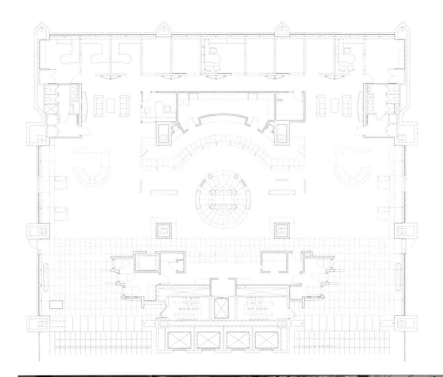

RIGHT The high level of finish and detail in this credenza and the private office it encloses evokes a feeling of warmth and comfort in chilly New England.

BELOW The adjacency of office cubicles and conference space in the financial services center of this Boston bank achieves a sense of privacy, security, and user-friendliness often missing from large banking halls.

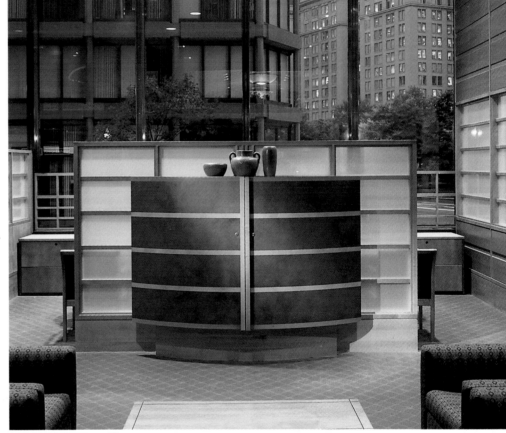

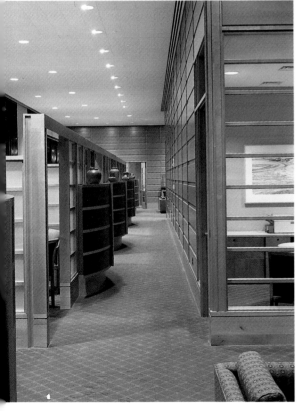

GARY LEE & PARTNERS

Established in 1993, Gary Lee & Partners has grown into a consortium of twenty architects and designers, each conversant with interior architecture, engineering, building construction, office technology, and the total interior environment. The firm subscribes to the belief that good design results from problem solving achieved through creativity, technical expertise, experience, and attention to detail. To ensure consistency, a core team of architects and designers is assembled to work directly and continuously with each client from project inception through completion. The final design expresses the culture of the client's organization, addresses the client's goals, and improves the client's efficiency and flexibility.

OPPOSITE Located on the office building's top floor, the sculptural stainless steel ceiling within the ceremonial Regents Room was raised to create a dramatic two-story volume.
PHOTO BY CHRIS BARRETT ©HEDRICH BLESSING

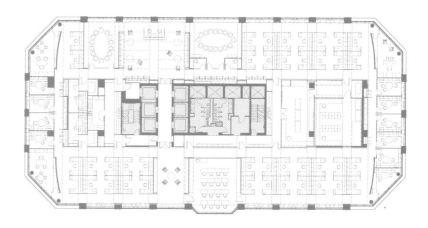

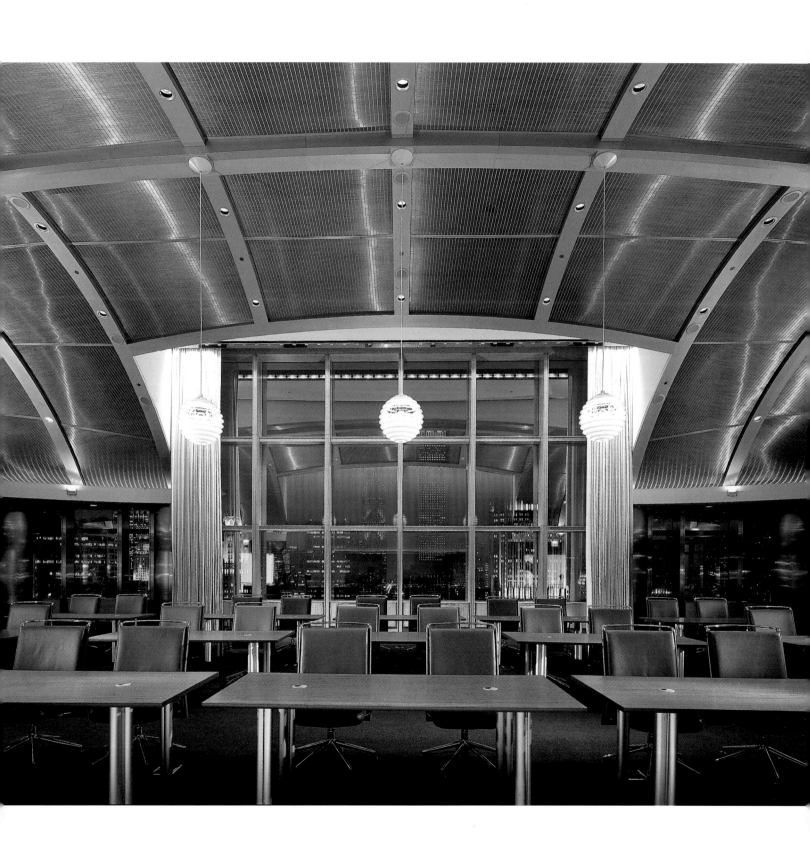

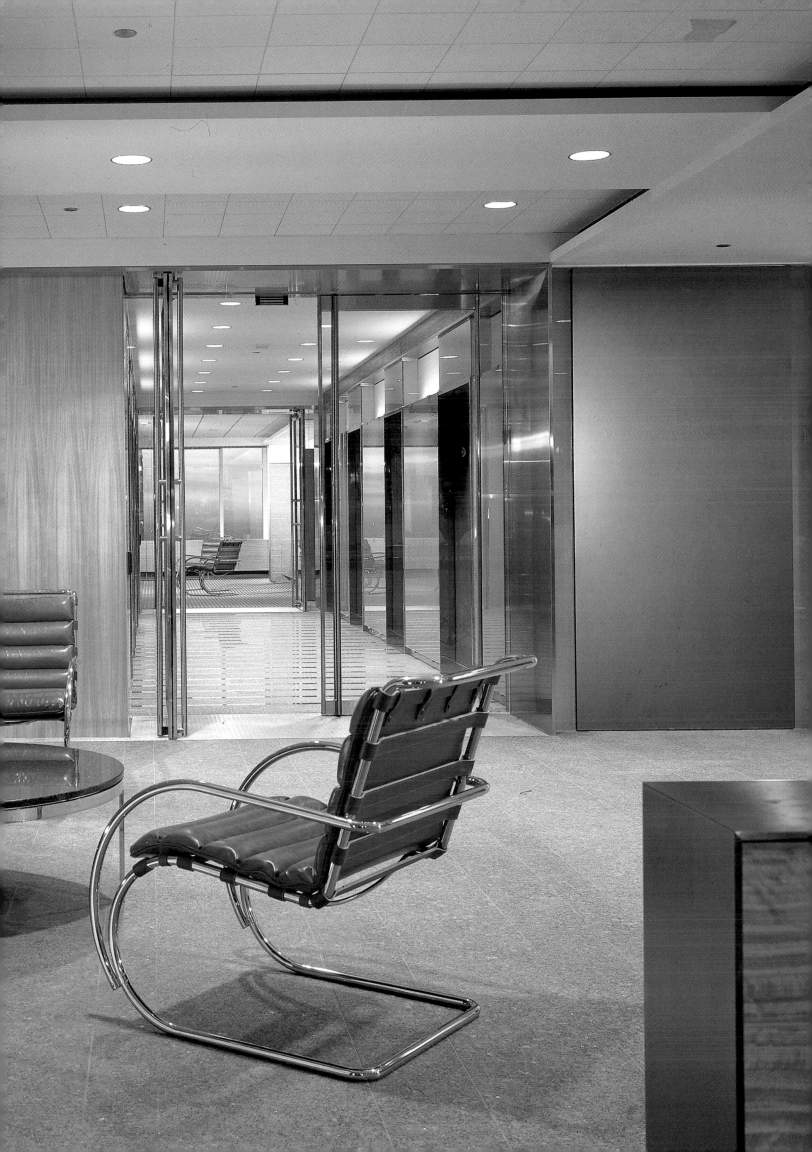

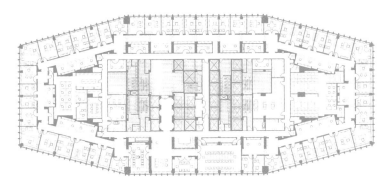

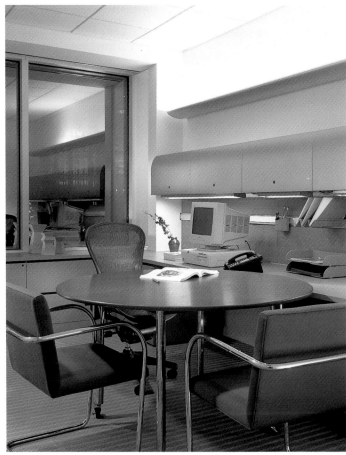

OPPOSITE Precise architectural detailing, refined finishes, and classic furnishings create a space that is commensurate with the image of this prestigious medical organization without overstating its prominence within the field of medicine.
PHOTO BY MARCO LORENZETTI
© HEDRICH BLESSING

ABOVE RIGHT Following the design principles of the workstations, custom desk units in private offices were designed to house ambient lighting, storage, and technology. Classic furnishings complement the design and foster a sense of timelessness.
PHOTO BY CHRIS BARRETT
© HEDRICH BLESSING

RIGHT Crisp simple lines impart a dramatic rhythm to the circulation passageways and internal stair.
PHOTO BY MARCO LORENZETTI
© KORAB HEDRICH BLESSING

FAR RIGHT Traditional styling was called for in this law firm's New York satellite office, where materials, patterns, and style combine to convey a strength of purpose appropriate to the firm image.
PHOTO BY MARCO LORENZETTI
© KORAB HEDRICH BLESSING

BELOW RIGHT Contemporary furniture hints at a classical influence, and art accents combine modern and historical elements to create a sophisticated setting.
PHOTO BY MARCO LORENZETTI
© KORAB HEDRICH BLESSING

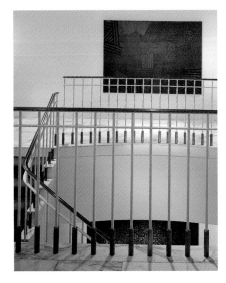

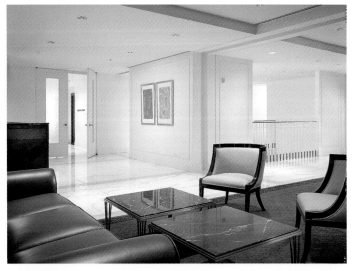

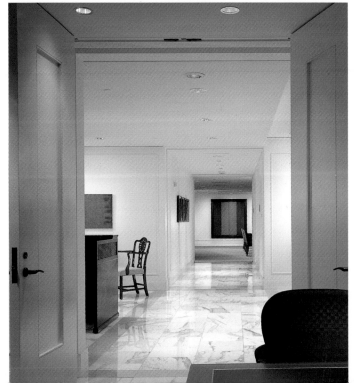

LEHMAN / SMITH / WISEMAN ASSOCIATES

Less than a decade after its founding in 1991, Lehman/Smith/Wiseman Associates has established itself as a leader in architecture and interior design. Principals who have collaborated for more than fifteen years on a broad range of projects manage the firm, which has a significant base of local, regional, and national clients. Projects are directly designed and managed by principals whose business philosophy is grounded in design excellence and client service. Lehman/Smith/Wiseman aims to design exceptional spaces that reflect the needs of the client, while rising above common solutions.

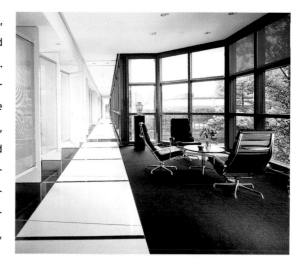

RIGHT Window bays projecting from the primary circulation spine at a large bank in Birmingham, Alabama, provide ideal informal meeting areas. Fritted glass screens allow light into the central office core, yet maintain a sense of privacy.

OPPOSITE A wavy ceiling of painted metal and stainless steel incorporates direct and indirect lighting to accent the servery in the bank's cafeteria, which occupies a 20,000-square-foot (1,800-square-meter) bridge that has become the company's gathering place.
ALL PHOTOS BY JON MILLER ©HEDRICH-BLESSING

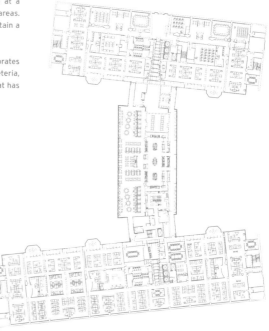

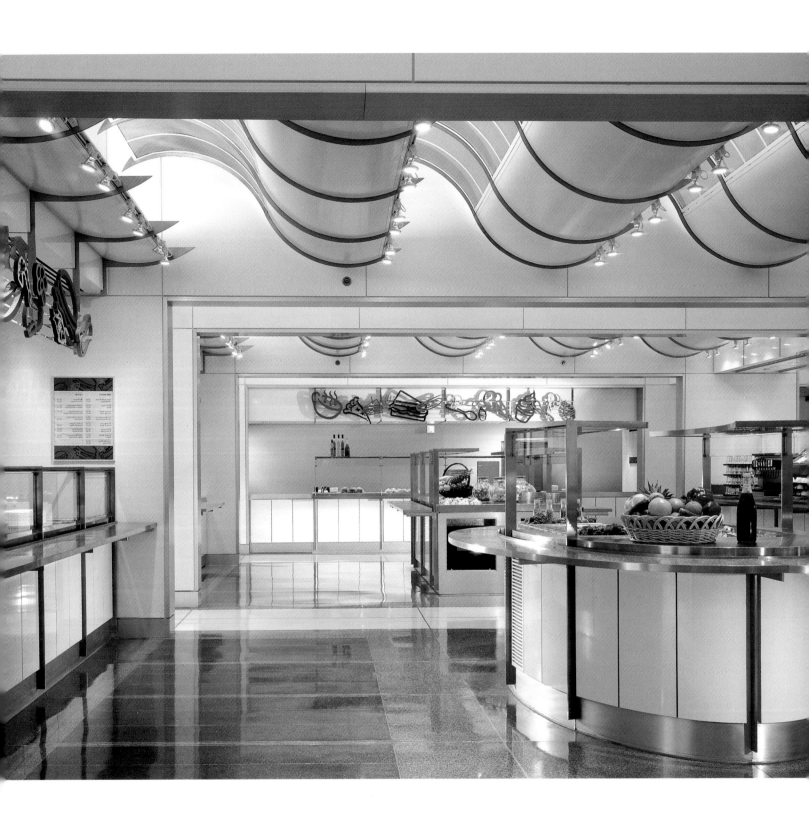

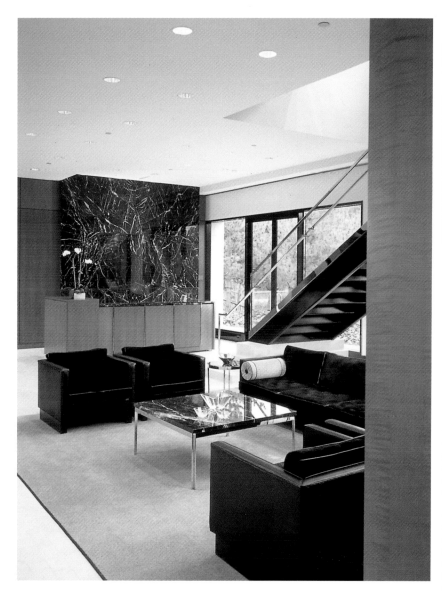

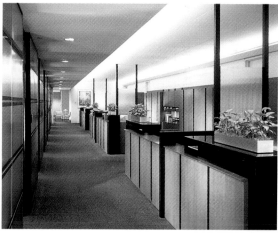

LEFT Limestone pavers, black St. Laurent marble, and pearwood paneling set the high tone of finish in the reception lobby of this Silicon Valley law office.

ABOVE The associate office features Translations systems furniture and a Montage moveable wall partition in pearwood, custom designed by Lehman/Smith/Wiseman.

BELOW For these executive offices in Houston, a high level of detail was warranted in the chairman's office, where the custom desk was built to match custom-figured maple wall panels. Leather lounge seating allows a more intimate alternative for private meetings.

OPPOSITE A conference room, wrapped in silk-covered walls and enclosed by a steel canopy, takes full advantage of natural light in the bright atrium of an investment trust in Rockville, Maryland. A natural cleft slate walkway leads from outside the building through the reception area to a grouping of Eames-designed chairs that doubles as informal meeting space.

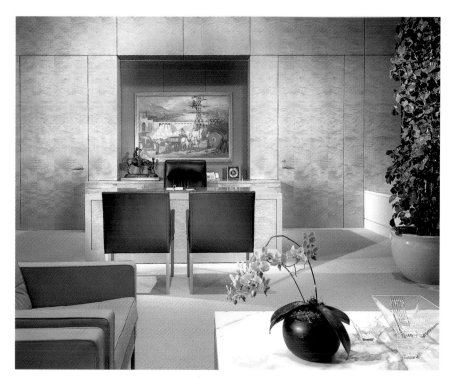

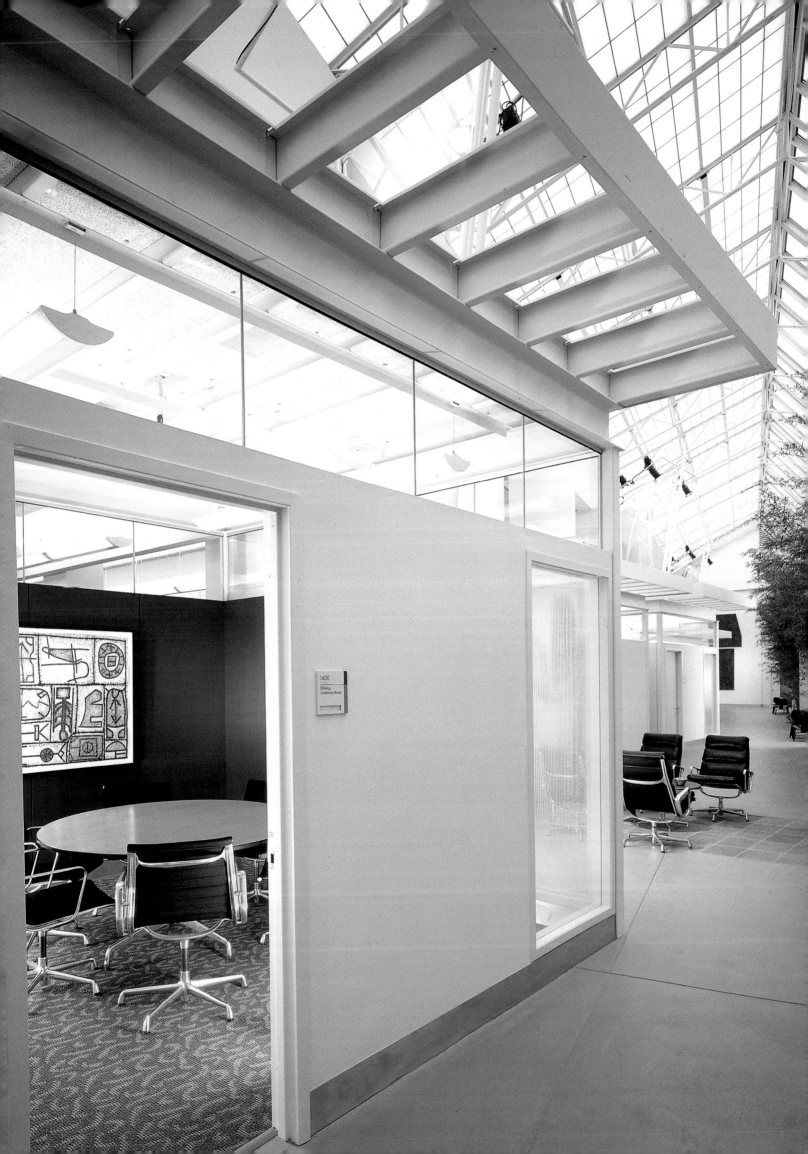

LIMINALITY LLP

LIMINALITY LLP is a full-service interior architecture firm that utilizes design to build a connection between workplace solutions and business strategies. For business owners and corporate executives looking to contain costs and maximize budgets, the firm offers a variety of services tailored to the needs of fast-growing companies. LIMINALITY's insight and experience with some of the country's most forward-thinking organizations allow the firm to complete assignments economically without sacrificing design integrity or the quality of the end product. As professional design consultants, the firm evaluates, analyzes, and provides options and solutions that are directly suited to clients' unique needs.

OPPOSITE The reception area for the corporate headquarters of a major aircraft manufacturer blends the influences of the company's European culture and its American location on the outskirts of Washington, D.C. PHOTO BY MICHAEL MORAN

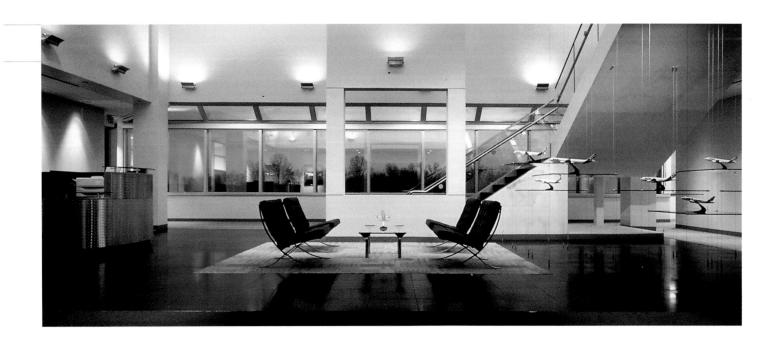

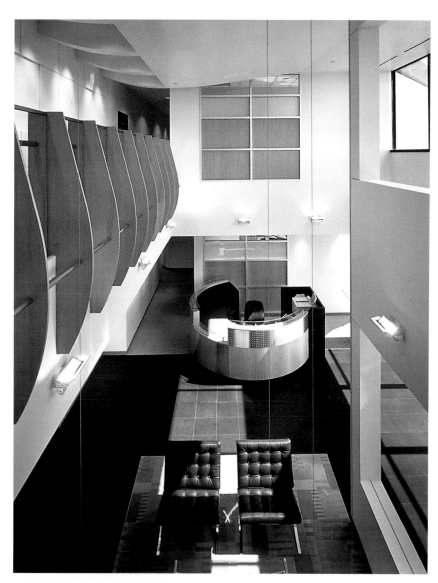

LEFT Striving to avoid trendiness in its design for this aircraft manufacturer's offices, the designers limited direct references to airplane vocabulary to shapes inspired by airfoils. These appear as signage elements, ceiling forms, and railing details.

BELOW The company's lunch room is located with access to prime views near the top of an interconnecting stairway to encourage informal meetings among employees.

PHOTOS BY MICHAEL MORAN

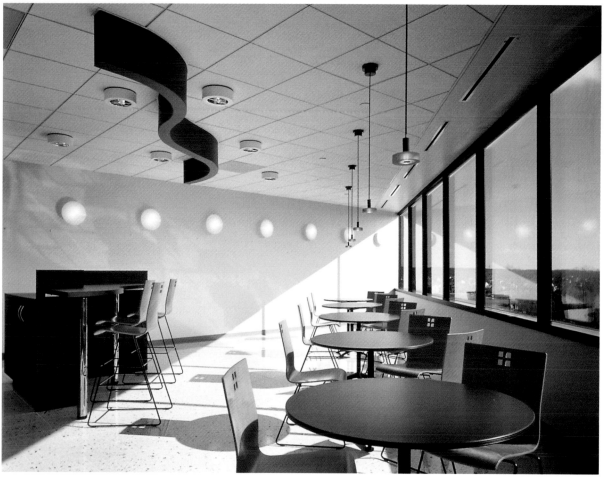

RIGHT In this Beverly Hills bank, a hanging soffit was introduced to visually connect three entries and provide an element that would house direct and indirect lighting fixtures.
PHOTO BY TOM BONNER

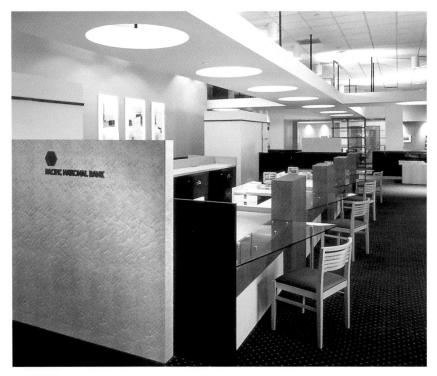

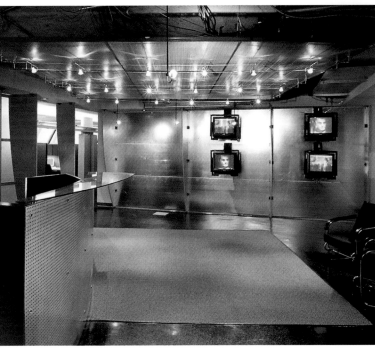

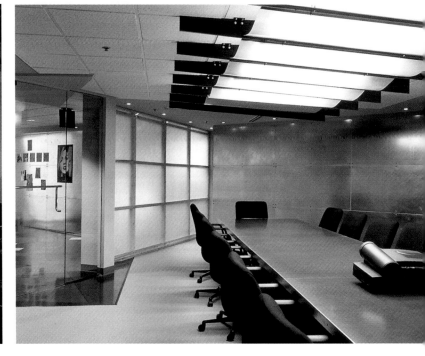

ABOVE LEFT Television monitors in the reception area of this Washington, D.C., ad agency air a steady stream of MTV and The Shopping Channel, lending a sense of irony and irreverence to the setting of a firm that eschews television advertising.
PHOTO BY MICHAEL MORAN

ABOVE RIGHT A wall of fiberglass panels and wood studs encloses the agency's conference room. Finland plywood was used in the construction of the reception desk and in elements such as the conference room light fixture.
PHOTO BY MICHAEL MORAN

MEYER, SCHERER & ROCKCASTLE, LTD.

Founded in 1981 by principals Thomas Meyer, Jeffrey Scherer, and Garth Rockcastle, Meyer, Scherer & Rockcastle, Ltd., (MS&R) regards interior design as equally important to architecture and strives to integrate the two in every project. This collaboration is most critical in the early phases of the work, so MS&R interior designers are involved from the very start. As the building footprint takes shape, the interior designers concentrate on meeting programmatic requirements. Furniture and equipment can then be test-fit into the space. In addition to furnishing and materials selection, MS&R's interior design staff is involved with programming, furniture layouts, millwork, and lighting design. This high level of involvement yields quality design and ensures harmonious and functional results.

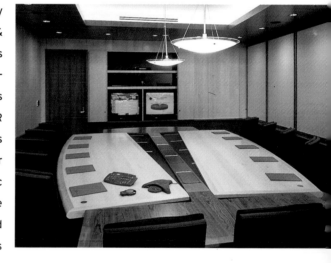

ABOVE RIGHT In the main conference room, the custom-made teak-and-maple table adjusts to meet demand: open for media-oriented sessions and closed for traditional meetings. Sliding screens made of sail fabric offer varying degrees of privacy.

OPPOSITE The identity wall for this Edina, Minnesota, investment firm is covered in hand-painted paper that is washed with light to set off the bronze lettering. In the waiting area, an area rug and lounge seating soften the hard flooring surface.

PHOTOS BY PHILIP PROWSE

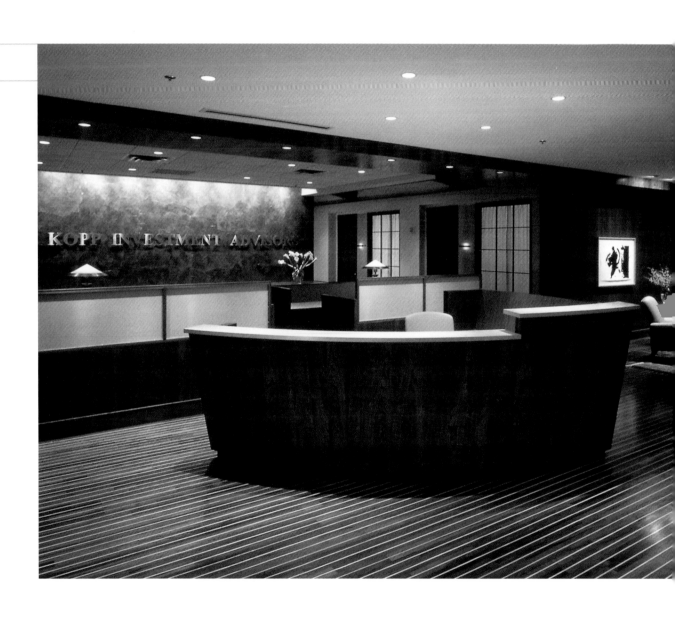

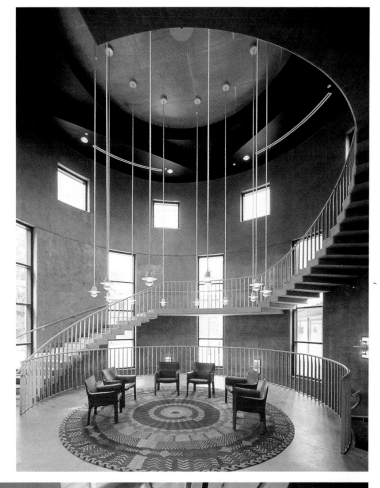

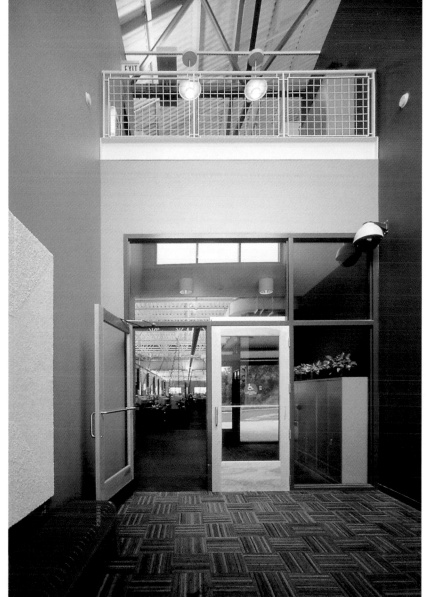

ABOVE A dramatic cylinder-shaped rotunda lies just beyond the lobby of this Pennsylvania investment company.

LEFT A typical building entry vestibule shows the playful use of color and exposed structure. Recycled materials, such as the rubber floor covering, are used extensively throughout the building.
PHOTOS BY TIMOTHY HURSLEY

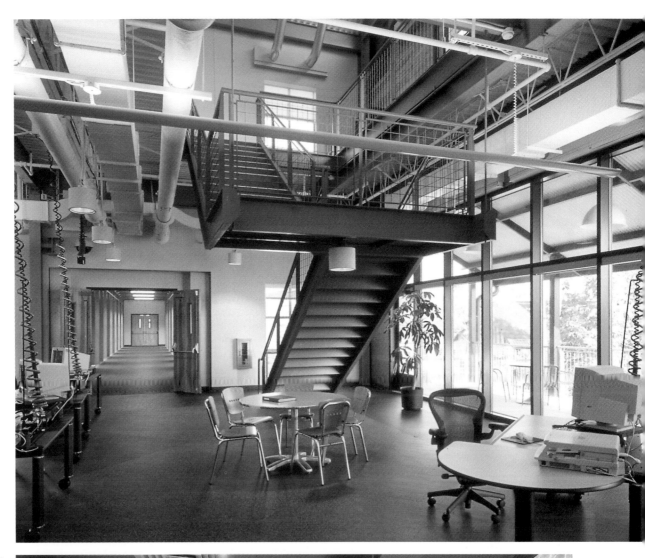

ABOVE RIGHT Because work teams are required to relocate quickly and adjust to changing market conditions, work stations were designed to be moved and reconfigured on a moment's notice.

RIGHT The company's training and seminar room is satellite-linked and fully interactive, with furnishings selected for flexibility and frugality.
PHOTOS BY TIMOTHY HURSLEY

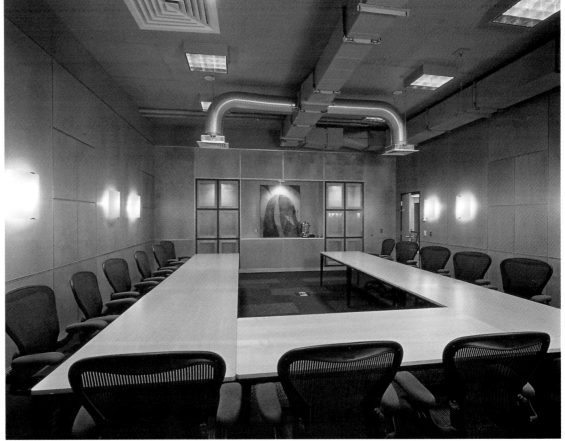

NBBJ

NBBJ is the world's fifth largest architecture firm with a staff of 800 and projects located throughout North America, South America, Asia, and Europe. Rigorously design-focused, the firm practices in twenty-one studios spread among six U.S. offices. Each studio is strongly committed to serving its clients and society through a balance of design, technology, process, and communication. No building or interior designed by the firm reflects a single style that defines the firm, but all are informed by the same set of complex principles. NBBJ is recognized for its innovative design solutions in corporate interiors, office buildings, mixed-use complexes, and a wide range of other building types.

OPPOSITE Tall birch panels surround the elevators beyond this software company's reception area. The lowered ceiling, distinct wood grains, and unique design elements contrast the raw and purposely exposed building structures.
PHOTO BY ASSASSI PRODUCTIONS

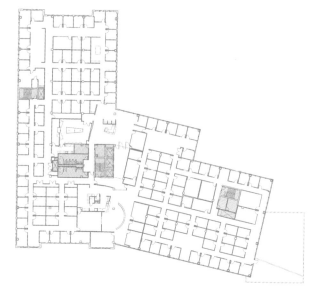

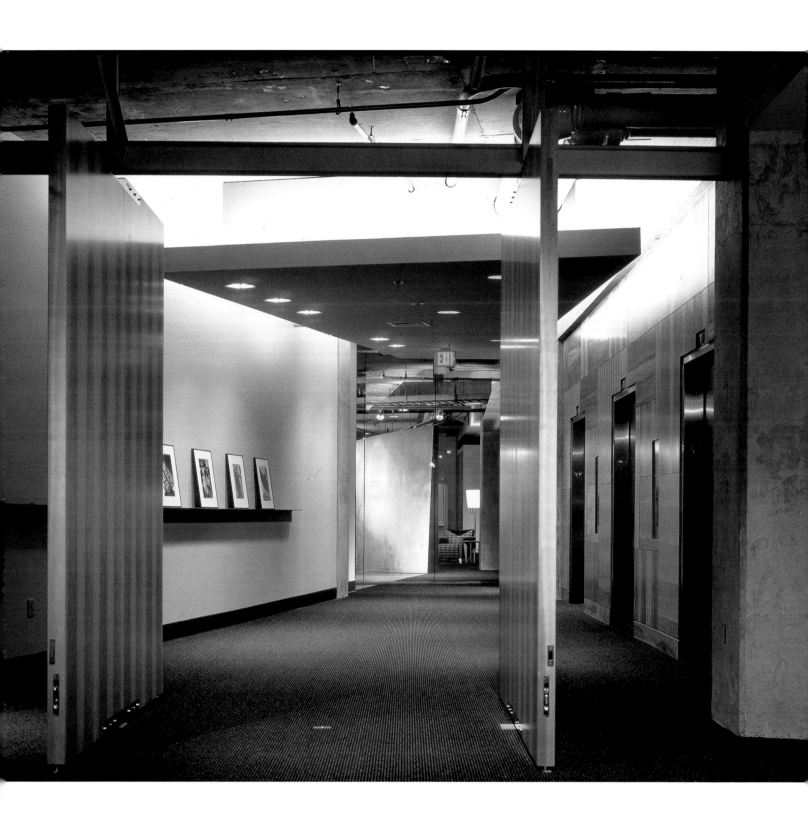

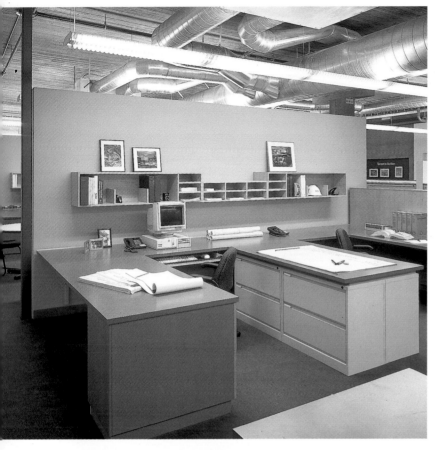

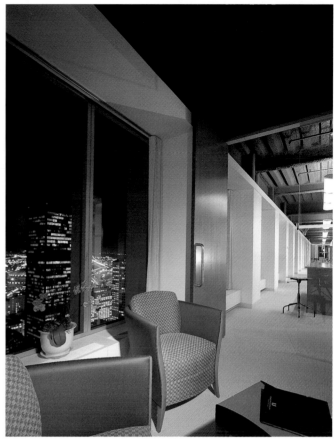

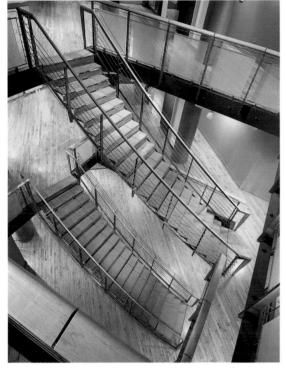

ABOVE LEFT Work areas with brightly painted walls are located in the office's central area and are furnished with expansive work surfaces, freestanding files, and custom storage elements.
PHOTO BY DICK BUSHER

ABOVE RIGHT The "great hall" of this property management company in Seattle serves as the main circulation path and houses administrative services. With flexible furniture configurations, the corridor strategically mandates social interaction and offers spectacular views of the Puget Sound accessible to all workstations.
PHOTO BY J. F. HOUSEL

LEFT The open floor stairways of this Seattle-based coffee company create a feeling akin to a warehouse loft and enhance ease of communication among employees.
PHOTO BY PAUL WARCHOL

RIGHT Lounge areas with inviting furniture along the primary circulation paths offer places for spontaneous meetings.
PHOTO BY PAUL WARCHOL

OPPOSITE This brand identity company's transparent conference room offers audio-privacy to occupants while allowing others to view the activities taking place within.
PHOTO BY ASSASSI PRODUCTIONS

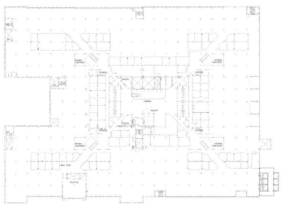

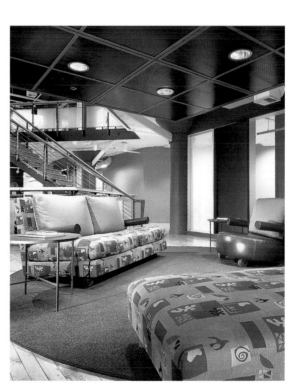

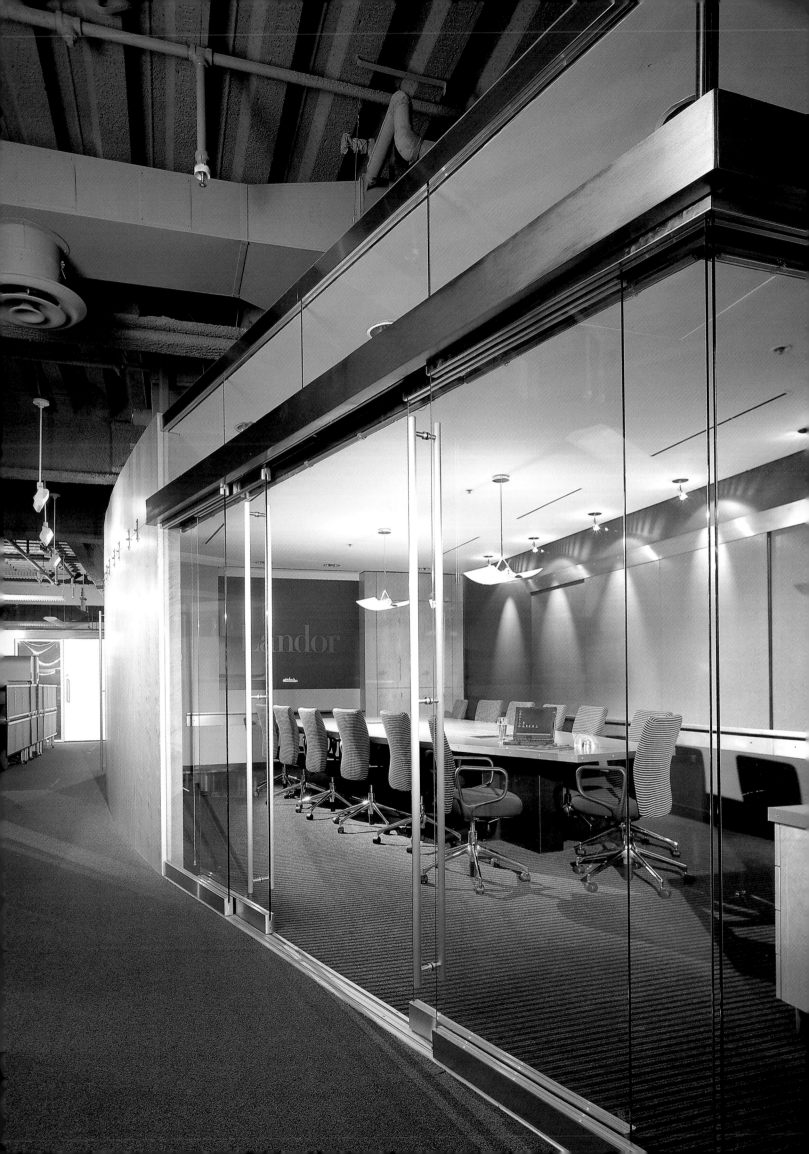

PERKINS & WILL

Founded in 1935, Perkins & Will is a professional service firm staffed with interior designers, architects, and planners. With offices in Chicago, New York, Atlanta, Charlotte, Los Angeles, Miami, Minneapolis, and Paris, the firm has completed projects in forty-nine states and thirty-seven countries. Perkins & Will's interiors department is dedicated to providing innovative service and value to accomplish clients' business goals, believing strongly in the synergistic relationship between an organization's business process and the arrangement of its space. To address this dynamic, Perkins & Will developed a unique project methodology that brings a strategic perspective to the design process. The result is intelligent interiors that enhance productivity, workflow, and communications.

OPPOSITE A simple black sisal carpet allows the spare planes of the architecture to frame the space in this Chicago law office. The interior designers fashioned the reception desk as a low meeting/greeting station for the reception and conference center. Stainless steel fins support a plane of Grecian marble with frosted glass modesty screens floating behind.
ALL PHOTOS BY MARCO LORENZETTI © HEDRICH BLESSING

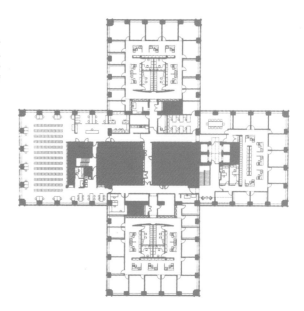

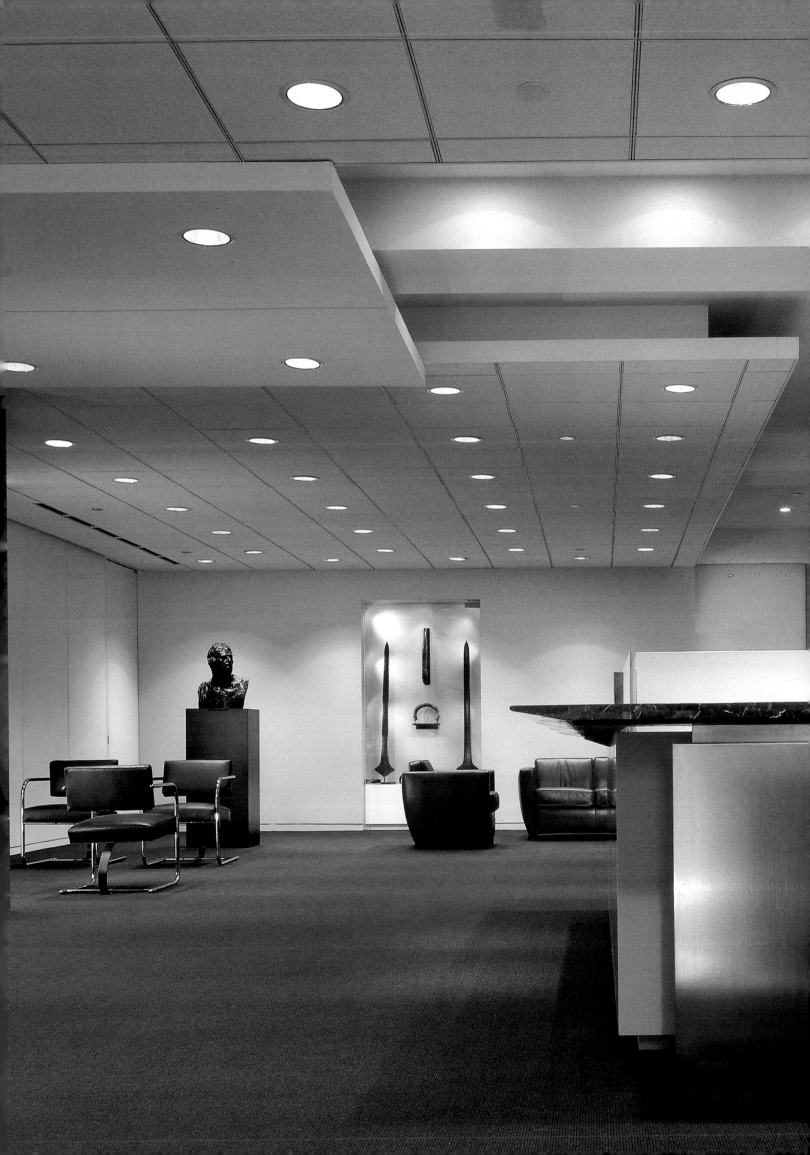

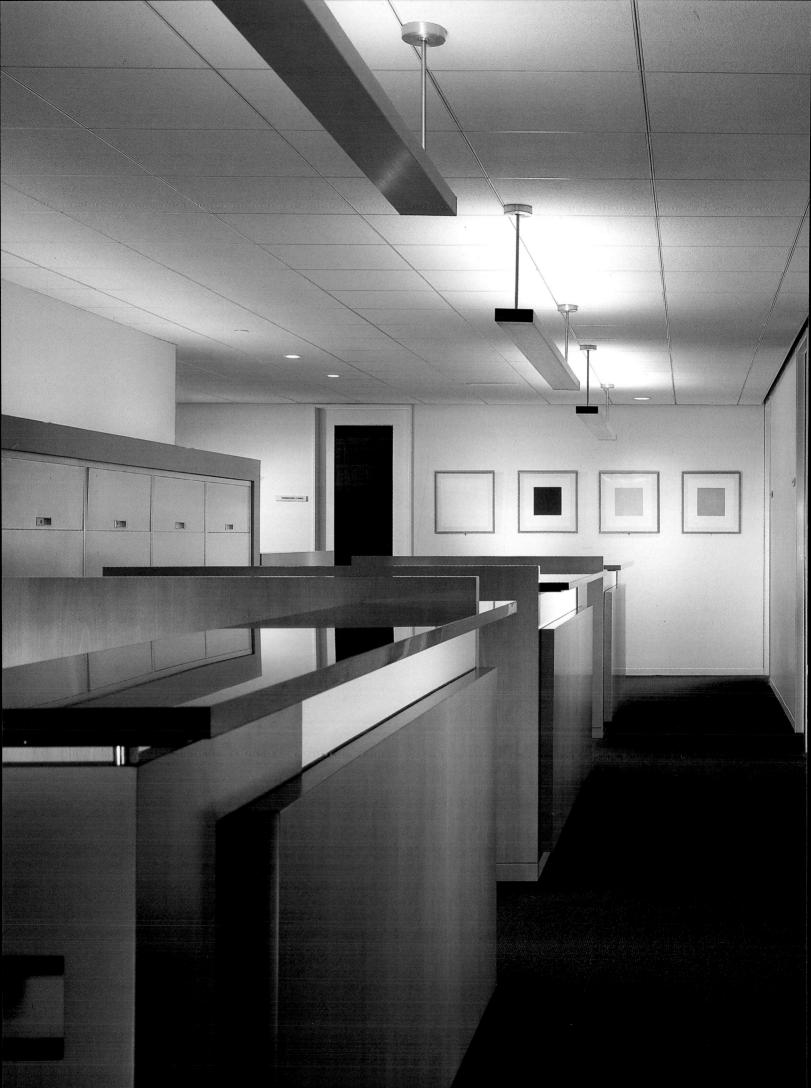

OPPOSITE Minimal forms were introduced in this office retrofit, including secretarial workstations with front and side panels of Northern European beech and a granite transaction shelf. The balance of the desk is made of lacquer panels. Indirect lighting is used throughout to minimize screen glare.

RIGHT Pivoting beech panels open to reveal a private caucus room featuring a granite conference table.

BELOW A typical screening element obscures utilitarian spaces in this New York office. Light eucalyptus veneers, backlit translucent onyx, a black granite shelf, and stainless steel insets provide a transitional setting for the somewhat more traditional furnishings and accessories.

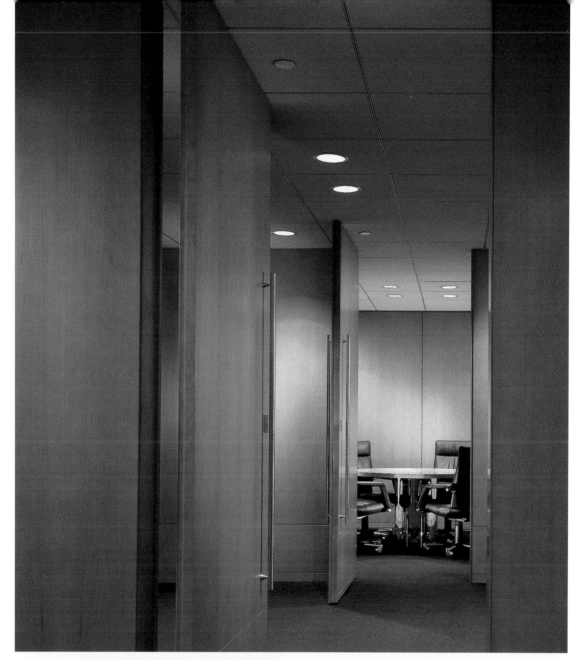

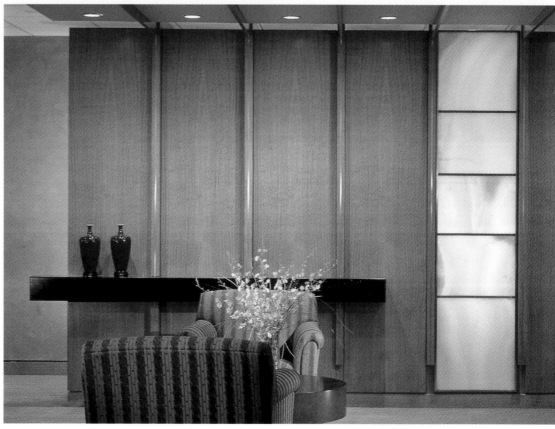

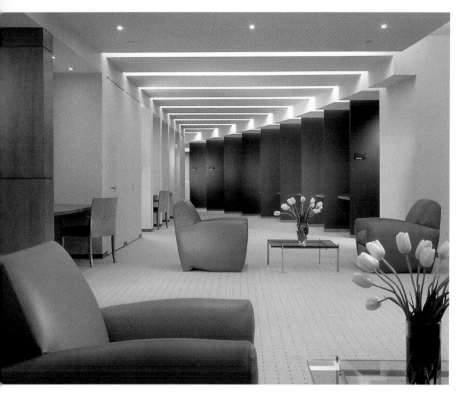

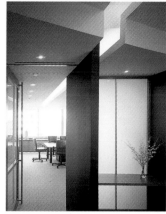

FAR LEFT Neutral tones in the floor and wall finishes enhance the drama of a stepped, curved wall in this reception area. Pear-stained maple veneer counters placed between the blue fins and against the opposite wall add richness and warmth.

LEFT A view through the curved blue wall into the conference room reveals wood-framed translucent glass panels that allow natural light to permeate the interior space and provide a soft glow.

BELOW LEFT The reception desk in the Chicago headquarters of an international consulting firm, seen here against the backdrop of the cleft slate wall behind it, combines two leather panels emphasizing a stainless steel joint that unifies the interior composition.

BELOW RIGHT This extra-wide, single-run stairway functions as a unique communication vehicle, accommodating personnel and encouraging staff interaction. Teaming areas such as conference rooms, training spaces, and the company café are spatially and visually connected to the atrium surrounding the stair.

OPPOSITE In this consulting firm's office, the boundaries between formal and informal meeting areas are intentionally blurred. A freestanding glass wall creates the seam between the conference room and break-out areas. Both the ceiling canopy and wood floor bridge between the spaces.

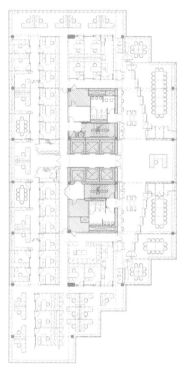

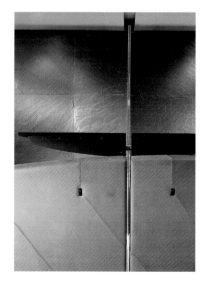

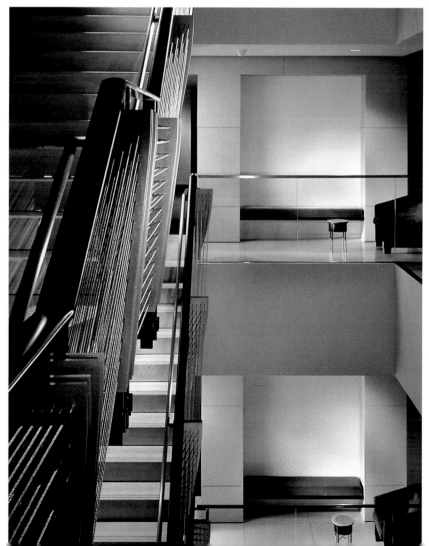

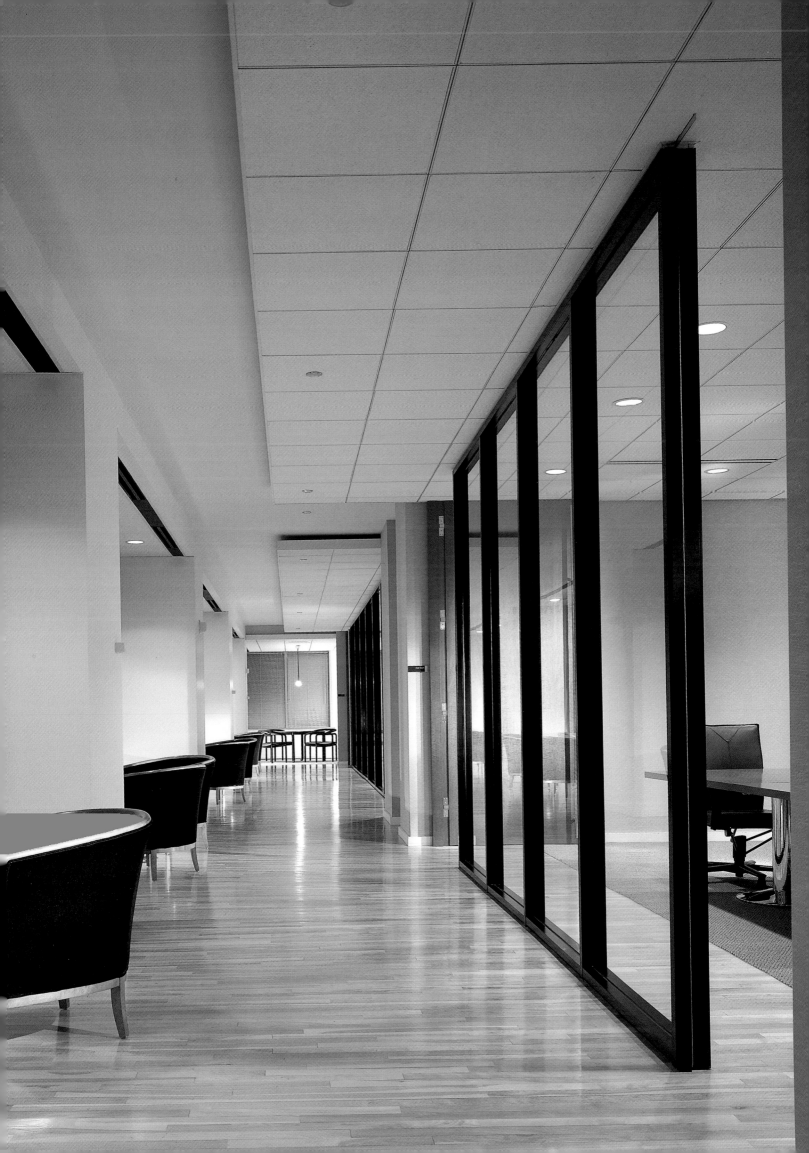

THE PHILLIPS GROUP

The Phillips Group, founded by James Phillips in 1979, is an architecture and interiors practice of approximately 170 employees. The firm's core business is corporate interiors, reflected in the fact that its designers plan and execute more than 5 million square feet (450,000 square meters) of office space per year. Ranked eleventh nationally in interior design sales volume and third in corporate office design by *Interior Design* magazine's 100 Giants, The Phillips Group is the largest New York City-based firm specializing in office interiors. The company believes in working hard on behalf of its clients and bringing value to an area of business that represents a major share of any company's capital and operating expenses.

OPPOSITE A glass grid wall outlines the private offices located on the perimeter of this printing and packaging company in New York City.
PHOTO BY NORMAN MCGRATH

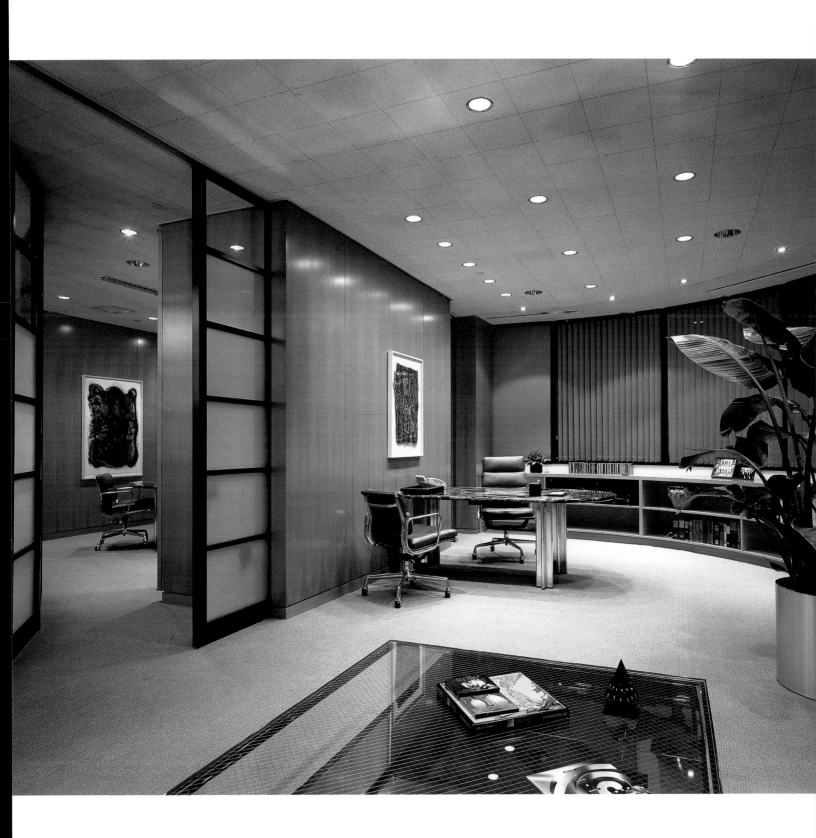

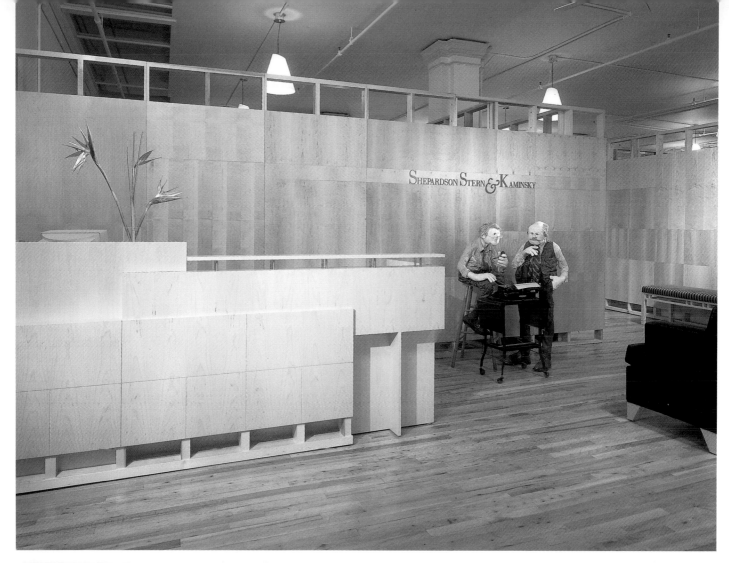

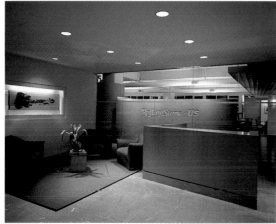

ABOVE The design intent was to enhance the loft-like qualities of this 5,400-square-foot (486-square-meter) space while creating a functional office. White maple partitions were finished with a natural stain to make maximum use of natural light, creating a distinctive and inviting place.
PHOTO BY WHITNEY COX

LEFT The reception area of this magazine publisher uses contrasting materials to create a distinctive mood. Inside, beyond the dimly lit space, the perimeter offices are glass-walled to maximize natural light.
PHOTO BY NORMAN MCGRATH

BELOW LEFT The 25,000-square-foot (2,250-square meter) office is designed to give an open, spacious feel with high ceilings and light-toned wood. Private offices surrounding the workstations provide ample space and privacy for each employee.
PHOTO BY WHITNEY COX

BELOW Coffered ceilings in this 90,000-square-foot (8,100-square-meter) international banking and trading institution in New York City were designed on a universal module to provide greater ceiling height and accommodate indirect lighting and acoustic panels.
PHOTO BY WHITNEY COX

OPPOSITE This highly secured reception area leads to the 110,000-square-foot (9,900-square-meter), state-of-the-art digital cable station facility, which includes four control rooms, twenty edit rooms, and a special effects/graphics department.
PHOTO BY BRIAN ROSE

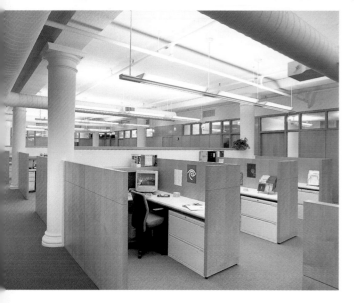

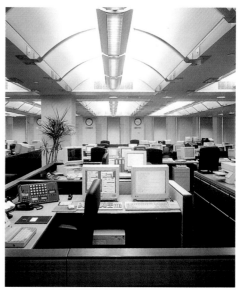

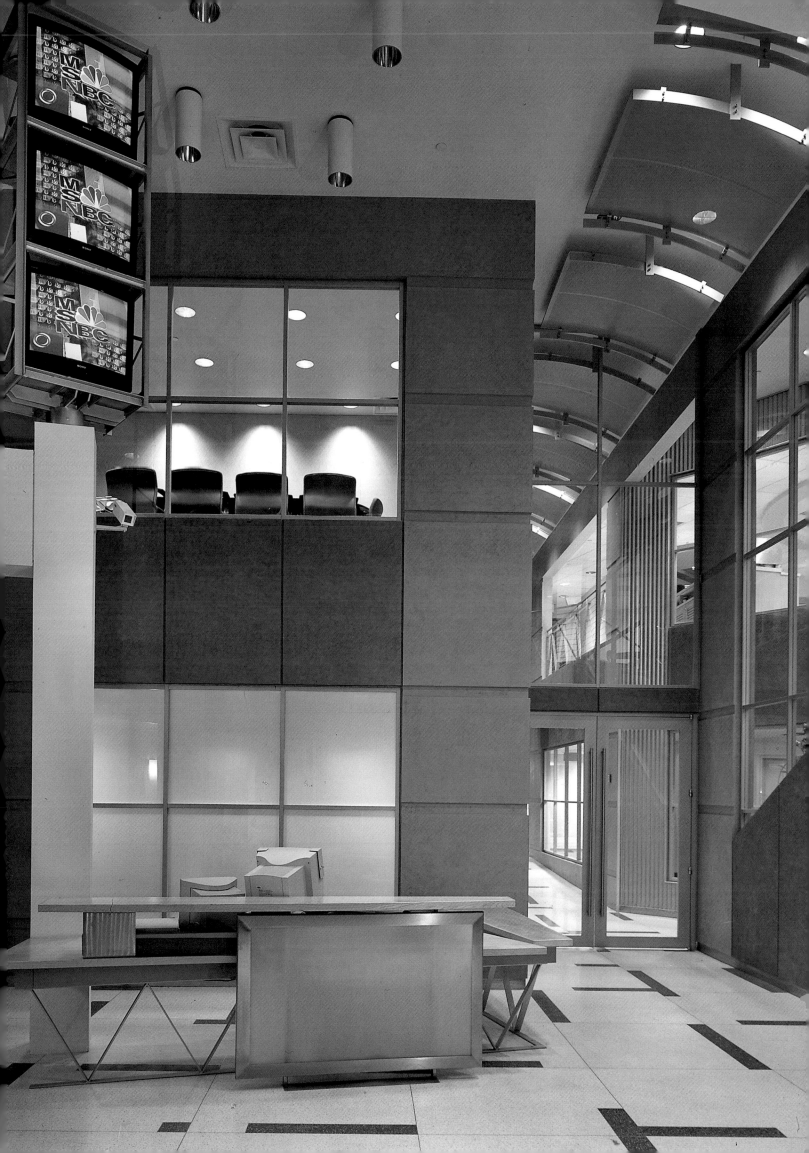

RICHARD POLLACK & ASSOCIATES

Richard Pollack & Associates (RPA) is dedicated to developing productive work environments. This mission has inspired significant research into measuring the impact of space on workers' productive capacity—benchmarking that is critical to the clients' continued economic success. This is a key differentiation for RPA. The firm believes that successful design is gauged by its responsiveness to the expressed and implied requirements of each client. RPA's design intent is to fulfill the necessary programmatic criteria and clearly communicate the client's philosophy, mission, character, function, and image. Through significant principal involvement, personal and proactive service, and quality design, RPA strives to create partnering relationships with its clients, leading to long-term collaboration. Established in 1985, RPA is a California corporation specializing in commercial interior design and architecture for corporate offices and facilities. RPA's staff of designers, architects, and administrative personnel offers a full range of services including building evaluation, programming, space planning, design, furniture selection and specification, construction drawings, contract administration, and tenant improvement.

OPPOSITE Double glazing and acoustical partitions separate the main conference room from the reception area in this commercial real estate brokerage, reducing disruption while taking full advantage of the natural light and the delightful view of the San Francisco Bay.
ALL PHOTOS BY JOHN SUTTON PHOTOGRAPHY

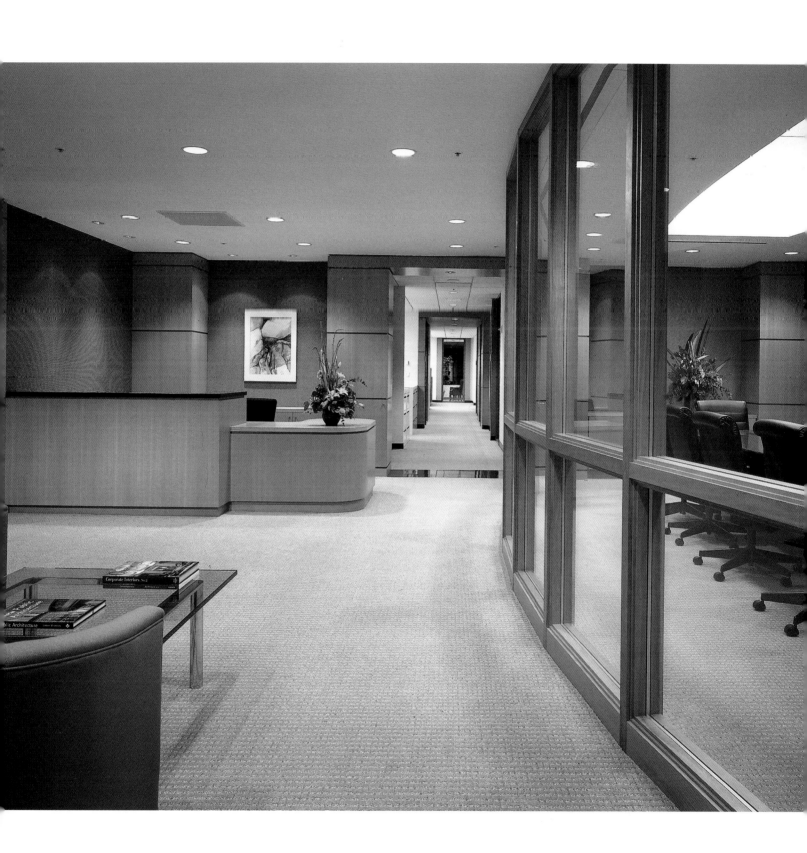

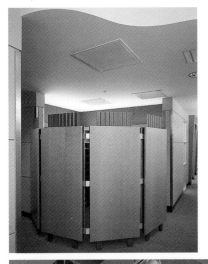

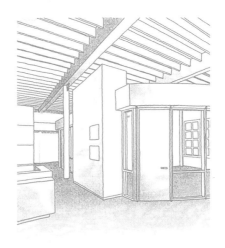

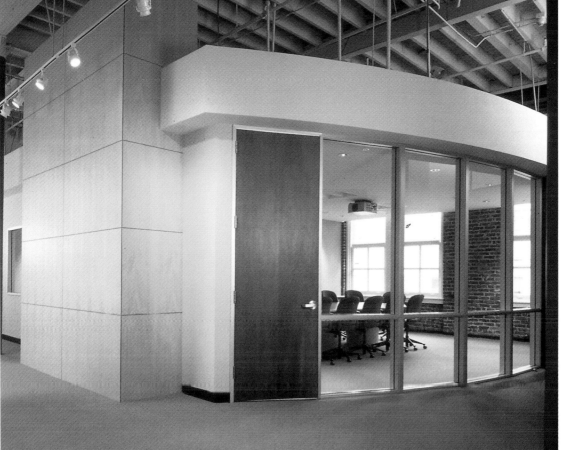

ABOVE LEFT Acoustical panels attached to the back of a cherry partition wall reduce noise and provide a tackable surface in the area assigned to coffee service and photocopying. Corrugated fiberglass panels fixed on top of the wall playfully recall found objects from a neighbor's carport.

LEFT This international advertising agency's San Francisco branch sought to return to its roots in a retrofitted brick-and-timber building. A neutral palette and generous amounts of glass allow natural light to highlight the sandblasted brick and whitewashed joists.

BELOW LEFT In this reception space for a financial services firm's in-house advertising division, cobalt blue Italian-plaster waves create a sense of enclosure and separate the public area from private work spaces.

BELOW RIGHT Two-story-high pillars and a sleek new staircase unite the two floors of this company's investment management division. The conference room in the background, equipped with built-in kitchen facilities, accommodates eighteen people.

OPPOSITE The break-out area in this advertising firm is designed as a waiting area to immerse visiting clients in the sights and sounds of ongoing creative work.

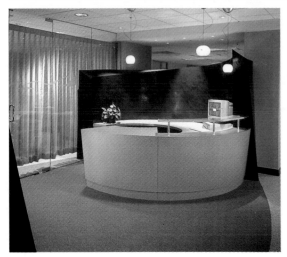

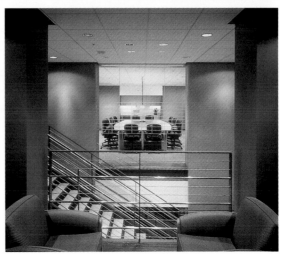

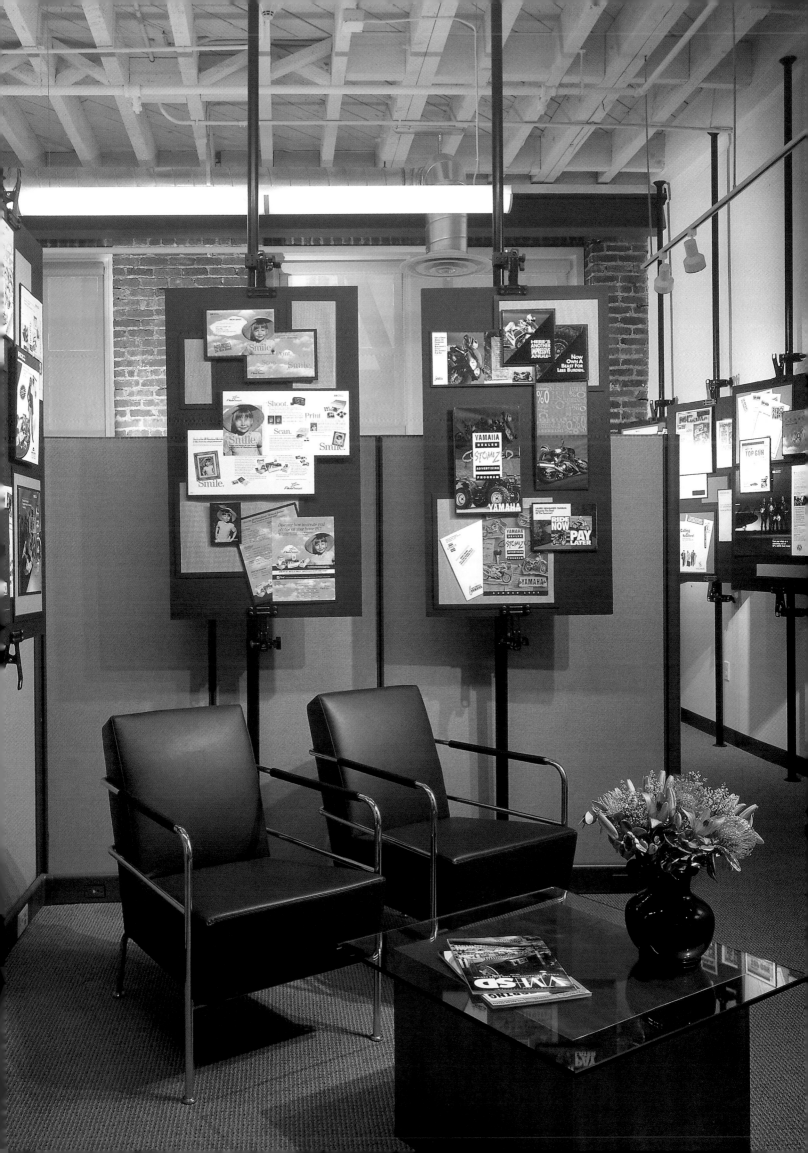

RTKL ASSOCIATES, INC.

Ranked by the *Washington Business Journal* as the second largest interior architectural firm in the Washington, D.C., area, the 125-person Washington office of RTKL provides architecture, interior architecture, engineering, planning, and landscape architecture services. The firm's portfolio of corporate projects reflects a design process that responds to the myriad forces confronting the private and public sector: changing business plans and real estate holdings, technology considerations, and new work concepts and methods. RTKL's corporate assignments range in scale from traditional interior design projects to ongoing historic renovations and office building repositionings. RTKL is also at the forefront of such nontraditional interior architectural services as facilities consulting, relocation and consolidation services, and property and building evaluations. Systems furniture design, selection, and specification are a major component of most of the firm's interior projects. Founded as a two-man office in 1946, RTKL has evolved into one of the world's largest multidisciplinary firms, with offices in Baltimore, Washington, Dallas, Los Angeles, Chicago, London, Tokyo, and Hong Kong.

OPPOSITE The reception area of this telecommunications firm conforms with the open space plan for the office, serving the dual function of informal meeting space. Purple accent walls highlight meeting areas throughout the interior. The designers arranged carpeting to signify changes in ceiling design and height; uplighting helps reduce the feeling of a low ceiling.
ALL PHOTOS BY MAXWELL MACKENZIE

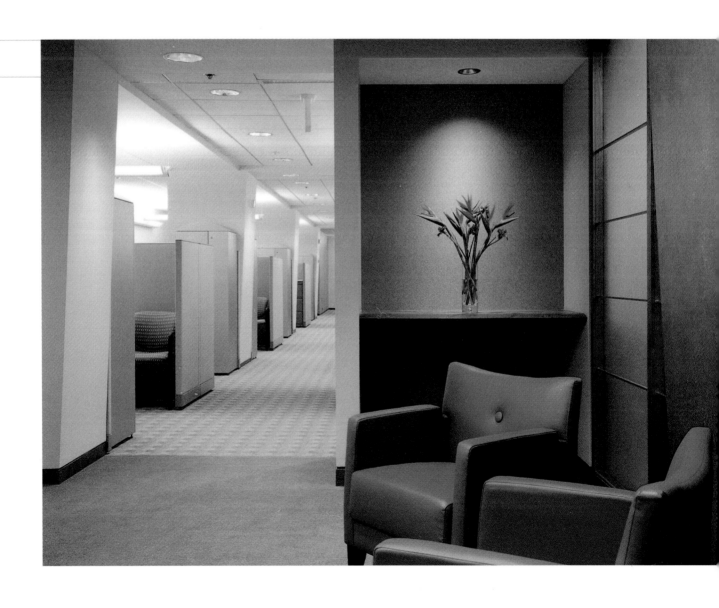

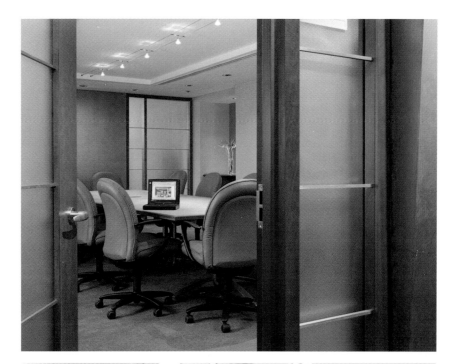

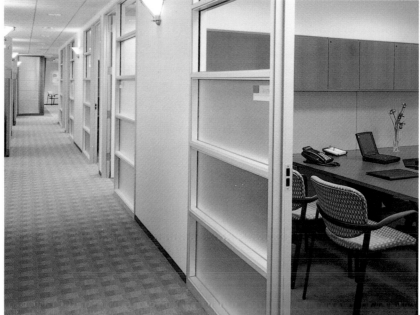

ABOVE Enclosed conference rooms and teaming areas support the open plan on each floor of this office in Washington, D.C. Fixed glass panels bracketed by purple accent walls are used to designate conference rooms and meeting areas. Horizontal metal rods in the glass panels form continuous threads that tie the interior together.

LEFT Although the design concept relies primarily on open office space, a limited number of private offices are strung in a row along the building perimeter. Textured glass partitions provide a degree of privacy, while clear glass was installed at eye level to maintain a feeling of openness.

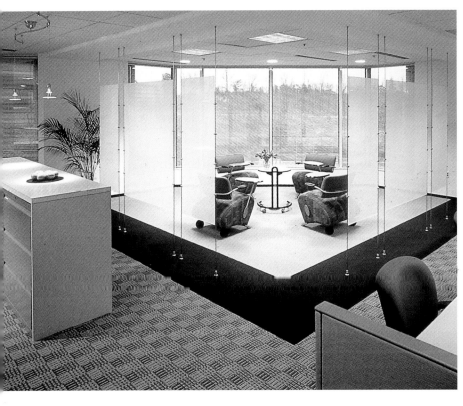

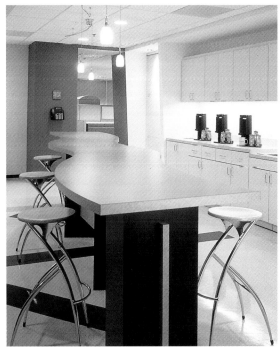

ABOVE LEFT This 44,000-square-foot (3,960-square-meter) expansion for a management firm in Reston, Virginia, incorporates readily accessible teaming areas delineated by floating glass partitions.

ABOVE RIGHT The office layout features central "pub" areas where copying facilities, food service, and multimedia displays are concentrated to create hubs of activity.

RIGHT Ninety-five percent of the offices are configured in an open plan around the building perimeter, allowing workers the benefit of natural light.

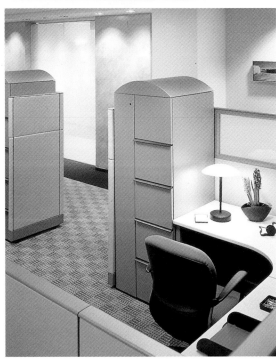

SASAKI ASSOCIATES, INC.

For more than forty-five years, Sasaki Associates has combined creativity and problem solving to provide clients with exceptional planning and design services. The approach is an outgrowth of founder Hideo Sasaki's belief that the most successful planning and design is accomplished by experienced professionals from an array of design disciplines who work closely with the client to achieve the best solution. The firm's interior design group provides comprehensive services to corporate and institutional clients for both new construction and renovation projects. The corporate focus has been on downtown and high-end suburban office space and large administrative/operations space, primarily in New England.

OPPOSITE This 110,000-square-foot (9,990-square-meter) operations center includes a large open office landscape focused on a three-story atrium that provides an orientation point for occupants.
PHOTO BY PETER VANDERWARKER

LEGEND
1 Atrium
2 Open Office
3 Private Office
4 Data Center
5 Training Room
6 Cafeteria
7 Servery

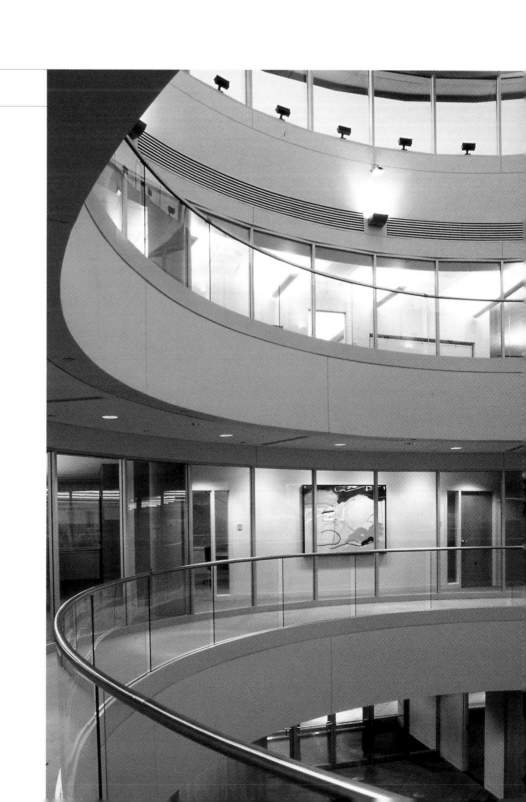

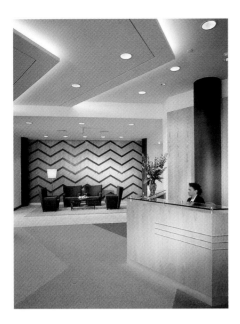

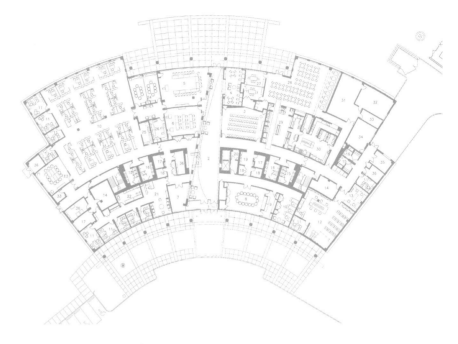

ABOVE The lobby of these health plan offices in a renovated 1920s building follows a contemporary vocabulary based on the forms and patterns of Art Deco.

BELOW LEFT Materials in the lobby of this New Hampshire service center highlight the contrast between the building's dominant radial geometry and a diagonal cut that creates the lobby space on each floor.

BELOW RIGHT Rich colors and simple furnishings in the cafeteria strike the right balance in creating a professional but understated atmosphere.

PHOTOS BY RICHARD MANDELKORN

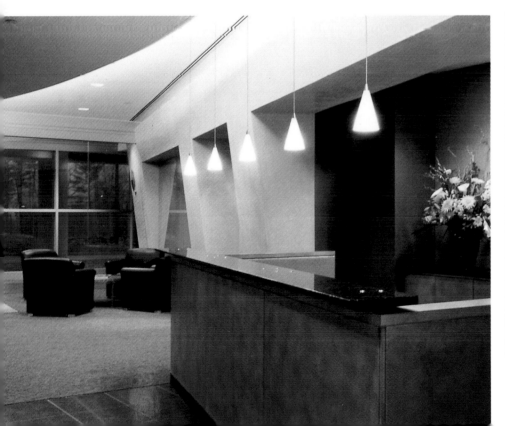

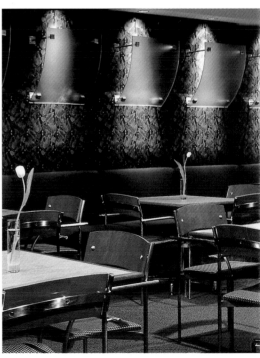

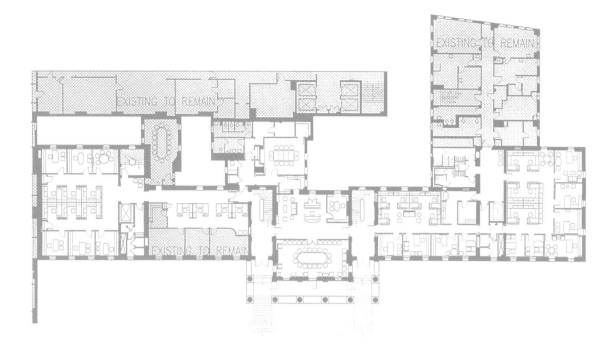

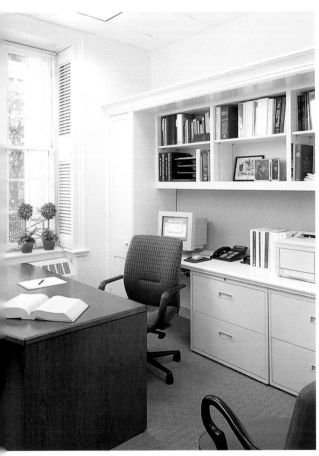

ABOVE A typical private office in this national landmark hospital includes appropriate elements, such as painted millwork and raised panel doors.

RIGHT Traditional styling was maintained in the executive conference room of this historic Boston hospital, designed by Charles Bulfinch in the early 1800s.
PHOTOS BY LUCY CHEN

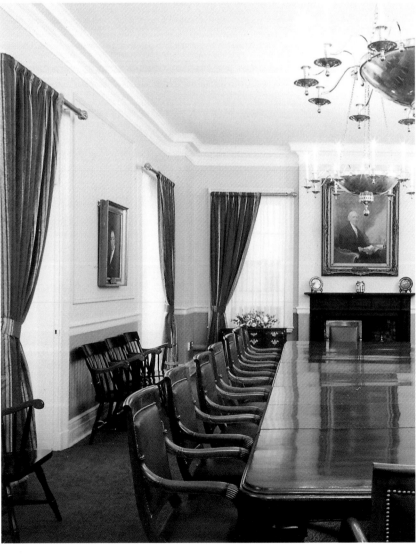

SIPSON GRAY ASSOCIATES

Sipson Gray Associates is a medium-sized practice of architects and designers in Hampshire, England, serving large commercial clients as well as smaller businesses. Other specialties of the firm include housing, education, and work for public authorities. Steady pressure from clients to control expenses and receive value for their design investment has led Sipson Gray to keep a constant eye on the bottom line while trying always to provide visual and tactile stimulation to a project. The firm now believes that cost is just another important discipline—imagination need not be expensive.

BELOW In the guest dining area, crystal chandeliers conceal the return air ducts. Crystal was specified because it enhances the quality of light and doesn't tarnish.

OPPOSITE To add visual interest to the cafeteria, Sipson Gray designed a fiber optic globe light fitted with color wheels to achieve a constantly changing appearance.
PHOTOS BY DAVID CHURCHILL

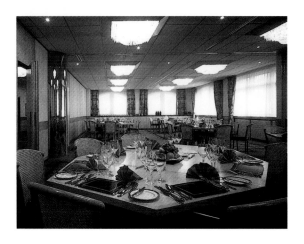

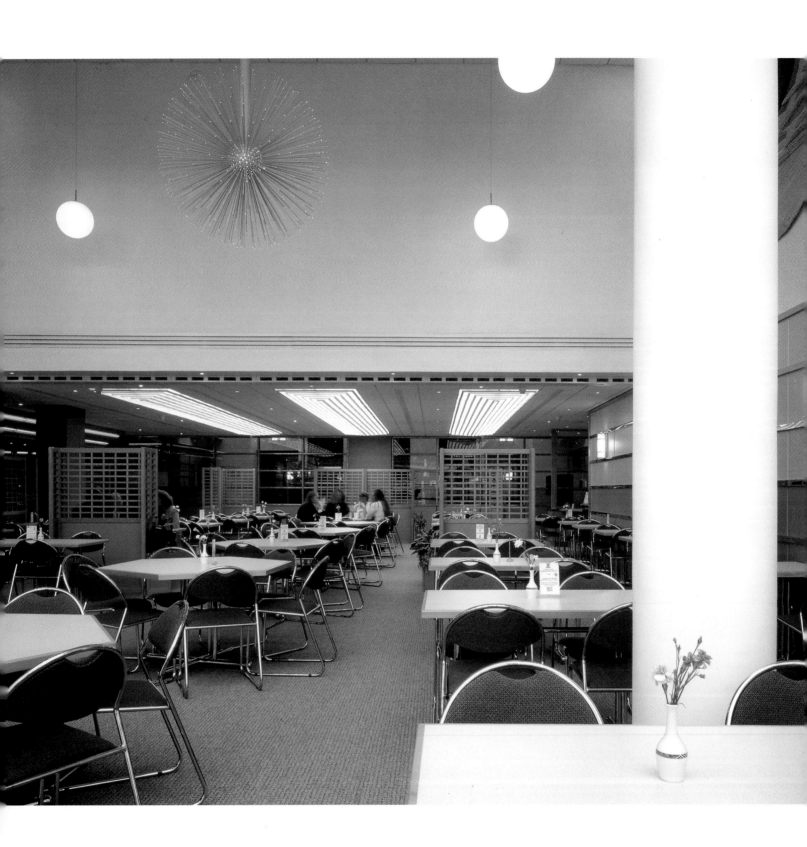

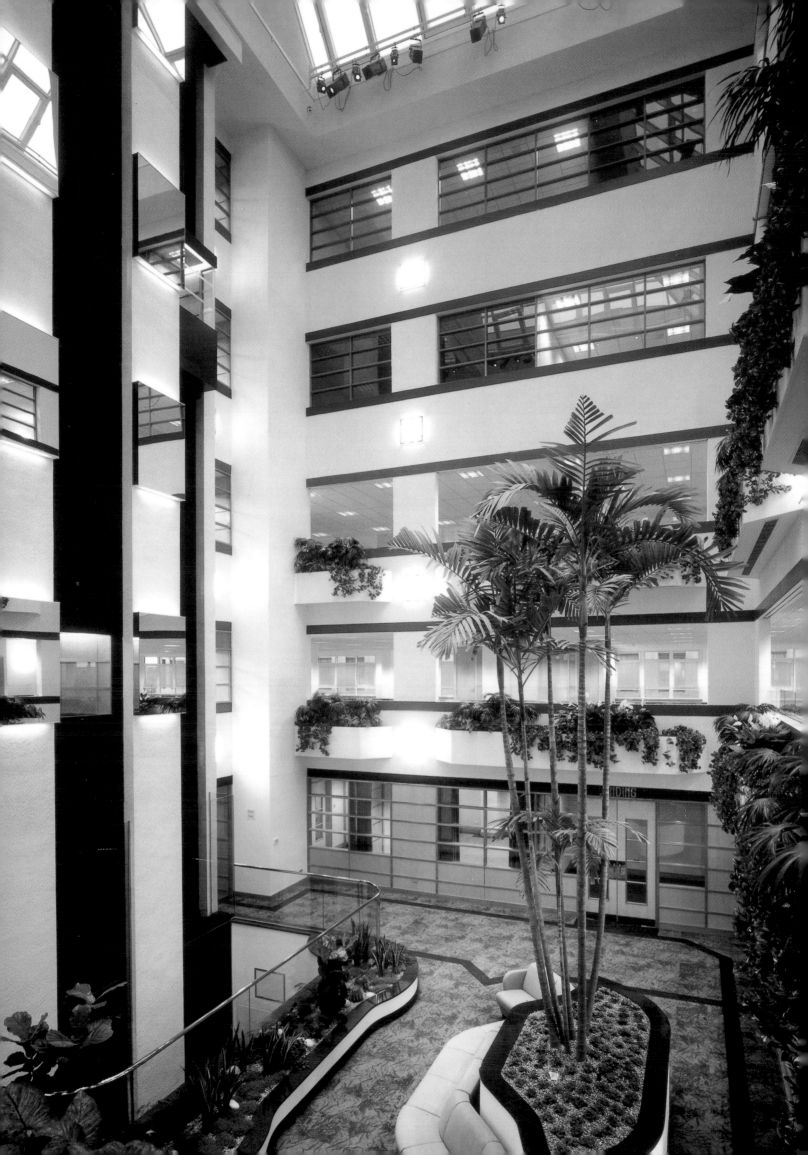

OPPOSITE In this skylit atrium, users of the building pass from the elevators at left to the cafeteria entrance at right.

RIGHT The intimate reception area is tucked beneath a series of steeped catwalks that cross overhead through the full-height atrium space.

FAR RIGHT The reception area occupies a pedestrian bridge above a main highway and connects two office buildings, one on each side of the highway. Lower glass panels in the outer wall are partially obscured with scenes of the local countryside fritted to the glass surface.

BELOW The reception area features a desk designed by Sipson Gray, as was the carpeting, which is laid in a radial pattern.

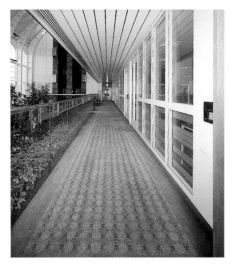

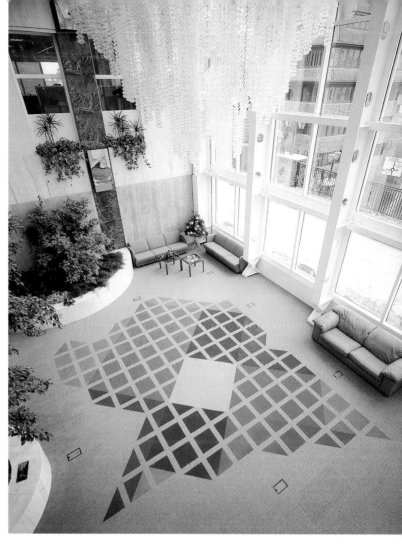

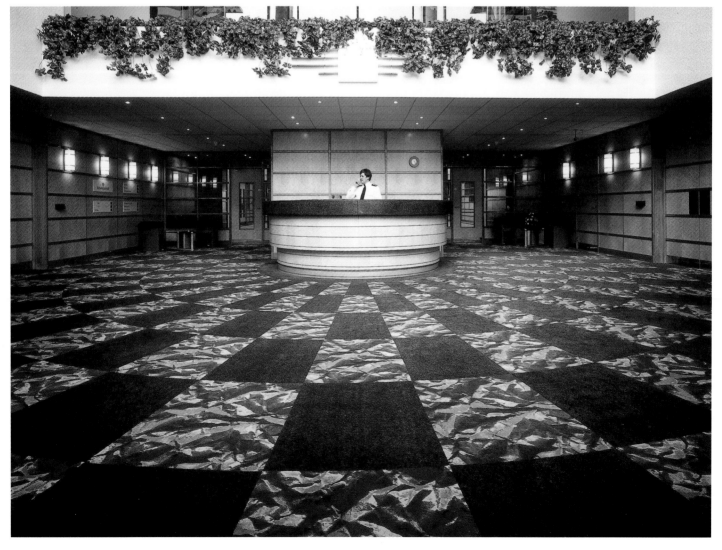

SKIDMORE, OWINGS & MERRILL LLP

Since its inception in 1936, Skidmore, Owings & Merrill (SOM) has undertaken a variety of commissions in the United States and in more than fifty countries throughout the world. SOM is renowned for the successful completion of challenging and complex assignments within strict time frames and budget constraints. The firm's track record in projects of all sizes and types gives clients confidence that they are hiring highly trained and experienced professionals. SOM's commitment to excellence results in the completion of visionary, functional, and noteworthy buildings. Its roster of completed projects is highly diversified, ranging from offices and hotels to educational buildings and airports. Interior design is an integral part of SOM's practice, as is a broad range of urban planning projects. In 1996, the American Institute of Architects recognized SOM with the highest honor given to architecture firms, the Architecture Firm Award. This decision was unprecedented inasmuch as SOM was the first recipient of the award in 1962 and is the first firm to win the award a second time.

OPPOSITE The employee cafeteria of this Chicago firm uses a series of rotating grids on the ceiling and floor to place it on axis with Michigan Avenue. Preferred seating in the cafeteria has become the Adirondack chairs that offer views of Lake Michigan.
PHOTO BY MARCO LORENZETTI ©HEDRICH BLESSING

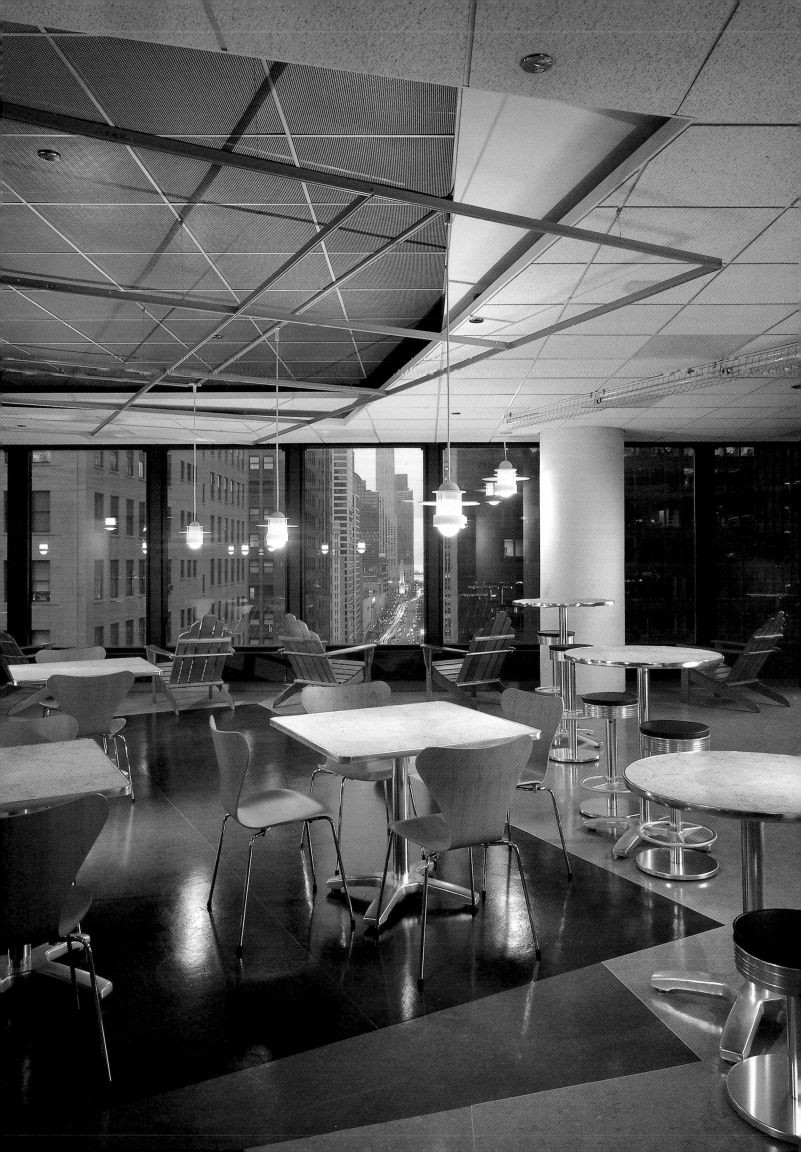

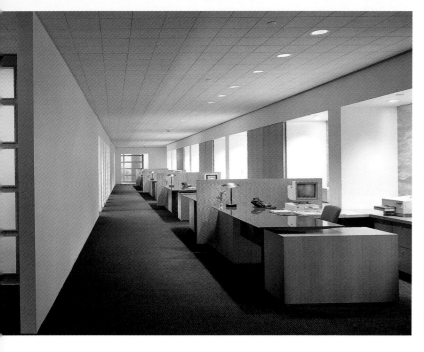

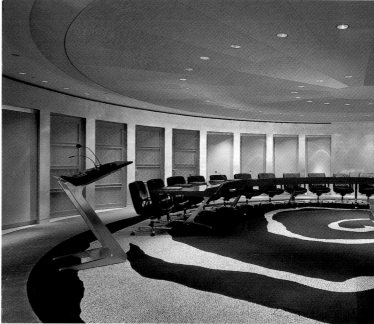

ABOVE LEFT Modular work stations are arranged at the north and south of the core along spine walls, which support furniture elements and contain all electrical, communications, and wiring.
PHOTO BY NICK MERRICK
© HEDRICH BLESSING

ABOVE RIGHT The main design concept was flexibility to allow the organization to change and evolve and for people, rather than walls, to move. A typical template floor plan was developed, with accommodation made for special spaces such as this conference room.
PHOTO BY NICK MERRICK
© HEDRICH BLESSING

BELOW LEFT Efficient utilization of space was achieved in this New York law firm by reassessing areas typically associated with storage. An unused elevator lobby, normally relegated to storage, became the firm's centerpiece—a two-story library housing a custom glass-and-stainless steel staircase.
PHOTO BY MICHAEL MORAN

BELOW RIGHT Major design challenges for this law firm included devising a method for alleviating the psychological barrier of impenetrable perimeter office walls. Natural illumination in the central work area was increased 50 percent by placing large expanses of laminated glass in the perimeter walls.
PHOTO BY MICHAEL MORAN

OPPOSITE Wooden trellises mark the entry into each of the open office areas that are defined by the spine walls of this Detroit office interior. A similar theme is repeated in special areas such as the elevator lobbies.
PHOTO BY NICK MERRICK
© HEDRICH BLESSING

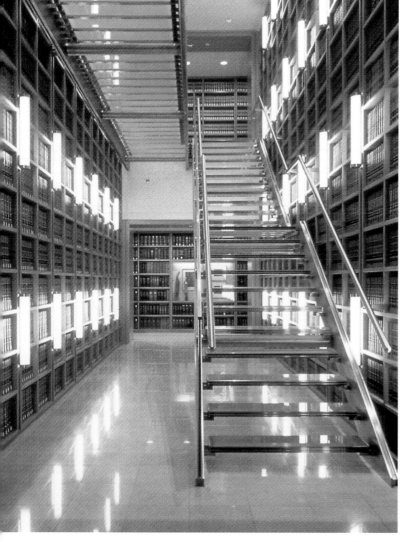

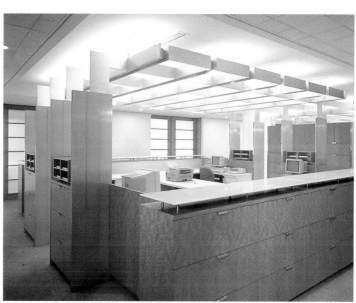

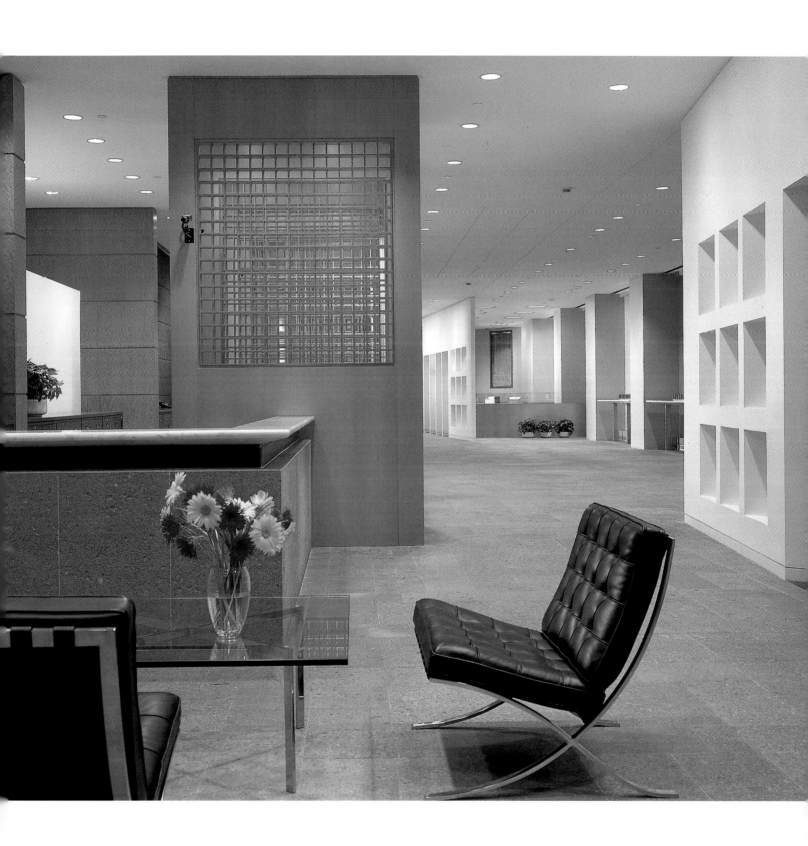

SPECTOR GROUP

The Spector Group strives to produce buildings that possess energy and a sense of presence. Recognized nationally for design excellence, the firm embraces a philosophy that "man's behavior is inspired by his life space." For thirty-five years, Spector Group has been defining environments where people live and work, pray and play, learn and heal. Founded in 1965 by Michael Harris Spector, the firm has combined creative and technical expertise to win more than fifty architectural design awards.

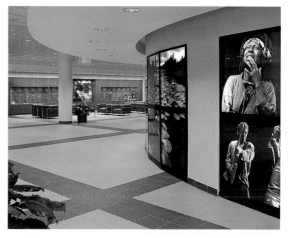

ABOVE RIGHT Glass cabinetry lines the perimeter of this corporate lobby. An arcing wall of backlit display photography draws visitors into this camera maker's lobby and exhibition space.

RIGHT Visitors to this publishing/entertainment company are welcomed into a reception area enveloped by a custom-designed curly maple desk, arced wall, and sleek corridors capped by curved, stainless steel ceilings.

OPPOSITE An executive conference room that links the president's and vice president's offices is filled with ambient lighting typical of the office design. Etched glass set in steel frames offers privacy while admitting natural light into the corridors.
ALL PHOTOS BY COLIN MCRAE

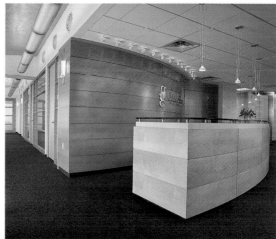

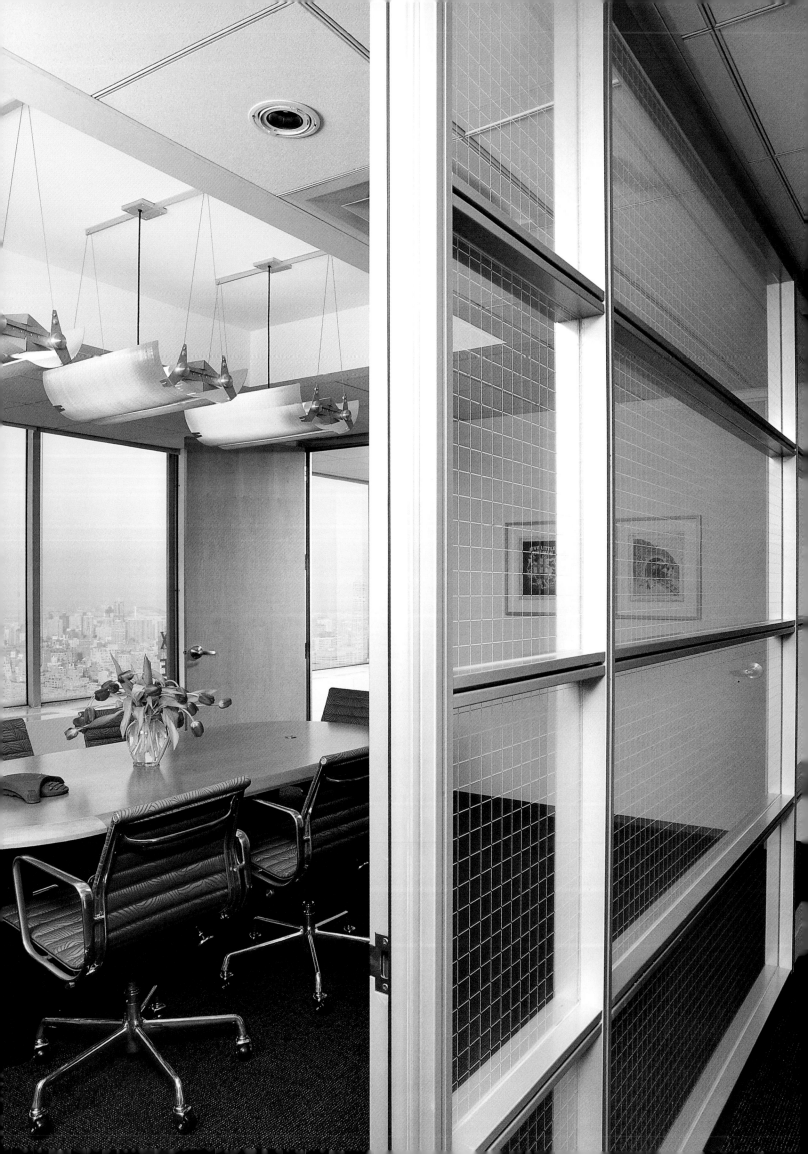

STUDIOS ARCHITECTURE

STUDIOS is committed to communicating the philosophy, character, and image of its clients. While the practice has produced a wide variety of architectural expressions, the firm has earned recognition for design excellence in many project types, including corporate headquarters, high-technology facilities, research and development facilities, universities, and law firms. This broad range of experience demonstrates that STUDIOS can effectively convey the character of its clients through unique and highly functional environments. STUDIOS Architecture is an international architecture firm that provides services in architecture, master planning, and interior architecture and design. With more than 130 employees located in offices in San Francisco, Washington, New York, London, and Paris, STUDIOS has forged long-term relationships with clients throughout the United States, Europe, and Asia. The firm's global presence provides its architects with opportunities to observe and implement design trends worldwide.

OPPOSITE Break-out spaces with full coffee bars are strategically located throughout the 500,000-square-foot (46,450-square-meter) campus for this Silicon Valley high-tech firm. Tabletops are surfaced with whiteboards for note-taking during brainstorming sessions that often occur spontaneously when employees from different departments encounter each other.
PHOTO BY MICHAEL O'CALLAHAN

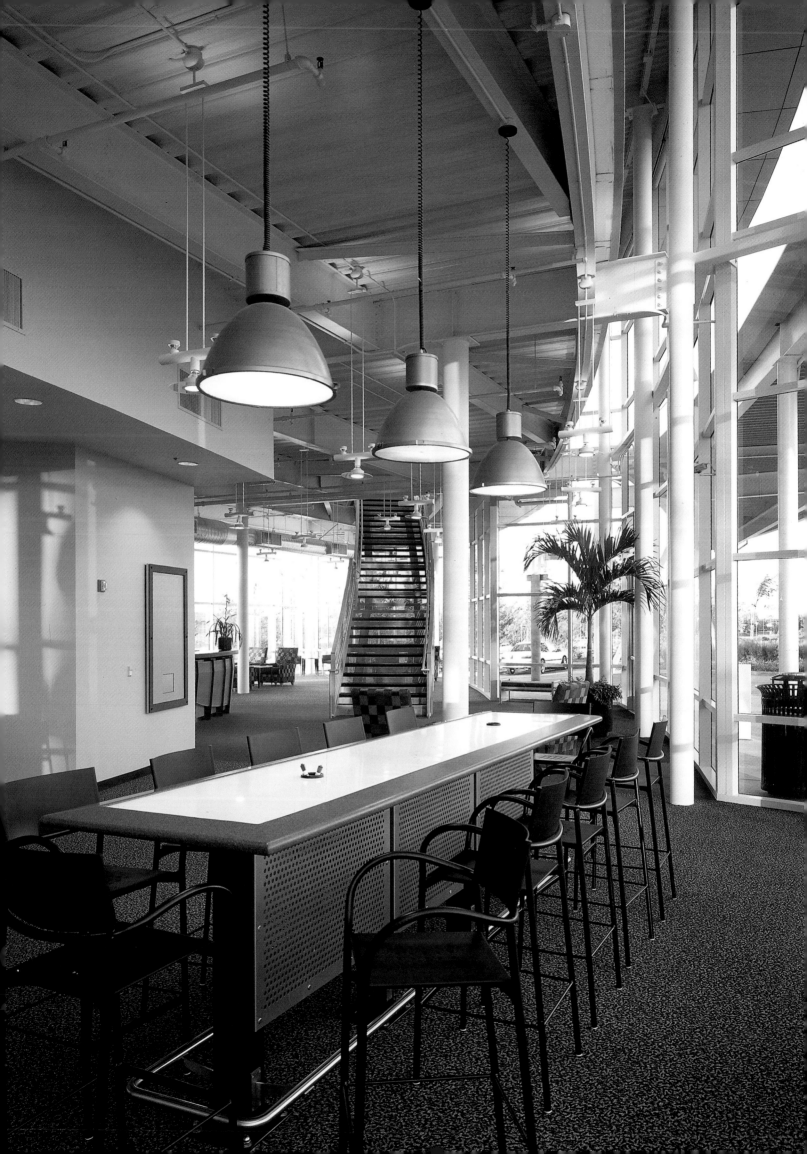

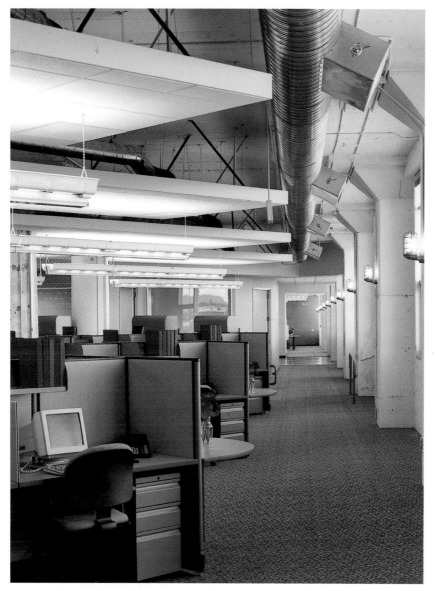

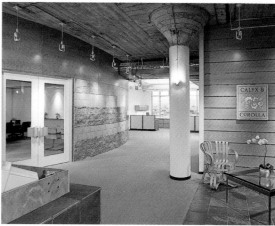

LEFT This call center for a high-end mail order floral company is flexible enough to accommodate staff sizes varying from thirty-five to 125 people. A 200-foot-long (20-meter-long) run of windows retained from the original warehouse supplements suspended strip fluorescent lighting. Neutral materials form the backdrop for floral samples.

PHOTO BY MICHAEL O'CALLAHAN

ABOVE A melding of new and old and raw and finished materials greets visitors to this San Francisco-based mail order flower company. Green carpeting suggests grass, while stonework hints at a garden wall and slate walkway. Where possible, the ceiling of the former warehouse is left exposed to lend contrast and textural interest to the new space; curly beech used on the reception desk and walls adds warmth.

PHOTO BY MICHAEL O'CALLAHAN

BELOW LEFT This computer manufacturer's European VIP marketing center in Paris had to be the architectural equivalent of the company. STUDIOS designed a minimalist space whose sensuality is ensured by the quality of the lighting. Luminescent curved walls convey the elegance, sobriety, and sophistication characteristic of the firm.

PHOTO BY JEAN-PHILIPPE CAULLIEZ

OPPOSITE A catwalk fashioned from unfinished timber breaks up the 27-foot-high (8.1-meter-high) warehouse space occupied by this Internet company in Redwood City, California. The catwalk connects mezzanine-level meeting areas with a two-level space on the opposite side of a preexisting four-hour rated concrete block wall. At right, the circular room straddling the concrete wall houses the heart of the business, a large mainframe computer system.

PHOTO BY MICHAEL O'CALLAHAN

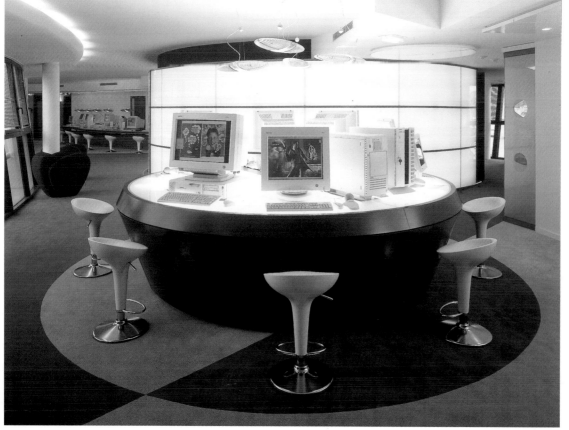

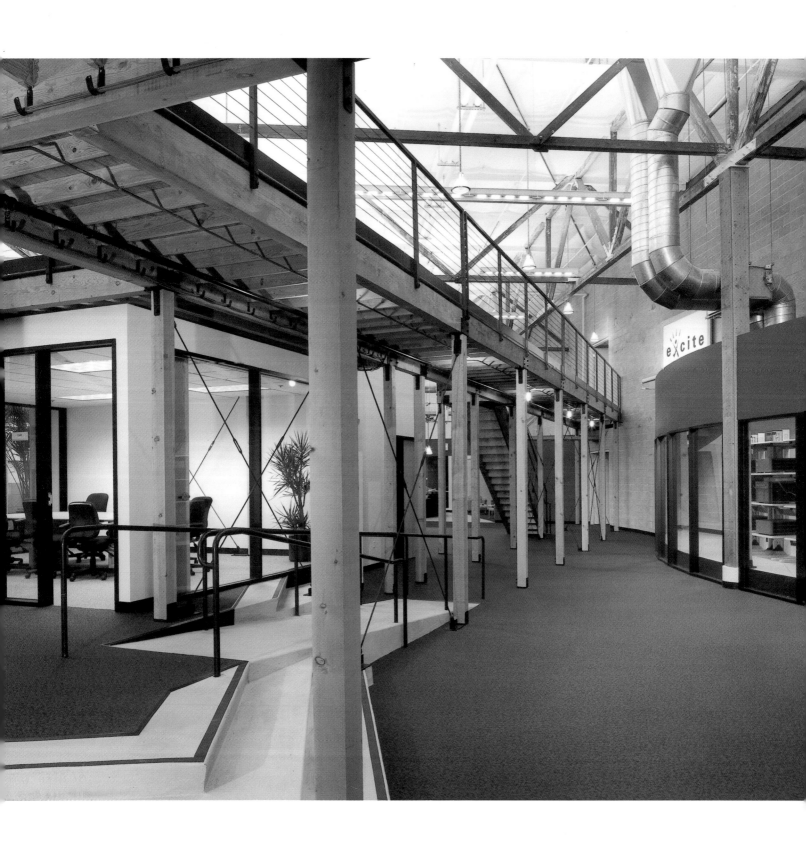

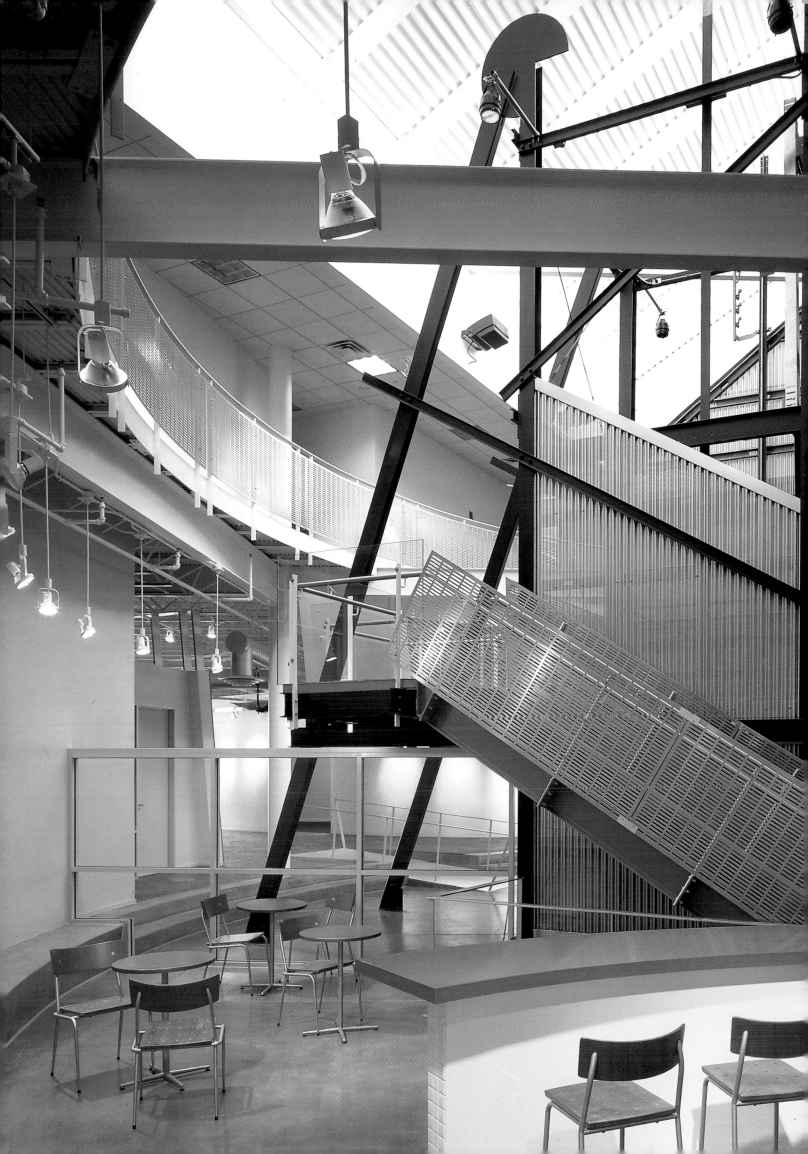

OPPOSITE Monumental stairwells inspired by Appalachian coal tipples are at the heart of each of three buildings on this high-tech campus in Warrendale, Pennsylvania. Aligned with a circulation spine that connects the buildings is an expressive steel construction supporting an open elevator shaft and stair. This café space pays homage to the prosaic beauty of everyday structural steel, proudly exposing round pipe columns, braced frames, open web joists, and decking.
PHOTO BY RICHARD BARNES PHOTOGRAPHY

RIGHT The atrium space of this London high-tech company serves as both a greeting area for visitors and an all-hands meeting space for employees. The three-story stair rises to the upper floors, where research and design teams are located. A low, translucent glass panel defines the boundary between secured and public areas.
PHOTO BY MICHAEL O'CALLAHAN

BELOW RIGHT In the reception area of this San Francisco-based wireless communications company, a custom-designed cable and hardware display uses images and text to illustrate the company's story. Portuguese limestone floors, granite stairs, eucalyptus wood panels, and fabric panels create a modern and sophisticated image that will remain timeless.
PHOTO BY CHAS MCGRATH

BELOW The company's private demonstration room features a curved, multi-screen media wall used in sales and marketing presentations. The wall is fabricated of a metallic ribbed laminate.
PHOTO BY CHAS MCGRATH

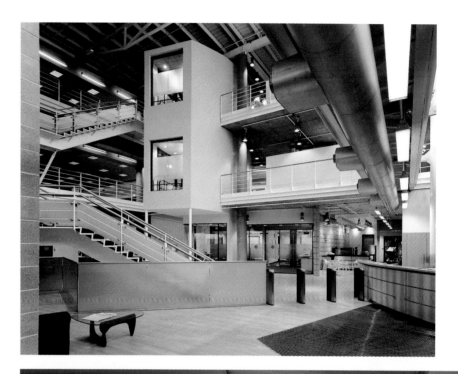

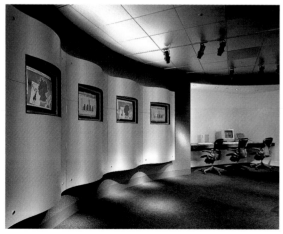

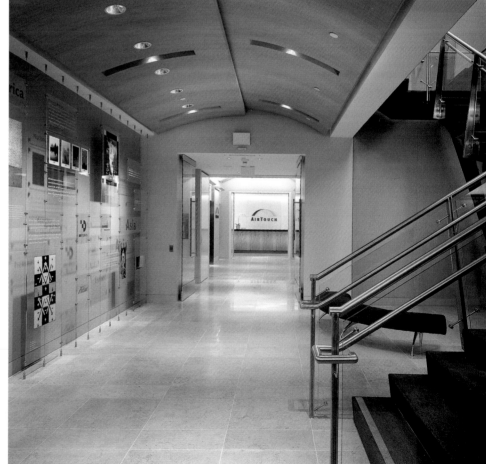

VOA ASSOCIATES, INC.

Founded in 1969, VOA is a Chicago-based organization of 285 employees with offices located in Orlando,
Miami, and Jacksonville, Florida; Washington, D.C.;
and Sao Paulo, Brazil. VOA Associates offers comprehensive services embracing the disciplines of architecture, space planning, interior design, facility programming, and master planning. VOA's diversified
practice includes corporate headquarters and offices,
college and university facilities, institutional master
plans, hotels and hospitality-related projects, institutional and health care facilities, and municipal and
transportation-related structures.

OPPOSITE The reception desk and bold backdrop at the entrance to this
Chicago financial firm introduce the metaphorical curve of stock market
volatility as a primary motif.
PHOTO BY STEVE HALL ©HEDRICH BLESSING

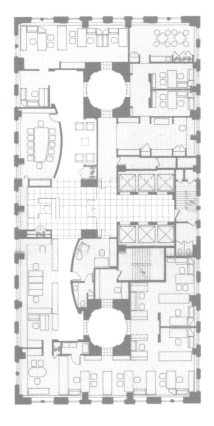

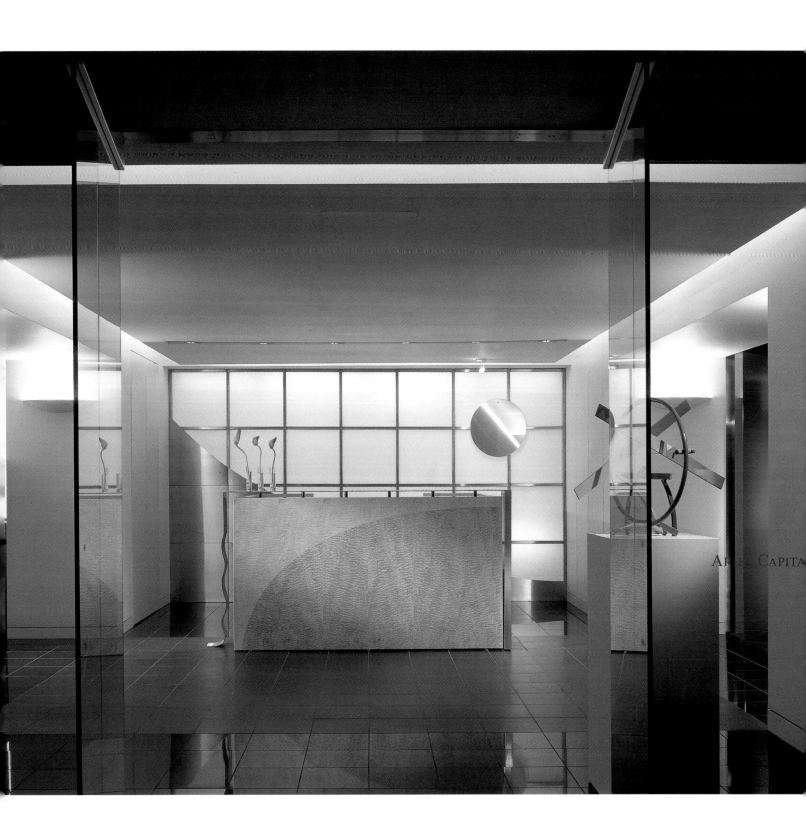

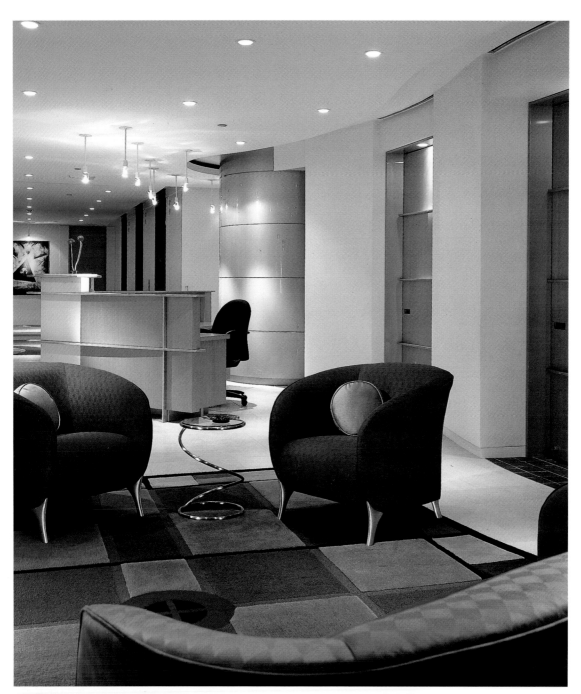

LEFT Training rooms, meeting rooms, and lounge areas at this Chicago insurance company are clustered around the reception area. All function separately, yet can be joined by moving three pivot doors into one expansive receiving space for annual meetings or other large gatherings.

BELOW LEFT Private offices are located at the building core in an effort to flatten the company's hierarchical structure.

PHOTOS BY STEVE HALL
© HEDRICH BLESSING

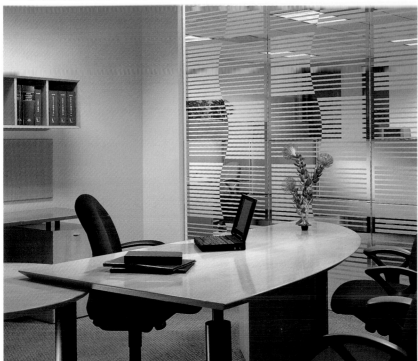

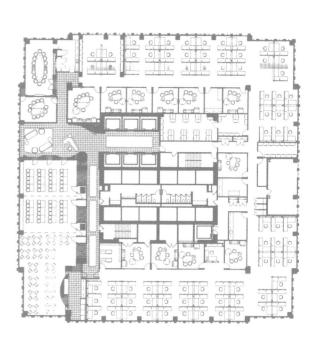

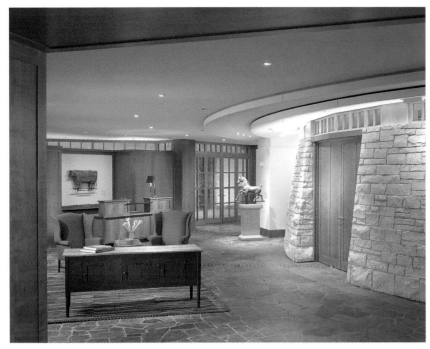

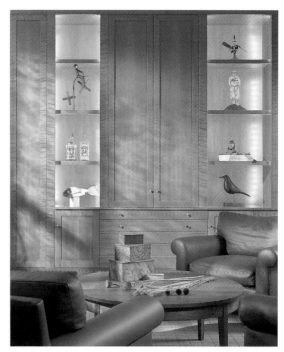

ABOVE LEFT For this Chicago insurance company's executive offices, the client's directive was to use Shaker philosophy and style as a theme to establish a warm, simple, and authentic space. In the reception and conference areas, split-face limestone and heavy timber construction recall an East Coast Shaker barn.

ABOVE RIGHT Coordinated features include customized furnishings, antique finishes on new millwork to match existing furniture, and a museum-like presentation of period artwork.

RIGHT Created below grade, a stimulating on-site training facility features state-of-the-art access to food/phone/fax/data equipment and break out areas for social and business interaction.

PHOTOS BY NICK MERRICK
©HEDRICH BLESSING

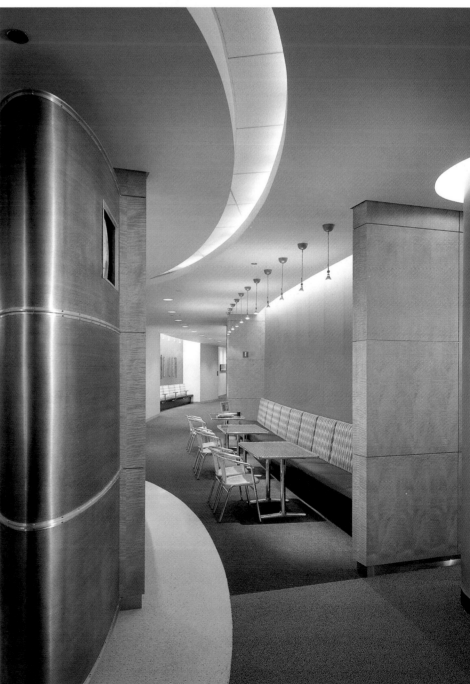

WARD-HALE DESIGN ASSOCIATES, INC.

From its inception in 1980, Ward-Hale Design Associates, Inc. has had a commitment to quality design resulting in a distinguished clientele and extensive repeat referral business. The firm has been recognized for design innovation by the former Institute for Business Design when it received two outstanding achievement awards in a single year—one for The Discovery Channel and the other a special recognition award.

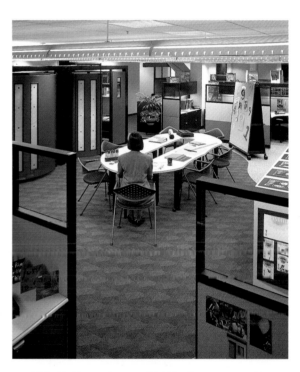

RIGHT The quality of work spaces ranges from formal to informal to allow for creative interaction while maintaining various degrees of acoustical privacy. In addition to providing open-plan workstations and managers' offices, the design incorporated three "activity tables" to host group work. Personal Harbors are available on reserve for solo efforts.

BELOW RIGHT High-tech drama charges the entry hall of an entertainment corporation in Bethesda, Maryland, which is lined with undulating stainless-steel mesh panels backlit with vertically mounted cold cathode tubes.

OPPOSITE Meeting spaces vary from living-room style areas to the traditional conference room, but the most popular new space is the open cappuccino bar.

PHOTOS BY PRAKASH PATEL

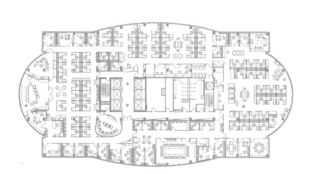

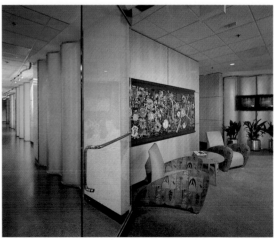

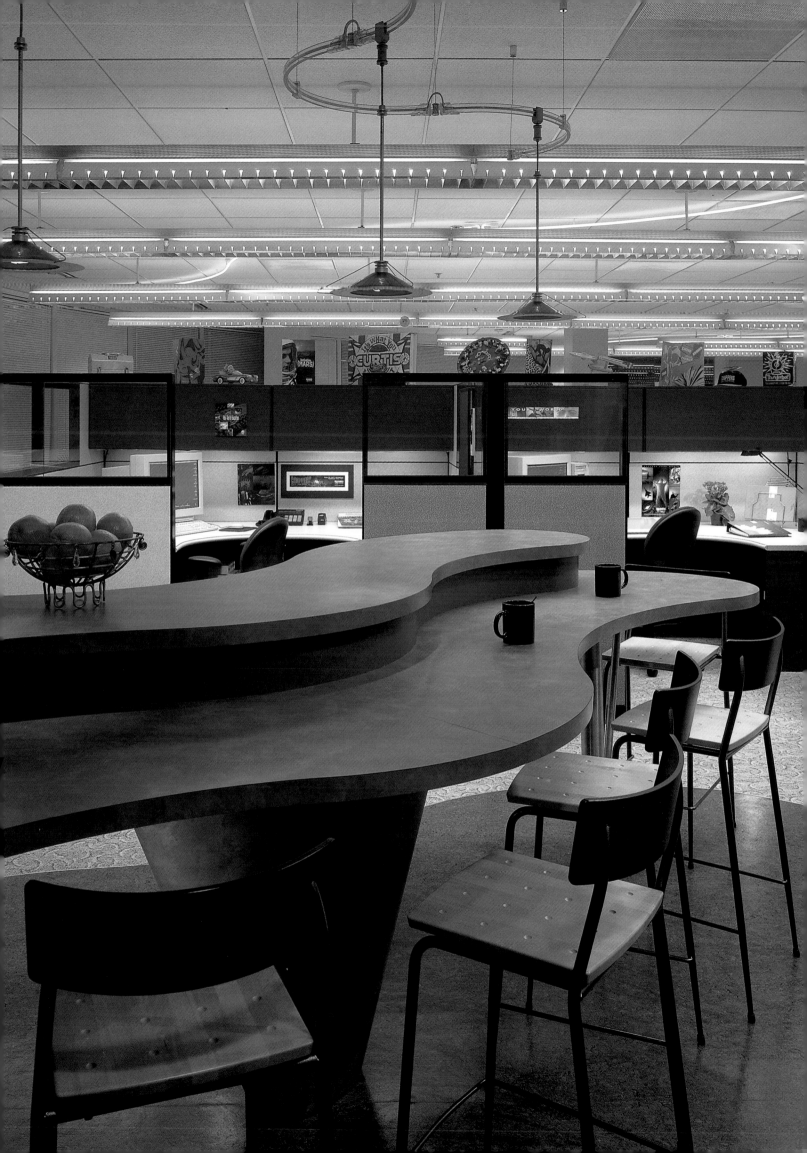

YABU PUSHELBERG

Yabu Pushelberg is a Canadian-based international design practice established in 1980 by creative director George Yabu and managing partner Glenn Pushelberg. From its headquarters in Toronto, the firm undertakes corporate, retail, and hospitality projects throughout North America, Europe, and the Far East. Yabu Pushelberg provides an array of design and project administration services as well as architectural and engineering services, graphic design and communications consultation, marketing strategies, and visual merchandising concepts. The firm's portfolio includes retail, hospitality, entertainment, and restaurant projects. The firm also has created a range of furnishings and carpets as an outgrowth of the custom designs that are frequently incorporated into its projects.

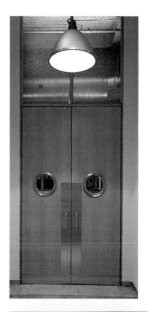

ABOVE RIGHT In keeping with the strong lines and refined industrial finishes used throughout the design, cafeteria doors are finished in honey-colored oak detailed with brushed stainless steel hardware.

RIGHT A vintage Knoll table and Saarinen armchairs in this meeting room complement the building's Modern architecture. The glazed partition wall, door, and transom ensure the greatest penetration of natural light into meeting and administrative areas, respecting the client's desire for an open, nonhierarchical design.

OPPOSITE The progression of doors and windows along the main corridor in these Toronto offices gives the impression of a streetscape. The polished concrete floor, natural wood finishes, and industrial light fixtures are inspired by the building's industrial character. PHOTOS BY EVAN DION

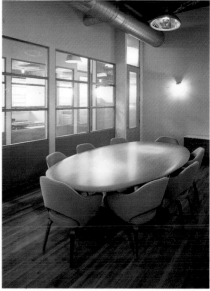

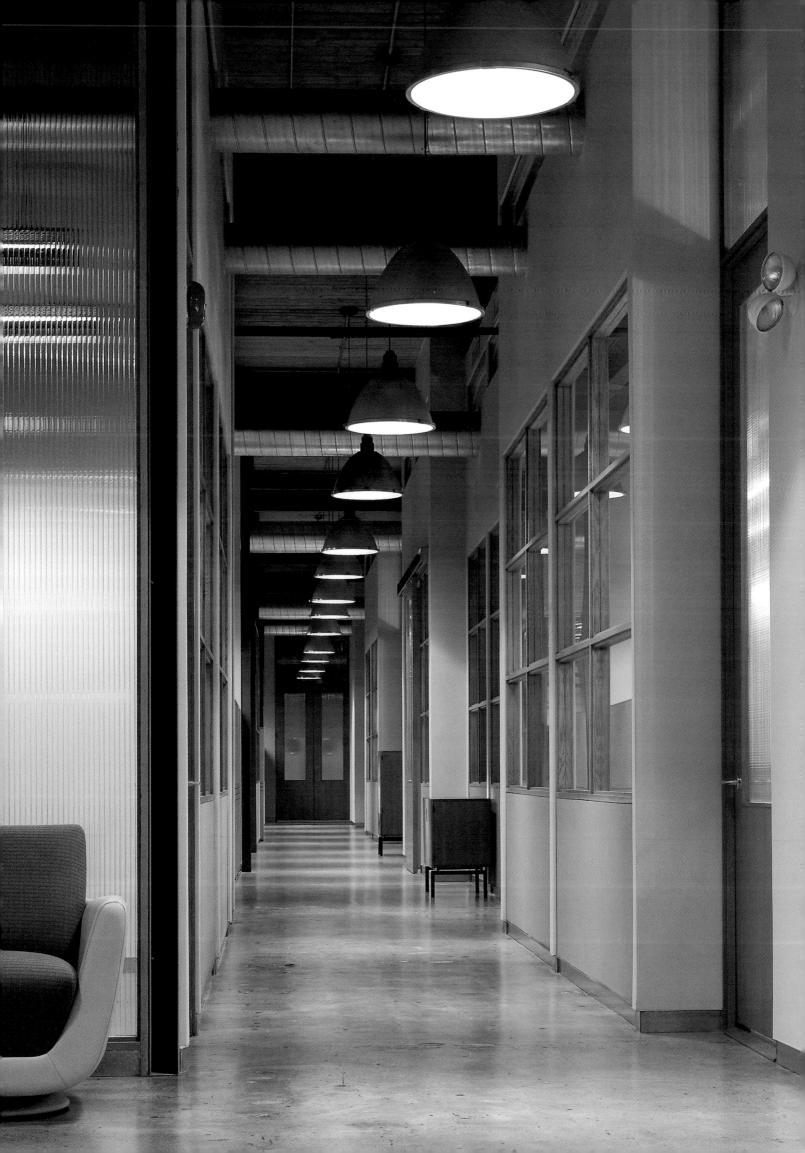

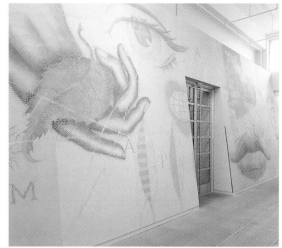

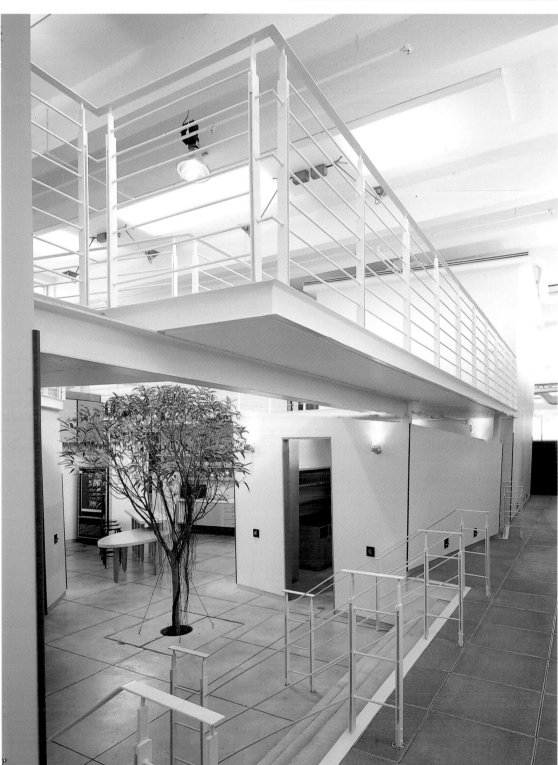

ABOVE A hand-painted mural, rendered in colors that complement the office pastels, covers the wall that separates the design group space and an adjacent auditorium. The mural features icons inspired by the five senses and communication-related themes.

LEFT Layers of dropped ceilings and non-loadbearing walls were removed in these Ottawa, Canada, offices and the visual environment energized by the combination of natural light with a light, bright color palette and spacious, multilevel plan.

OPPOSITE The meeting and display rooms off the central plaza are entered via sliding wood doors mounted with playful steel-framed portholes. The raised walkway around the periphery of this space creates a conduit for computer and telecommunications wiring.

PHOTOS BY ROBERT BURLEY,
DESIGN ARCHIVE

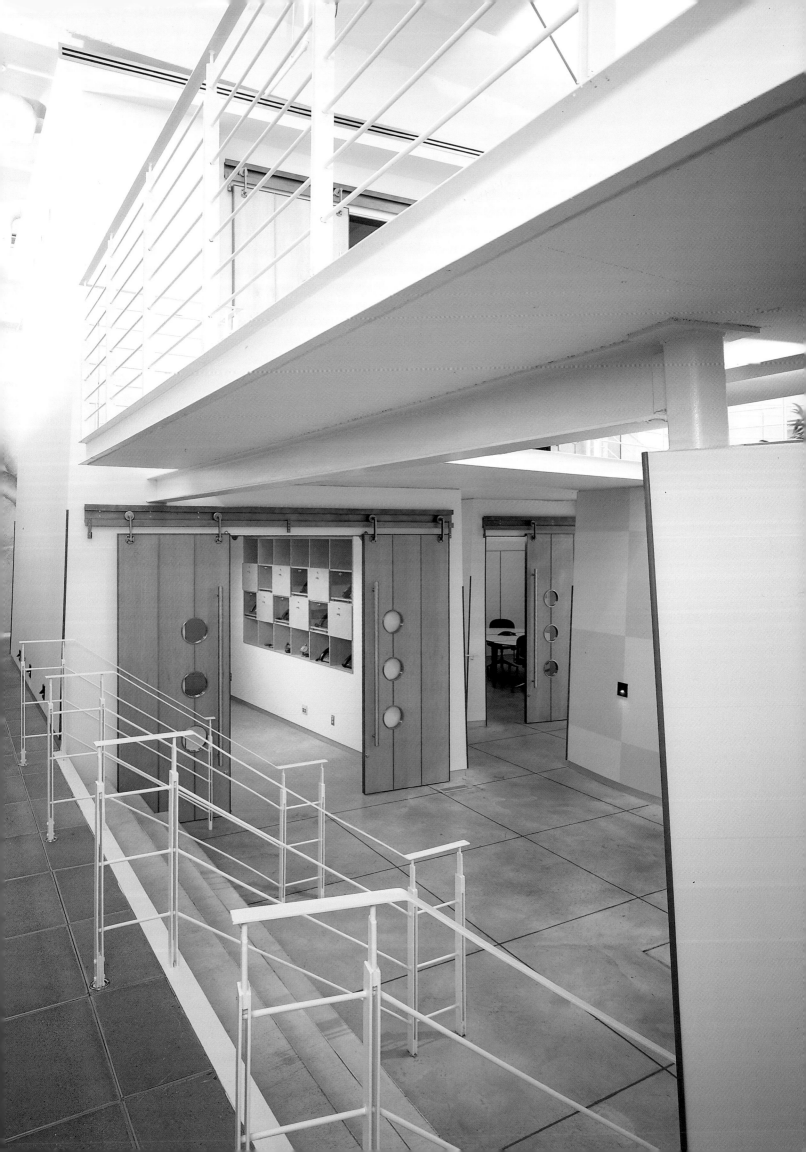

ADD Inc
80 Prospect Street
Cambridge, Massachusetts 02139
617-661-0165
Fax: 617-661-7118
www.addarch.com
E-mail: add@addarch.com

Ai
1445 New York Avenue, NW
Suite 400
Washington, D.C. 20005
202-737-1020
Fax: 202-737-0879

Architectural Alliance
400 Clifton Avenue South
Minneapolis, Minnesota 55403
612-871-5703
Fax: 612-871-7212

AREA
550 South Hope Street
Floor 18
Los Angeles, California 90071
213-623-8909
Fax: 213-623-4275

Bergmeyer Associates, Inc.
286 Congress Street
Boston, Massachusetts 02210
617-542-1025
Fax: 617-338-6897
www.bergmeyer.com

The Bommarito Group/Graeber, Simmons & Cowan
100 Congress Avenue
Suite 2200
Austin, Texas 78701
512-480-8898
Fax: 512-480-9451

Brayton & Hughes Design Studio
250 Sutter Street
Suite 650
San Francisco, California 94108
415-291-8100
Fax: 415-434-8145

Brennan Beer Gorman Monk/Interiors
515 Madison Avenue
New York, New York 10022
212-888-7667
Fax: 212-935-3868
www.bbg-bbgm.com

Callison Architecture, Inc.
1420 5th Avenue
Suite 2400
Seattle, Washington 98101
206-623-4646
Fax: 206-623-4625
www.callison.com

Camas Associates Architects PA
100 N. Tryon Street
Suite 3660
Charlotte, North Carolina 28202
704-372-0491
Fax: 704-372-5615

Cannon
2170 Whitehaven Road
Grand Island, New York 14072
716-773-6800
Fax: 716-773-5909

CDFM² Architecture Inc.
1015 Central
Kansas City, Missouri 64105
816-471-1080
Fax: 816-471-4362
E-mail: cdfm2@cdfm2.com

CORE
1010 Wisconsin Avenue NW
Suite 405
Washington, D.C. 20007
202-466-6116
Fax: 202-466-6235
www.coredc.com

Elkus/Manfredi Architects Ltd
530 Atlantic Avenue
Boston, Massachusetts 02210
617-426-1300
Fax: 617-426-7502

The Environments Group
303 E. Wacker Drive
Chicago, Illinois 60601
312-644-5080
Fax: 312-644-5299

Fox & Fowle Architects
22 West 19th Street
New York, New York 10011
212-627-1700
Fax: 212-463-8716
www.foxfowle.com

G.A. Design International
4 Delancey Passage
Delancey Street
London NW1 7NN
England
44 171 387 4002
Fax: 44 171 387 4003

Gensler
600 California Street
San Francisco, California 94108
415-433-3700
Fax: 415-627-3737

Greenwell Goetz Architects, P.C.
2000 L Street, NW
Suite 410
Washington, D.C. 20036
202-682-0700
Fax: 202-682-0738
www.gga.com

Griswold, Heckel & Kelly Associates, Inc.
55 West Wacker Drive
6th Floor
Chicago, Illinois 60601
312-263-6605
Fax: 312-263-1228

Hammel, Green and Abrahamson, Inc.
1201 Harmon Place
Minneapolis, Minnesota 55403-1985
612-337-4100
Fax: 612-332-9013
www.hga.com

Atelier Christian Hauvette
16 bis Avenue Parmentier
75011 Paris
France
33 1 43 70 2990
Fax: 33 1 43 70 8617

Herbert Lewis Kruse Blunck Architecture
202 Fleming Building
Des Moines, Iowa 50309
515-288-9536
Fax: 515-288-5816
E-mail: arch@hlkb.com

HKS Inc.
1919 McKinney Avenue
Dallas, Texas 75201
214-969-5599
Fax: 214-969-3397

Interior Architects Inc.
350 California Street, Suite 1500
San Francisco, California 94104
415-434-3305
Fax: 415-434-0330

Jung/Brannen Associates, Inc.
34 Farnsworth Street
Boston, Massachusetts 02210
617-482-2299
Fax: 617-482-4886
www.jb2000.com

Gary Lee & Partners
1743 Merchandise Mart
Chicago, Illinois 60654
312-644-1744
Fax: 312-644-1745
E-mail: glpartners@aol.com

Lehman/Smith/Wiseman Associates
1150 18th Street, NW
Suite 350
Washington, D.C. 20036
202-466-5660
Fax: 202-466-5069

LIMINALITY LLP
1627 K Street, NW
5th Floor
Washington, D.C. 20006
202-463-2340
Fax: 202-822-3650
www.liminality.com
E-mail: LIMINALITY@liminality.com

Meyer, Scherer & Rockcastle, Ltd.
119 North 2nd Street
Minneapolis, Minnesota 55401
612-375-0336
Fax: 612-342-2216

NBBJ
111 South Jackson
Seattle, Washington 98104
206-223-5555
Fax: 206-621-2300
www.nbbj.com

Perkins & Will
330 North Wabash
Suite 3600
Chicago, Illinois 60611
312-755-0770
Fax: 312-755-0775
www.perkinswill.com

The Phillips Group
11 West 42nd Street
New York, New York 10036
212-768-0800
Fax: 212-768-1577
www.thephillipsgroup.com

Richard Pollack & Associates
214 Grant Avenue
Suite 450
San Francisco, California 94108
415-788-4400
Fax: 415-788-5309
www.RPAarch.com

RTKL Associates Inc.
1250 Connecticut Avenue, N.W.
Washington, D.C. 20036
202-833-4400
Fax: 202-887-5168
www.rtkl.com

Sasaki Associates, Inc.
64 Pleasant Street
Watertown, Massachusetts 02472
617-926-3300
Fax: 617-924-2748
www.sasaki.com
E-mail: info@saski.com

Sipson Gray Associates
Campbell House
294 High Street
Aldershot, Hampshire GU12 4LT
United Kingdom
44 1252 331248
Fax: 44 1252 316989

Skidmore, Owings & Merrill LLP
224 South Michigan Avenue
Suite 1000
Chicago, Illinois 60604
312-554-9090
Fax: 312-360-4545
www.som.com

Spector Group
3111 New Hyde Park Road
North Hills, New York 11040
516-365-4240
Fax: 516-365-3604
www.spectorgroup.com

STUDIOS Architecture
99 Green Street
San Francisco, California 94111
415-398-7575
Fax: 415-398-7763

VOA Associates, Inc.
224 S. Michigan Avenue
Suite 1400
Chicago, Illinois 60604
312-554-1400
Fax: 312-554-1412
www.voa.com

Ward-Hale Design Associates, Inc.
1444 I Street, N.W.
Suite 1100
Washington, DC 20005
202-337-4702
Fax: 202-337-2739

Yabu Pushelberg
55 Booth Avenue
Toronto, Ontario
Canada
416-778-9779
Fax: 416-778-9747
E-mail: design@yabupushelberg.on.ca

ABOUT THE AUTHOR

Vernon Mays is editor of *Inform*, the architecture and design magazine of the Virginia Society AIA. He was formerly a senior editor of *Progressive Architecture* before returning to his native Virginia in 1989. Mays also served as architecture critic for the *Hartford Courant,* and today, he is a contributing editor to national magazines, including *Architecture and Landscape Architecture,* and has written about design for *Preservation, World Architecture, Residential Architect,* and *WIRED.* Educated as both a journalist and an architect, he lives with his wife and two children in Richmond, Virginia.